Ghost Hunter's Guide
to the
San Francisco
Bay Area

Ghost Hunter's Guide
to the
San Francisco
Bay Area
Revised Edition

Jeff Dwyer

PELICAN PUBLISHING COMPANY
Gretna 2011

To my children, Sam, Michael, and Sarah Dwyer.

All houses wherein men have lived and died are haunted houses.
—*Henry Wordsworth Longfellow*

First edition, April 2005
Second edition, October 2011

The word "Pelican" and the depiction of a pelican are trademarks of Pelican Publishing Company, Inc., and are registered in the U.S. Patent and Trademark Office.

ISBN 9781589809680
E-book ISBN 9781455615520

Printed in the United States of America
Published by Pelican Publishing Company, Inc.
1000 Burmaster Street, Gretna, Louisiana 70053

Contents

Acknowledgments

I am grateful to my literary agent, Sue Janet Clark, for invaluable support and guidance, and endless patience. I owe many thanks to the staff of Pelican Publishing Company, especially Heather Green, John Scheyd, Nina Kooij, and Katie Szadziewicz for invaluable advice, guidance, and expertise in the production and marketing of my books.

My thanks go to ghost hunting colleagues Norene Balovich, Nancy Bowman, Karen Adamski, and Jackie Ganiy for sharing their knowledge with me, and to the Morning Show cast at radio KFOG in San Francisco for the many opportunities to speak to their listening audience.

Many thanks to Loyd Auerbach whose writing and scholarship have inspired and enlightened me.

Finally, special thanks to Darlene, Sam, Michael, and Sarah Dwyer for making everything worthwhile.

Introduction

Who believes in ghosts? People from every religion, culture, and generation believe that ghosts exist. The popularity of ghosts and haunted places in books, television programs, and movies reflects a belief held by many people that other dimensions and spiritual entities exist.

In 2000, a Gallup poll discovered a significant increase in the number of Americans who believe in ghosts since the question was first asked in 1978. Thirty-one percent of respondents said they believed ghosts existed. In 1978, only 11 percent admitted to believing in ghosts. Less than a year later, Gallup found that 42 percent of the public believed a house could be haunted, but only 28 percent believed that we can hear from or mentally communicate with someone who has died. A 2003 Harris poll found that an astounding 51 percent of Americans believed in ghosts. As with preceding polls, belief in ghosts was greatest among females. More young people accepted the idea of ghosts than older people. Forty-four percent of people aged 18 to 29 years admitted a belief in ghosts compared with 13 percent of those over 65. In 2005, a CBS News poll reported that 22 percent of respondents admitted they had personally seen or felt the presence of a ghost. In this same year, Gallup pollsters reported that 75 percent of Americans believed in at least one paranormal phenomenon including ESP, reincarnation, spirit channeling, ghosts, and clairvoyance. More recently, in 2007, an Associated Press survey reported that 34 percent of Americans believed in ghosts.

Polls and surveys are interesting, but there is no way of knowing how many people have seen or heard a ghost only to feel too embarrassed, foolish, or frightened to admit it. Many ghost hunters and paranormal investigators believe a vast majority of people have seen or heard something from the other world, but failed to recognize it.

Today, many visitors and residents of the San Francisco Bay Area believe that ghostly phenomena can be experienced there. This is evidenced by the increased popularity of tours of cemeteries and historic districts in the cities and quaint towns of the region, the large number of paranormal investigations staged by local organizations, and television shows produced at places alleged to be haunted.

Broadcast and cable television channels recognize the phenomenal nationwide interest in paranormal phenomena. The SyFy channel airs a weekly 1-hour primetime program called *Ghost Hunters*. The popularity of this show has been so great that a spin-off, *Ghost Hunters International*, also airs in primetime. Cast members of these documentary shows have achieved celebrity status. In December of 2007, the Arts and Entertainment Channel premiered a new series called *Paranormal State* that follows a group of Pennsylvania State University students as they conduct investigations of ghosts and demons. On Friday evenings, the Travel Channel also offers two documentary programs that feature ghost investigations. *Most Haunted* follows a British cast of psychics, historians, and parapsychologists as they explore locations in the UK. An American cast of three investigators is featured in *Ghost Adventures*. Discovery Channel, Animal Planet, Biography Channel, and History Channel also offer documentary programs that often include dramatic recreations of ghostly activity.

The major networks offer fact-based dramas that portray ghost encounters experienced by sensitives. CBS recently ended the long-running weekly primetime drama called *Medium* that follows the true-life experiences of psychic Allison DuBois of Arizona, who communicates with ghosts in order to solve crimes. For five years, CBS aired the most popular show in this genre called *Ghost Whisperer* that portrays the experiences of sensitive Mary Ann Winkowski of Ohio. This show is now in syndication on several cable channels.

Internet users will find more than 4.0 million references to ghosts, ghost hunting, haunted places, and related paranormal phenomena. Search engines such as Google can aid ghost hunters in tracking down reports of ghostly activity in almost any city in America, locating paranormal investigative organizations they can join or consult, and purchasing ghost hunting equipment or books that deal with the art and science of finding ghosts.

The recent worldwide interest in ghosts is not a spin-off of the New Age movement of the 1980s, the current popularity of angels, or the manifestation of some new religious movement. The suspicion or recognition that ghosts exist is simply the reemergence of one of mankind's oldest and most basic beliefs: there is a life after death. Ancient writings from many cultures describe apparitions and a variety of spirit manifestations that include tolling bells, chimes, disembodied crying or moaning, and whispered messages. Legends and ancient books include descriptions of ghosts, dwelling places of spirits, and periods of intense spiritual activity related to seasons or community events such as festivals and crop harvests.

Vital interactions between the living and deceased have been described. Many ancient cultures included dead people or their spirits in community life. Spirits of the dead were sought as a source of guidance, wisdom, and protection for the living. Many followers of the world's oldest religions agree that non-living entities may be contacted for guidance or may be seen on the earthly plane. Among these are visions of saints, the Virgin Mary and angels.

Ancient sites of intense spiritual activity in Arizona, New Mexico, and Central and South America are popular destinations for travelers seeking psychic or spiritual experiences. More modern, local sites, where a variety of paranormal events have occurred, are also popular destinations for adventurous living souls. Amateur and professional ghost hunters seek the spirits of the dearly departed in the Bay Area's mansions, old theatres, historic bars and inns, firehouses, stores, and countless other places including graveyards and famous ships. Modern buildings, city parks, restaurants and bars, numerous historic sites such as Alcatraz Prison, and seldom-traveled back country roads also serve as targets for ghost hunters.

Throughout the past two millennia, the popularity of belief in ghosts has waxed and waned, similar to religious activity. When a rediscovery of ghosts and their role in our lives occurs, skeptics label the notion a fad or an aberration of modern lifestyles. Perhaps people are uncomfortable with the idea that ghosts exist because it involves an examination of our nature and our concepts of life, death, and afterlife. These concepts are most often considered in the context of religion, yet ghost hunters recognize that acceptance of the reality of ghosts, and a life after death, is a personal decision, having nothing to do with religious beliefs or church doctrine. An intellectual approach enables the ghost hunter to explore haunted places without religious bias or fear.

The great frequency of ghost manifestations in the San Francisco Bay Area, as evidenced by documentary reports on TV and other news media, reflects the success of amateur and professional ghost hunters who research and seek paranormal encounters in the region. Ghost hunting is a popular weekend pastime for many adventurous souls. Advertisement of haunted inns, restaurants, sips, and historical sites is commonplace. It is always fun, often very exciting, and may take ghost hunters places they had never dreamed of going.

ABOUT THIS BOOK

The first edition of *Ghost Hunter's Guide to the San Francisco Bay Area* was published in May of 2005. It represents information I gathered over the preceding 20 years from research and my paranormal investigations. Since then, I have received hundreds of reports of continuing and new ghostly activity in the Bay Area. So much new information accumulated in a short period of time that I decided to write a second edition of this popular book. Many of the haunted places described in the first edition have been retained in the second edition if recent investigations indicated that paranormal phenomena have persisted.

Chapter 1 of this book will help you, the ghost hunter, to research and organize your own ghost hunt. Chapters 2 through 5 describe several locations at which ghostly activity has been reported. Unlike other collections of ghost stories and descriptions of haunted places, this book emphasizes access. Addresses of each haunted site are included along with other information to assist you in locating and entering each location. Several appendices offer organizational material for your ghost hunts, including a Sighting Report Form to document your adventures, lists of suggested reading and videos, Internet resources, and organizations you may contact about your experiences with ghosts.

GHOST HUNTING IN THE BAY AREA

The very word, ghost, immediately brings to mind visions of ancient European castles, foggy moors, dark streets, and spooky cemeteries. The fact is that ghosts are everywhere. A history based in antiquity that includes dark dungeons, hidden catacombs, or ancient ruins covered with a veil of sorrow and pain is not essential, but contemporary versions of these elements are common in many American cities, however. Indeed, several of the central cities of the San Francisco Bay Area and many outlying communities have all the ingredients necessary for successful ghost hunting.

Indians who inhabited the region for a thousand years, or more, frequently engaged in inter-tribal warfare while practicing a spiritual lifestyle that included communication with the dead. Discovery and desecration of their graves during construction of modern roads and buildings have led to reports of spirit activity and disturbing paranormal events.

Since the 1770s, the region has been populated with people from a variety of cultures who experienced tremendous changes in their lives. Changes and challenges that were, at times, overwhelming were created by transition of the region in 1820 from a Spanish colony to a province under the tenuous control of Mexico, and then, in 1846, to a nearly lawless American territory. The calamity of the Gold Rush from 1849 to 1858 brought thousands of people to the San Francisco Bay Area before they embarked for the gold fields and diggings of the Sierra Nevada creating even more turmoil in the region. The growing wealth of the region's cities and towns, and the admission of California to the Union in 1850 as the thirty-first state, did little to dampen criminal activity, reduce civil disobedience, dissipate racism, or civilize those who had abandoned the best qualities of their character to seek quick riches. Other cataclysmic changes were brought about by armed conflicts, including skirmishes between Indians and white settlers,

Yankees who confronted Mexican soldiers in the 1846 Bear Flag Revolt, and San Francisco's vigilante mobs and criminals.

Epidemics that swept through the Bay Area brought tragedy to many families, ending lives at a young age and filling many pioneer cemeteries. In 1855, the SS *Sam* arrived in San Francisco Bay carrying immigrants from the Far East. Within a few days, a cholera epidemic broke out, eventually filling several makeshift cemeteries. In 1900, ships that moored at San Francisco's piers discharged rats infected with bubonic plague. The epidemic that followed was not eradicated until 1905. Fear that the many corpses prolonged the epidemic prompted city leaders to establish new cemeteries far beyond city limits. Graves of plague victims were exhumed from city cemeteries and the bodies transported to Colma and other locations on the San Francisco peninsula. The Spanish flu epidemic of 1918 that killed 100 million people world-wide left 2,220 dead in San Francisco. In fascinating cemeteries, such as the Mission Dolores graveyard in San Francisco, the National Cemetery of the Presidio of San Francisco, and the Columbarium of San Francisco, some grave markers list specific epidemics as the cause of death. Many also reveal that death came at a young age, creating spirits who have yet to let go and move on.

In the 1880s, San Jose and Fremont suffered devastating fires but they were minor compared to more contemporary disasters. Following the San Francisco earthquake of 1906, ruptured gas mains created thirty fires that swept through the city, accounting for 90 percent of the destruction and causing more than 3,000 deaths. Four hundred and ninety city blocks were affected culminating in the destruction of 25,000 buildings including a San Francisco landmark, the Palace Hotel.

On October 17, 1989, the Loma Prieta earthquake killed 63 people but left as many as 12,000 people homeless after fires swept through San Francisco's Marina District. Much of the destruction in the neighborhood was attributed to the construction of houses on rubble from the 1906 earthquake.

The Oakland Hills Firestorm of 1991 served as a gruesome reminder that even modern construction is not immune to the kind of fires that destroyed many Gold Rush era towns in regions surrounding the Bay Area. The fire killed twenty-five people and consumed 3,354 single-family homes and 437 apartments. Many who died in the firestorm were overcome by heat and smoke as they fought flames with a garden hose. Others were caught by the fiery blast as they attempted to navigate roads obscured by smoke and burning debris.

Fires that swept through rural and suburban areas of the late nineteenth century also destroyed thousands of wooden grave markers in town cemeteries. During ensuing periods of rapid rebuilding and expansion of Oakland, San Francisco, San Jose, and Palo Alto, spirits became restless when buildings were constructed over their unmarked graves. In the 1990s, during construction of parks, homes, businesses, and streets, several graves were discovered and inadvertently desecrated, leading to reports of ghostly activity in modern structures. Most recently, graves have been discovered during sewer reconstruction under the streets of Los Gatos, in Fairfield, and in the Presidio of San Francisco.

With three major airports and numerous military facilities in the Bay Area, aviation and naval disasters have become a prominent part of local history. On July 17, 1944, the Port Chicago Naval Magazine was nearly wiped from the face of the earth by a massive explosion that sank two cargo ships laden with munitions, several smaller vessels, and killed more than 300 dock workers. It has been estimated that 10,000 tons of explosives were ignited by a heavy shell or bomb that had been dropped on a steel deck. The force of the 10:19 p.m. explosion awoke people in Oakland, more than 20 miles away. Debris weighing as much as 200 pounds was blasted as far as five miles from the site of the disaster.

On February 11, 1968, two Navy aviators died when their T-33b jet departed from the Alameda Naval Air Station and hit the Bay Bridge. Tragedy struck the bridge again in 1989 when the Loma Prieta earthquake caused part of the roadbed to collapse, killing two people. The nearby Cypress Freeway collapsed adding forty two to the death toll.

On February 7, 1973, a Navy Corsair jet fighter crashed into an apartment building a few blocks from my home in Alameda. The 8:13 p.m. crash was heard all over the island city. Aside from the pilot, ten people were killed while twenty-six were injured. The crash site, at 1814 Central Avenue, has been rebuilt and nothing remains to mark the disaster except the spirits who walk through the new building. Another airplane crash, at Sun Valley Mall in Concord, on December 23, 1985, left seven dead. Environmental remnants of this disaster have been detected by psychics on the third floor of the mall.

Several disasters dating before 1920 have contributed to the restless spirits of the Bay Area. These include the San Francisco cable car explosion of February 1887, Alameda Masonic temple gas explosion of 1904, sinking of the ferry boat *Contra Costa* in 1859, fire aboard the steamship *Columbia* in 1907, and the Mare Island (Vallejo) navy yard explosion in 1892.

All of these tragic events add to the region's paranormal legacy and have left powerful emotional imprints created by spirits of the dearly departed who felt a need to stay on. A common factor in the creation of a ghost is the loss of life by a sudden, violent event, often at a young age, leaving their souls with an inextinguishable desire to achieve their life's objectives, or with a sense of obligation to offer protection to a particular place or person.

Some ghosts remain on the earthly plane for revenge or to provide guidance for someone still alive. Many of those who came to California for gold were caught up in their dreams of great wealth but met with only frustration and failure before dying alone and in poverty. Their restless spirits still roam the streets of Gold Rush era towns such as Benicia and Clayton and the back roads of rural areas searching for the elusive yellow metal.

Communities of the San Francisco Bay Area have had their share of criminal activities and social injustice. From October 1966 to May 1981, Bay Area communities lived in the fear of the Zodiac Killer. Credited with forty-nine possible victims, this mass murderer has yet to be caught. The Zodiac left victims in Vallejo, Lake Berryessa, Presidio Heights in San Francisco, Benicia, Richmond, and other areas that may include four western states.

On July 1, 1993, Gian Luigi Ferri entered the law offices of Pettit and Martin, at 101 California Street in San Francisco and opened fire with two pistols. After the smoke cleared, six lay injured among eight who were killed. Ferri shot himself as police arrived at the scene.

Ghost hunters who are fascinated by criminals will want to visit Alcatraz Island. Before the tiny island in San Francisco Bay was transformed into a prison, the "rock" was known by Native Americans as a place occupied by evil spirits. In spite of Indian legends, the U.S. Army established a fort on the island in 1850. During construction between the wharf and guardhouse, a landslide buried two men and renewed Indian warnings that the place was haunted by evil spirits. During the ensuing fifty years, an untold number of prisoners— deserters, southern sympathizers of the Civil War era, criminals, and escapees from other prisons--died in their cells. In 1907, the Army vacated the island as a Bay Area defense installation, making way for its transformation to the Western U.S. Military Prison. Ultimately, the place became a federal prison for some of America's most famous criminals including Al Capone, Public Enemy Number One Alvin Carpis, Machine Gun George Kelly, and the Birdman of Alcatraz, Robert Stroud. It is believed that during its twenty-nine years of operation, no prisoners escaped from the Rock. Official records reveal that thirty-six men were involved in fourteen attempts. Six escapees were shot and killed on the rocks at water's edge while two were unaccounted for and believed drowned in the bay.

Four hundred and twelve victims of one of the most horrendous cult-related crimes in American history are interred in Oakland's Evergreen Cemetery. On November 18, 1978, at the urging of cult leader Jim Jones, 918 people died by mass suicide in a Guyana village. Since many of the victims were once residents of the Bay Area, a large plot was made available for burial in the East Bay. Electronic voice phenomena (EVP) and other paranormal experiences have been reported at this location.

The activities of criminals have produced many used, abused, confused, and forlorn spirits who may remain with us after their death. The spirits of these victims may still seek lost dreams while they remain attached to what little they gained during their difficult lives. Many ghosts who harbor deep resentment, pain, or a desire to complete their unfinished business, still roam the darkened halls of court houses, jails, prisons, hotels, theatres, cemeteries, modern buildings, and many other places throughout the region that are accessible to the public.

WHAT IS A GHOST?

A ghost is some aspect of the personality, spirit, consciousness, energy, mind, intelligence, or soul that remains after the body dies. When any of these are detected by the living—through sight, sound, odor, or movement—the experience is called a paranormal encounter by parapsychologists. Most of us call it a ghost. How the ghost manifests itself is unknown. There seems to be a close association, however, between aspects of the entity's life and the mode it uses to manifest itself as a ghost. These include a sudden, traumatic death, strong ties to loved ones who survived the entity or to a particular place, unfinished business, strong emotions such as hatred and anger, or a desire for revenge.

Ghosts differ from other paranormal phenomena by their display of intelligent interaction with a witness or the environment. This includes interaction with the living by touching, speaking, gestures, facial expressions, and sounds such as tapping in response to questions, creation of sounds or signals on audio recorders, or light anomalies on photographic media. When any of these are made in response to questions, directions, requests, or movement made by the living, it may be said that a ghost is present. The ghost's activity is often an effort to communicate. Ghosts may speak to the living to warn of an unforeseen accident or disaster, to protect a cherished place or object, to give advice, or to express their love, anger, remorse, or disappointment. They may also be trying to complete some project or duty they failed to finish before death.

A ghost may be present if an unseen entity interacts with the environment by performing purposeful activity, or responds to a change in the environment. Unexplained movement of objects such as books, a pipe, eye glasses, tools, weapons, door knobs, bedding, etc., that cannot be attributed to normal or natural processes often indicates the presence of a ghost. Some ghosts have been known to rearrange furniture and room decorations or the like to suit their preferences. If new objects are placed in a ghost's favorite room they may be found moved outside the room, broken, or hidden in another location. Common ghostly activities are movement of a rocking chair, turning of doorknobs, activation of light switches and electronic equipment such as TVs, and disheveling bedding.

Most ghosts make their presence known through sound or movement of objects, without creating an image that can be seen or captured on photographic media. In contrast, some ghosts may appear completely life-like because they are unaware they are dead and possess the energy to create an apparition. Others appear as partial apparitions—a hand, a foot, or head—because they are confused about their transition from life to death or lack the energy to create an image of their entire body.

Occasionally, paranormal activity attributed to ghosts is bizarre, frightening, or dangerous. Witnesses may see objects fly about, hear strange sounds, or experience accidents. This kind of activity is often attributed to a "poltergeist" or noisy ghost. In spite of the widely used term, most authorities believe that a living person, not the dead, causes these manifestations. Generally, someone under great emotional stress releases psychic energy that creates subtle or spectacular changes in the environment.

Noises commonly associated with a poltergeist include loud tapping on walls or ceilings, heavy footsteps, shattered glass, ringing telephones, and running water. Objects may move about on tables or floors or fly across a room. Furniture may spin or tip over. Dangerous objects, such as knives, hammers, or pens, may hit people. These poltergeist events may last a few days, a year, or more. Discovery and removal of the emotionally unstable, living person often stops the poltergeist.

HAUNTINGS

Hauntings and ghostly activity appear to be similar but they are not the same thing. Many professional ghost hunters and parapsychologists are careful to make a clear distinction between these two kinds of paranormal phenomena. They share a lot of the same features in terms of what witnesses see, feel, or smell, but a haunting may occur without the presence of a spiritual entity or the consciousness of a dead person. People have reported seeing pale, transparent images of a deceased person walking in hallways, climbing stairs, sitting in rocking chairs, or sitting on airplanes, trains, buses, and even in restaurants. Some have been seen sleeping in beds, hanging by a rope from a tree, or walking through walls. Most commonly, a partial apparition of a single entity is seen, but witnesses have reported seeing entire armies engaged in battle. Unlike ghosts, hauntings do not display intelligent action with respect to their location—they do not manipulate your new computer—and they do not interact with the living.

A haunting may be an environmental imprint or recording of intense, repetitive emotion experienced by a living person during an event or activity at a specific location. As such, they tend to be associated with a specific place or object, not a particular person. The ghostly figures tend to perform some kind of repetitive task or activity. Sometimes the haunting is so repetitive that witnesses feel as though they are watching a video loop that plays the same brief scene over and over. A good example is that of a deceased grandmother who makes appearances seated in her favorite rocking chair. If the chair does not move, this is a haunting, not a ghost.

Typically, a ghostly figure will perform the same repetitive task or activity without variation for a few seconds; rarely more than a minute. A haunting is created when the energy of the emotion associated with the repetitive activity or event is imbedded in the electromagnetic field of the environment. Like a file recorded on a computer disk, the recording may be quite durable, lasting decades. It may be triggered to "play" by local physical conditions and captured on surveillance recorders when no living person is present. This indicates that the haunting is associated with a specific place or object, not a particular living person.

There is a lot of evidence that living people can trigger and experience these environmental recordings by visiting the particular site, touching an object that was a key element of the event, and psychically connecting with the event. The location of strong environmental imprints can also be discovered through devices such as electromagnetic field detectors. Higher magnetic field readings have been found at locations where psychics frequently experience hauntings.

HOW DOES A GHOST MANIFEST ITSELF?

Ghosts interact with our environment in a variety of ways that may have something to do with the strength of their personality, desire to communicate, or level of confusion concerning their transformation by death. The talents or skills they possessed in life, their personal objectives, or frustrations arising from the end of life may underlie their efforts in getting our attention. Some ghosts create odors or sounds, particularly those associated with their habits, such as cigar smoke or signature perfumes or whistling. Many reports mention the odors of tobacco, oranges, and hemp as most common. Sounds, including voice messages, may be detected with an audio recorder (see Electronic Audio Phenomenon). Ghost hunters have recorded greetings, warnings, screams, sobbing, and expressions of love.

One of the most common ghostly activities is moving objects. Ghosts like to knock over stacks of cards or coins, turn doorknobs, scatter matchsticks, and move your keys. For many it appears easy to manipulate light switches and TV remotes, open and close windows and doors, or push chairs around. Some ghosts have the power to throw objects, pull pictures from walls, or move heavy items. As a rule, ghosts cannot tolerate disturbances within the place they haunt. If you tilt a wall-mounted picture, the ghost will set it straight. Obstacles placed in the ghost's path may be pushed aside. These seemingly minor indications of ghostly activity should be recorded for future reference on the Sighting Report Form in Appendix A.

Ghosts can also create changes in the physical qualities of an environment. Ice-cold breezes and unexplained gusts of wind are often the first signs that a ghost is present. Moving or stationary cold spots, with temperatures several degrees below surrounding areas, have been detected with reliable instruments. Temperature changes sometimes occur with a feeling that the atmosphere has thickened as if the room was suddenly filled with unseen people.

In searching for ghosts, some people use devices that detect changes in magnetic, electrical, or radio fields. However, detected changes may be subject to error, interference by other electrical devices, or misinterpretation. Data from these instruments that comprises convincing evidence that a ghost is present may be difficult to capture on a permanent record.

Ghosts may create images on still cameras (film or digital) and video recorders such as luminous fogs, balls of light called orbs, streaks of light, or the partial outline of body parts. In the 1860s, this was called spirit photography. Thousands of images reputed to be paranormal may be viewed on the Internet but modern digital photographs are easily edited and make it difficult to produce convincing proof of ghostly activity.

Humanoid images of ghosts or hauntings are the prized objective of most ghost hunters but they are also the least produced. When such images occur, they are often partial, revealing only a head and torso with an arm or two. Feet are seldom seen. Full body apparitions are extremely rare. Some ghost hunters have seen ethereal, fully transparent forms that are barely discernible. Others report seeing ghosts who appear as solid as a living being.

WHY DO GHOSTS REMAIN AT A PARTICULAR PLACE?

Ghosts remain in a particular place because they are emotionally attached to a room, a building, or special surroundings that profoundly affected them during their lives, or to activities or events that played a role in their death. A prime example is the haunted house inhabited by the ghost of a man who hanged himself in the master bedroom because his wife left him. It is widely believed that death and sudden transition from the physical world confuse a ghost. He or she remains in familiar or emotionally stabilizing surroundings to ease the strain. A place-bound ghost is most likely to occur when a violent death occurred with great emotional anguish. Ghosts may linger in a house, barn, cemetery, factory, or store waiting for a loved one or anyone familiar that might help them deal with their new level of existence. Some ghosts wander through buildings or forests, on bridges, or alongside particular sections of roads, but they rarely travel far. Some await enemies, seeking revenge. Others await a friend for a chance to resolve their guilt.

UNDER WHAT CONDITIONS IS A SIGHTING MOST LIKELY?

Although ghosts may appear at any time, a sighting may occur on special holidays, anniversaries, birthdays, or during historic periods (for example, July 4 or December 7), or calendar periods pertaining to the personal history of the ghost. Halloween is reputed to be a favorite night for many apparitions, while others seem to prefer their own special day or night, on a weekly or monthly cycle.

Night is a traditional time for ghost activity, yet experienced ghost hunters know that sightings may occur at any time. There seems to be no consistent affinity of ghosts for darkness, but they seldom appear when artificial light is bright. Perhaps this is why ghosts shy away from camera crews and their array of lights. Ghosts seem to prefer peace and quiet, although some of them have been reported to make incessant, loud sounds. Even a small group of ghost hunters may make too much noise to facilitate a sighting. For this reason, it is recommended that you limit your group to four persons and oral communication be kept to a minimum.

IS GHOST HUNTING DANGEROUS?

Ghost hunting can be hazardous, but reports of injuries inflicted by ghosts are rare and their veracity suspect. Movies and children's ghost stories have created a widespread notion that ghosts may harm the living or even cause the death of persons they dislike. In 2006, a popular television program showed a fascinating video of a ghost hunter being struck down by his camera equipment. The man's heavy equipment moved suddenly from a position at his waist and struck him on the side of the face. Video of this event was interpreted as evidence of a ghost attack, but no apparition or light anomaly was visible.

Many authorities believe that rare attacks by ghosts are a matter of mistaken identity, i.e., the ghost misidentified a living person as a figure the ghost knew during his life. It is possible that encounters that appear to be attacks may be nothing more than clumsy efforts by a ghost to achieve recognition. Witnesses of ghost appearances have found themselves in the middle of gunfights, major military battles, and other violent events, yet sustained not the slightest injury.

Persons who claim to have been injured by a ghost have, in most cases, precipitated the injury themselves through their own ignorance or fear. Ghost hunters often carry out investigations in the dark or subdued light and may encounter environmental hazards that lead to injury. Fear may trigger an attempt to race from a haunted site, exposing the ghost hunter to injury by tripping over unseen objects or making contact with broken glass, low-hanging tree limbs, exposed wiring, or weakened floorboards, stairways, or doorways.

The ghost hunter will be safe if he keeps a wary eye and calm attitude and sets aside tendencies to fear the ghost or the circumstances of its appearance. Safety may be enhanced if you visit a haunted location while it is well illuminated, during daylight hours for instance. Potential hazards in the environment can be identified and, perhaps, cleared or marked with light-reflecting tape.

Most authorities agree that ghosts do not travel. Ghosts will not follow you home, take up residence in your car, or attempt to occupy your body. They are held in time and space by deep emotional ties to an event or place. Ghosts have been observed on airplanes, trains, buses, and ships: however, it is unlikely that the destination interests them. Something about the journey, some event such as a plane crash or train wreck, accounts for their appearance as travelers. In some cases, it is the conveyance that ties the ghost to the physical plane. A vintage World War II B-17 bomber may be haunted by the ghost of a man who piloted that type of aircraft in the 1940s. A ship, such as the USS *Hornet* in Alameda, California, may be an irresistible attraction for the ghost of a sailor who once served on aircraft carriers.

HOT SPOTS FOR GHOSTLY ACTIVITY

Numerous sites of disasters, criminal activity, suicides, devastating fires, and other tragic events abound in the San Francisco Bay Area, providing hundreds of opportunities for ghost hunting. You may visit the locations described in Chapters 2-5 to experience ghostly activity discovered by others, or discover a hot spot to research and initiate your own ghost investigation.

Astute ghost hunters often search historical maps, drawings, and other documents to find the sites of military conflicts, buildings that no longer exist, or sites of tragic events now occupied by modern structures. For example, maps and drawings found online or displayed in museums such as the Oakland Museum, the Wells Fargo History Museum, and historic locations such as Fort Point in San Francisco may be a good place to start.

People who died in earthquakes, train wrecks, or stage coach robberies, of epidemics or infections that ensued after minor injuries, who succumbed to the hard life of a fisherman or farmer, and who were displaced by other tragic events such as fires, may haunt the site of their graves, favorite bars or restaurants, workplaces, or cherished homes.

In some of the Bay Area's older neighborhoods, homes of many well-known residents, such as agricultural pioneer William Meek (1869), in Hayward, and the father of the National Park Service, John Muir, in Martinez (1875), are reputed to harbor ghosts. Fascinating histories and ghostly atmospheres may be found in historic homes such as the Ignacio Peralta house (1901) in Oakland, the Captain Walsh house (1849) in Benicia, the Captain Robert Dollar mansion, Falkirk (1888), in San Rafael, the Faxon Atherton mansion (1881) in San Francisco, the Haas-Lilienthal House (1886) in San Francisco, the William Ralston mansion (1864) in Belmont, the Coleman mansion (1880; now the Peninsula School) in Menlo Park, and the world-famous Sarah Winchester mansion (1884) in San Jose.

In Oakland, sixteen grand Victorian mansions built between 1870 and 1911 at various locations throughout the city were moved to grounds near the historic city center to create Preservation Park. The project saved many of these mansions from demolition as freeways and commercial districts grew. Some of the homes have a history of paranormal activity, especially the Remillard house (1887) and the Nile Hall (1911). Nearby, the Enock Pardee mansion (1869), home of a Gold Rush immigrant, and the Camron-Stanford house (1875) on the shores of Lake Merritt, are well-known as haunted places.

Many of these historic buildings are popular weekend destinations for ghost hunters. Access is easy since many are open as historic sites or museums.

Some towns have established historic districts and other venues, such as docks, squares, and parks that have been investigated by professional and amateur ghost hunters. These include the preserved and restored Victorian mansions of Oakland's Preservation Park, the historic Presidio of San Francisco, Saratoga Avenue in Saratoga, the Old Town section of Los Gatos, First Street in Benicia, China Camp Region Park in San Rafael, Fort Point in San Francisco, and world-famous Alcatraz Island in San Francisco Bay.

The Oldest churches in the San Francisco Bay Area are the Spanish missions. Founded June 26, 1776, San Francisco's Mission Dolores is the oldest intact building in the city. Initial successes of the Franciscan priests in converting local Indians to Catholicism led to the establishment of another mission at the south end of San Francisco Bay, the Mission Santa Clara. Founded on January 12, 1777, the mission is now part of the University of Santa Clara and still used for church services. Peaceful Indian tribes on the east side of the bay and abundant natural resources attracted the attention of the Franciscans who established Mission San Jose on June 11, 1797. This mission is now surrounded by the town of Fremont, named for explorer Colonel John Charles Fremont. The Mission San Rafael was dedicated on December 14, 1817, as a convalescent hospital for Indians at other missions who suffered from lingering illness. Located out of the Bay Area's fog-belt, this mission offered a warmer climate and easy access to vegetables most months of the year.

All the missions had graveyards filled with thousands of Indians who succumbed to diseases imported by travelers from Europe and South America. Today, many graves are covered by streets and parking lots.

Several of the Bay Area's nineteenth century churches are restored and accessible to visitors as points of historical interest in addition to serving as religious centers. Paranormal investigators have visited the St. Paul's Episcopal Church (1859) Benicia, St. Peter's Chapel (1901) on Vallejo's Mare Island, Christ Episcopal Church (1882) in Sausalito, St. Luke's Episcopal Church (1883) in Los Gatos, Memorial Church (1887) on the Stanford University campus in Palo Alto, Trinity Episcopal Church (1863) in San Jose, First Unitarian Church (1889) in Oakland, Old St. Hilary's Church (188?) in Tiburon, and St. Catherine of Siena Parish (1868) in Martinez. In the city of San Francisco, ghost hunters may want to visit the trinity Presbyterian Church (1892), St. Patrick Church (1872), and the old St. Mary's

Cathedral (1854). The grounds of some of these fascinating places contain graves of well-known Bay Area pioneers, in addition to mass graves of those who died in earthquakes and the epidemics of the nineteenth century.

Several cemeteries dating from the early-nineteenth century are scattered about the region and known by local ghost hunters as good places to experience paranormal phenomena. Many of them have fascinating architecture, epitaphs, and lists of occupants in addition to a spooky atmosphere. These cities of the dead include some unusual tombs and crypts marked by peculiar symbols.

The oldest cemetery in the region is San Francisco's Mission Dolores graveyard, which received its first occupant in 1777. Several of the original graves were removed in the 1880s to make way for the Sixteenth Street extension but as many as 446 bodies remain including recipient of vigilante justice, James Casey, and Don Luis Arquello (1784-1830), governor of Alta, California. Other Spanish missions in Fremont, Santa Clara, and San Rafael are surrounded by the unmarked graves of thousands of Indians who died during epidemics of imported diseases.

Today, the city of San Francisco has only three cemeteries within its borders. These include Mission Dolores, the National Cemetery at the Presidio, and the Neptune Society Columbarium reserved for interment of ashes only. Until 1901, several cemeteries were scattered throughout the city. Some of these were neglected and lost as fire destroyed wooden headstones or careless builders expanded roads and parks and erected buildings. In 1901, fearing that buried corpses of bubonic plague victims might prolong the epidemic, city officials ordered the exhumation of thousands of graves and reburial at distant locations such as the complex of cemeteries at Colma and Oakland's Mountain View Cemetery. The destruction of thousands of graves created a massive supply of broken marble and granite that was wisely used by the city in the construction of gutters, storm drains, and retaining walls. These remnants can be seen at Buena Vista Park and at several locations throughout Golden Gate Park.

A list of lost cemeteries can be found at www.sanfrancisco cemeteries.com. This Web site lists twenty-seven former graveyards now covered with streets, parks, and buildings. Among the most famous are cemeteries that once occupied grounds on Laurel Heights and Lone Mountain. From 1852 to the mid-1940s, Laurel Hill, Calvary, Masonic, and Odd Fellows cemeteries were known as the "big four" because they housed the remains of many of the city's foremost pioneers and developers, including the legendary Emperor Norton. Today, only the San Francisco Columbarium remains, marking the former entrance to the Odd Fellows Cemetery. Modern development covers the former burial grounds which, many believe, still contain remains overlooked by workers who were charged with relocating thousands of graves. Paranormal activity at the sites of several former cemeteries in San Francisco has aroused suspicions that the decades-long, grave-removal project failed to locate thousands of graves. The Civic Center Plaza, Powel Street at Filbert and Greenwich, and the grounds at First and Clementina Streets have been investigated by ghost hunters. The former Golden Gate Cemetery at Clement and 33rd Street was moved in 1909 but historians believe 11,000 may remain under the Lincoln Park Golf Course.

A tour of many of these former burial grounds is offered by San Francisco City Guides (see Appendix D: Special Tours and Events).

Since the early 1950s, several Indian burial grounds covered by modern structures have been discovered, usually during major renovations, replacement of older buildings with shopping centers, or reconstruction of sewers or streets. Mound Street, in Alameda, was named for the Indian burial and refuse mounds discovered during the construction of houses. Located a few blocks from my childhood home, I grew up hearing stories of ghostly Indians appearing in the kitchens and bedrooms of my friends' homes. These sightings persist today. Emeryville's Bay Street shopping center sits on one of the largest shell mounds ever discovered. Created by Ohlone Indians over hundreds of years and covering one million square feet, the mound included homes, areas where canoes were built, and burial grounds. Neglected and long-forgotten graves have been uncovered at the old Public Health Service Hospital at the Presidio in San Francisco, Village Oaks Shopping Center in Clayton, and the cluster of shops in Los Gatos, at Highway 9 and North Santa Cruz Avenue. All of these locations are currently under investigation by local ghost hunters.

Oakland's Mountain View Cemetery contains the remains of such luminaries as coffee magnate James Folger, architect Julia Morgan, and bank founder Charles Crocker. Murder victim Elizabeth Short, aka the Black Dahlia, is also buried there. The Evergreen Cemetery contains the remains of more than 400 victims of the Jones Town mass suicide.

Many paranormal investigators cite Rose Hill Cemetery, near Antioch, and Mare Island Cemetery in Vallejo as the most haunted graveyards in the Bay Area. Opened in the 1860s to serve the region's coal mining towns, Rose Hill Cemetery contains the remains of many who died at an early age from cave-ins, explosions, or black lung disease. The cemetery also contains the remains of Sarah Norton, known throughout the East Bay Area as the white witch. On Vallejo's Mare Island, the U.S. Navy established a cemetery in 1856 and filled it with American heroes and others, including eight Russian sailors who lost their lives in 1863 fighting a fire in San Francisco. Nine hundred graves fill this tiny cemetery of 2.4 acres while an uncounted number of ghosts wander the grounds. Spirits in these spooky cemeteries create orbs in photographs and digital images or create cold spots and that creepy feeling that you are being watched or touched by invisible hands.

The best way to see the historic cemeteries of the Bay Area and learn fascinating histories of those entombed, is to tour them with a knowledgeable guide. (See Appendix D: Special Tours and Events.) Some of these places are too spooky and possibly unsafe after dark unless you are accompanied by people who can ensure a pleasant visit.

Several historic ships moored on San Francisco Bay are haunted and open for tourists. At San Francisco's Maritime National Historical Park, the 1886 square-rigger *Balclutha* and the 1890 ferryboat *Eureka* harbor the ghosts of crew and passengers. Nearby, a phantom crew member haunts the engine room of the WWII submarine USS *Pampanito*. Across the bay, one of the most famous haunted vessels in America, the WWII aircraft carrier USS *Hornet*, is moored in Alameda. In Jack London Square in Oakland, the presidential yacht, USS *Potomac*, is haunted by ghosts from the Roosevelt era.

Astute ghost hunters keep an eye on San Francisco Bay when touring waterfront areas. Phantom vessels are often sighted gliding under the Golden Gate Bridge or approaching a wharf. The most famous sighting was made by the crew of the destroyer, USS *Kennison*

(DD-138). This WWII fighting ship entered fog-bound San Francisco Bay on the morning of September 15, 1942. Lookout Howard H. Brisbane alerted officers on the bridge to a large ship that lay ahead. As the fog lifted, several of the *Kennison's* crew were astounded to see a square-rigged ship, unpainted and heavily worn by years at sea. The event was recorded in the *Kennison's* log and widely accepted as a true account given the fact that the crew's skills in identifying ships, friend or foe, were sharpened by a long patrol in the Pacific Ocean.

LOCAL GHOST HUNTERS

Several local organizations dedicated to ghost hunting are active in the Northern California region. They can help you locate haunted sites, provide information about previous ghost investigations they have conducted, or sharpen your skills as a paranormal investigator. Foremost among these are the San Francisco Ghost Society, Haunted and Paranormal Investigations (HPI), Ghost Trackers, Paranormalzone TV, and Sonoma SPIRIT. The activities of these organizations have been featured in a variety of news media. Their investigators combine advanced high-tech approaches to ghost hunting with the insight of psychics to produce some amazing results. HPI and Ghost Trackers also host special events and offers classes and training seminars. The San Francisco Ghost Society offers a local web cast called Supernatural San Francisco that may be accessed through their website. Paranormalzone TV presents live-streams of these investigators on a cable TV channel. See Appendix F (Internet Sources) for contact information. Tours of haunted places are available in many cities throughout the San Francisco Bay Area. Some of these are staged only during the Halloween season, but San Francisco has several tours that are offered year round (see Appendix D).

THREE SIMPLE RULES

Three simple rules apply for successful ghost hunting. The first is to be patient. Ghosts are everywhere, but contact may require a considerable investment of time. Second, respect the boundaries of private property and the rights of property owners to restrict or deny access to places you may wish to investigate. The third rule is to have fun. Ghost hunting can be a fascinating and exciting experience. You may report your ghost hunting experiences or suggest hot spots for ghost hunting to the author via e-mail at Ghosthunter@jeffdwyer. com. Visit the author's Web site at www.jeffdwyer.com.

Chapter 1

How to Hunt for Ghosts

You may want to visit recognized haunted sites, listed in chapters 2 through 5, using some of the ghost hunting techniques described later in this chapter, or search for a new haunted site. If you are looking for a haunted place that has not yet been discovered, start with an old house in your neighborhood or a favorite bed-and-breakfast inn. You may get a lead from fascinating stories about ancestors that have been passed down through your family, rumors circulating among your friends and neighbors, or reports posted on the Internet.

Your search for a ghost or exploration of a haunted place starts with research. Summaries of obscure and esoteric material about possible haunted sites are available from museums, local historical societies, and bookstores. Brochures and booklets, sold at historical sites under the California State Park system, can be good resources, too.

Guided tours of historical sites such as Oakland's Preservation Park, the aircraft carrier USS *Hornet* in Alameda, old neighborhoods in towns such as Petaluma, San Rafael, and Saratoga, the historic Presidio in San Francisco, or old churches, theaters, and pioneer cemeteries throughout the San Francisco Bay Area are good places to begin your research. Tours can help you develop a feel for places within a building where ghosts might be sighted or an appreciation of relevant history. Bay Area ghost, cemetery, and history tours are popular and offer a good way to learn a lot about local paranormal activity in a short time.

By touring haunted buildings, you will have opportunities to speak with guides and docents who may be able to provide you with clues about the dearly departed or tell you ghost stories you can't find in published material. Docents may know people—old-timers in the area or amateur historians—who can give you additional information about a site, its former owners or residents, and its potential for ghostly activity.

Almost every city has a local historical society (see Appendix G). These are good places to find information that may not be published anywhere else. This could be histories of local families and buildings; information about tragedies, disasters, criminal activity, or legends; and myths about places that may be haunted. You may learn about secret scandals or other ghost-producing happenings that occurred at locations now occupied by modern buildings, roads, or parks. In these cases, someone occupying a new house or other structure could hear strange sounds, feel cold spots, or see ghosts or spirit remnants.

Newspapers are an excellent source of historical information as well. You can search for articles about ghosts, haunted places, or paranormal activity by accessing the newspaper's archives via the Internet and entering key words, dates, events, or names. Newspaper articles about suicides, murders, train wrecks, plane crashes, and paranormal phenomena can often provide essential information for your ghost hunt. Stories about authentic haunted sites are common around Halloween.

Bookstores and libraries usually have special-interest sections with books on local history by local writers. A few inquiries may connect you with these local writers who may be able to help you focus your research.

If these living souls cannot help, try the dead. A visit to a local graveyard is always fruitful in identifying possible ghosts. Often you can find headstones that indicate the person entombed died of suicide, criminal activity, local disaster, or such. Some epitaphs may indicate if the deceased was survived by a spouse and children, or died far from home. Grave markers that have been desecrated or damaged by weather, vegetation, erosion, or earthquakes are often haunted by spirits who seek help in restoring their final resting place. At the graves of children and young adults, ghost hunters may discover paranormal activity in the form of environmental imprints created by intense, repetitive emotions of grieving family members.

Perhaps the best place to start a search for a ghost is within your own family. Oral histories can spark your interest in a particular ancestor, scandal, building, or site relevant to your family. Old photographs, death certificates, letters and wills, anniversary lists in family Bibles, and keepsakes can be great clues. You can visit gravesites, work places, or homes of your ancestors to check out the vibes as you mentally and emotionally empathize with specific aspects of your family's history such as a fatal event that befell an ancestor.

Almost every family has a departed member who died at an early age, suffered hardships or emotional anguish, or passed away suddenly due to an accident or natural disaster. Once you have focused your research on a deceased person, you need to determine if that person remains on this earthly plane as a ghost. Evaluate the individual's personal history to see if he had a reason to remain attached to a specific place.

Was his death violent or under tragic circumstances?

Did he die at a young age with unfinished business?

Did the deceased leave behind loved ones who needed his support and protection?

Was this person attached to a specific site or building?

Would the individual be inclined to seek revenge against those responsible for his death?

Would his devotion and sense of loyalty lead him to offer eternal companionship to loved ones?

Revenge, anger, refusal to recognize the reality of transformation by death, and other negative factors prompt many spirits to haunt places and people. However, most ghosts are motivated by positive factors. Spirits may remain at a site to offer protection to a loved one or a particular place.

Also, remember that your investigation of the paranormal may reveal phantom images—the residual essence of a structure that no longer exists on the physical plane—such as ships, buildings, covered wagons, bridges, and roads. Many people have seen houses, cottages, castles, villages, and large ships that were destroyed or sunk years before.

BASIC PREPARATION FOR GHOST HUNTING

If you decide to ghost hunt at night or on a special anniversary, make a trip to the site a few days ahead of time. During daylight hours, familiarize yourself with the place and its surroundings. Note hazards such as broken glass, loose floor boards, barbed wire, or unsafe structures. If possible, tag these with light-reflecting tape so you can recognize them during a nighttime visit. Many historical sites are closed after sunset or crowded at certain times by organized tours.

TWO BASIC METHODS FOR FINDING GHOSTS

Based partly on the kind of paranormal activity reported at a site, the ghost hunter must decide which method or approach will be used. Some will feel competent with a collection of cameras, electromagnetic field detectors, digital thermometers, computers, data recorders, and other high-tech gadgets. These ghost hunters prefer to use the Technical Method. Others may discover they have an emotional affinity for a particular historic site, a surprising fascination with an event associated with a haunting, or empathy for a deceased person. These ghost hunters may have success with the Psychic Method. Another consideration is the ghost hunter's goal. Some desire scientific evidence of ghostly presence while others simply want to experience paranormal activity.

THE TECHNICAL METHOD

Professional and advanced amateur ghost hunters often use an array of detection and recording devices that cover a wide range of the electromagnetic spectrum. This approach can be complicated, expensive, and require technically skilled people to operate the devices. Ghost hunters who want to keep their investigations simple may get satisfying results with common audio and video recording devices and other low-tech methods.

EQUIPMENT PREPARATION

A few days before your ghost hunt, purchase fresh film for your camera and tape for audio recording devices or clear the media of previous recordings. Test your batteries and bring new backup batteries and freshly charged power packs to the investigation site. You should have two types of flashlights: a broad-beam light for moving around a site and a penlight-type flashlight for narrow-field illumination while you make notes or adjust equipment. A red lens will help you avoid disruption of your night-adapted vision. A candle is a good way to light the site in a way that is least offensive to a ghost.

STILL-PHOTOGRAPHY TECHNIQUES

Many photographic techniques that work well under normal conditions are inadequate for ghost hunts. That's because ghost hunting is usually conducted under conditions of low ambient light. This requires the use of long exposures. Some investigators use a strobe or flash device but these can make the photos look unauthentic or create artifacts.

If you use film-based photography, practice taking photos with films of various light sensitivities before you go on your ghost hunt. Standard photographic films of high light sensitivity should be used— ASA of 800 or higher is recommended. At a dark or nearly dark location, mount the camera on a tripod. Try several exposure settings, from one to 30 seconds, and aperture settings under various low-light conditions. Your equipment should include a stable, light-weight tripod. Hand-held cameras may produce poorly focused photographs when the exposure duration is greater than ⅟₆₀ of a second.

Make notes about the camera settings that work best under various light conditions. Avoid aiming the camera at a scene where there is a bright light such as a street lamp or exit sign over a doorway. These light sources may "overflow" throughout your photograph.

Some professional and advanced amateur ghost hunters use infrared film. You should consult a professional photo lab technician about this type of film and its associated photographic techniques. Infrared photography can reveal yield some amazing pictures of spirits not detected by other means. It has been theorized that spiritual entities exist at a frequency that lies below that of the visual spectrum of humans. By using a camera filter that blocks out visible light while admitting infrared light, images of ghosts may be obtained. Infrared film has become scarce, and expensive, since 2007 when manufacturers such as Kodak encountered a significant decline in the demand for the product. However, digital cameras are inherently sensitive to infrared light, and minor adjustments allow users to take pictures that may reveal entities that would not be seen with conventional photographic techniques. In some digital cameras, these adjustments are quite easy, requiring nothing more than selecting a "night vision" mode.

Ghost hunters have also used Polaroid-type cameras with interesting results. The rapid film developing system used by these cameras gives almost instant feedback about your technique and/or success in documenting ghost activities. Ghosts have reportedly written messages on Polaroid film.

If you use digital photographic methods, practice taking pictures under conditions of low ambient light, with and without artificial lighting. Most digital cameras have default automatic settings that might not well work during a ghost investigation. These settings may not be easily changed as ambient conditions change at the haunted site unless you have practiced the procedures. Many cameras have features that enable automatic exposures at specific intervals, e.g., once every minute. This allows a hands-off remote photograph record to be made. Repetitive automatic exposures also allow a site to be investigated without the presence of the investigator.

While every ghost hunter armed with a camera wishes to capture the full-bodied image of a ghost, most have to settle for light anomalies. These may be amorphous, luminescent clouds, narrow streaks of light resembling a shooting star. The light anomaly most frequently captured on film and in digital images is the orb. An orb is a symmetrical white disk that appears most often in photographic and digital images made under low-light conditions. It may appear hovering near a ceiling, over a bed, or inside a car. A photograph may contain a single orb or show so many of varying sizes that they cannot be counted. Impressive pictures of light anomalies may be viewed at several Web sites.

Many ghost hunters claim that orbs are spirit manifestations without explaining why the spirit of a human would appear as a disk of light. Some of these have a humanoid shape but fail to convince critics and skeptics that the image is that of a ghost because the image is so perfectly illuminated that it appears fake. Software for processing digital images has reduced the power of proof that was once attributed to photographs. Critics and skeptics point out that orbs may be the result of bugs, dust particles, or water droplets suspended in the air close to the lens or inside the camera. Excited ghost hunters have displayed pictures of light anomalies that turn out to be the result of wisps of hair, a camera strap, a finger, cigarette smoke, light reflected from jewelry, or smudges on the lens.

It is interesting to note that orbs were virtually unheard of in the field of paranormal investigation until digital cameras became available. Consequently, many people suspect that orbs may be the result of operating characteristics of the camera. Under conditions of low light, pixels of a digital camera may not fill in completely. This has been called under-pixelation. As a result, no image information or electronic signal is generated. The lack of a signal is detected by the camera's software which then fills in the missing spot in the picture's signal array with white light. The result is an orb.

Is it possible that a spirit will manifest as an orb? Yes, although many experts suggest that as many as 99 percent of orb pictures do not represent anything paranormal. I've seen some very impressive orbs, however. Ghost hunter Jackie Ganiy, president of Sonoma SPIRIT, captured a picture of an orb hovering over the flight deck of the aircraft carrier USS *Hornet* in Alameda, CA. This orb was symmetrically rounded but a skull was visible within it. Books by Melvyn Willin and Troy Taylor present fascinating collections of the best pictures of ghosts and other paranormal light anomalies, including orbs.

Generally, light anomalies should not be readily accepted as evidence of spirit manifestation unless there is corroborating evidence from other technical devices. This includes audio phenomena, changes in electromagnetic field, isolated changes in air temperature, or other still or video images. Evidence might also be found in psychic impressions experience at the time and place that the orb picture was created. Psychic impressions of intense emotions, sobbing, and cries for help, or screaming might be obtained while standing in an old hospital room as a photographer captures a picture of an orb hovering over the bed.

AUDIO RECORDING TECHNIQUES

Tape or digital recorders provide an inexpensive way to obtain audio evidence of ghostly activity. The popular term for this is *Electronic Voice Phenomena* or EVP. The American Association for EVP defines the process as any intelligible voice detected on recording media that has no known explanation. Most ghost hunters accept a wider definition which includes the sound of moving objects, such as doors, windows, or glass objects, whistling, sobbing, laughter, screams, humming, gun shots, footsteps, explosions, musical notes, or tapping and knocking. Given this wide variety of sounds, I've proposed that the term EVP be replaced by EAP, *Electronic Audio Phenomena* and defined as any audio recording that cannot be attributed to normal phenomena.

EAP are obtained as a ghost hunter operates an audio recording device while investigating an allegedly haunted place. The ghost hunter may record an EAP while remaining stationary at a site, such as next to a grave, or while walking around. This is called an EAP or EVP sweep. Generally, questions are asked to which spirits may respond. These questions should be simple and follow an invitation for any spirit to communicate, even if only by a non-vocal sound. Typical questions include the following:

"What is your name?"

"Did you die here?"

"How old are you?"

"Do you want me to leave?"

"Why are you here?"

Your research may indicate specific questions you can use in your EAP investigations. If you seek a ghost of a farm worker who committed suicide by hanging himself in a barn, you may ask, "Did you die in this barn?" And, "Did you hang yourself?" The ghost hunter may also provoke a spirit through verbal confrontation or insult.

In most cases, spirit responses cannot be heard by the ghost hunter but they may be discovered on the audio recording during playback. Typically, responses are brief, rarely lasting more than a few seconds. Vocalizations sometimes have amazing clarity but most often they are unintelligible and, as with other sounds, rarely repeated in subsequent recordings. If the spirit's response comprises a clear and reasonable answer to the question, the recording may be called a "specific" EAP. Other responses, whether they are vocalizations or other sounds, must be labeled "random" EAP and scrutinized as the result of processes that are not paranormal. For example, the sound of a conversation between two living people may be carried a long distance across a body of water. A ghost hunter who is unaware of others in the area may ask, "What is your name?" The response discovered during playback may be "I am cold." This may be a random EAP or a non-paranormal recording of words spoken by a living person. Random EAP may be created by natural or normal processes, such as the wind against a window or drafts in an old house, and there is high likelihood that they do not reflect a spirit's intelligent interaction with the investigator. Specific EAP has greater value as evidence of ghostly presence because clear and reasonable responses to specific questions are not likely to be created by random conversations among living people nearby or natural processes.

Often, EAP consists of non-vocal sounds. Musical instruments, slamming doors, gun shots, footsteps, and tapping sounds may be evoked by the ghost hunter's questions. Ghosts that are unable to generate vocalizations may resort to these sounds as the only means of communication. These may be random EAP but still comprise good evidence of a ghostly presence. You may ask, "Why are you here?" On playback, the recording may reveal the sound of footsteps moving away from the microphone. In this instance, the ghost may have been troubled by the question and decided to leave.

While EAP are seldom heard through the human auditory sense, they may be captured on recording media by one of two ways. Spirits may encode their intention or effort to create sound telepathically onto the magnetic tape or electronics of the recording device by manipulation of its internal electromagnetic fields. Or, a vocalization, musical note, or other sound that was previously imprinted on the electromagnetic field of the environment may be triggered to "play" by the ghost hunter and detected by the recording device. In the case of the latter, the EAP is typically random, suggesting no spirit is present, but the experience is still paranormal. Ghost hunters who have exceptional luck in acquiring paranormal audio recordings have been called "EVP magnets."

Before you begin your EAP sweep, test your recorder under conditions you expect to find at the investigation site in order to reduce audio artifact and ensure optimal performance of the device. Does your recorder pick up excessive background noise? This may obscure ghostly sounds. If so, consider upgrading the tape quality or select a high-quality digital audio recorder. Also, consider using a wind guard on the microphone.

Consider using two or more recorders at different locations within the site. This allows you to verify sounds such as wind against a window and reduce the possibility of ambiguous recordings or misinterpretation of an EAP.

Allow time, at least 15 to 60 seconds, for a response. EAP can be heard only during playback, so ghost hunters should review recordings every 5-10 minutes during the investigation rather than waiting until it is completed. This will enable the identification of hot spots for spirit activity that may be investigated more thoroughly.

You can use sound-activated recorders at a site overnight. They will automatically switch on whenever a sound occurs above a minimum threshold. Be aware that tape recorders may yield recordings that start with an annoying artifact, the result of a slow tape speed, at the beginning of each recorded segment. The slow tape speed could obscure the sounds made by a ghost.

Remote microphones and monitor earphones allow you to remain some distance from the site and activate the recorder when ghostly sounds are heard. If this equipment is not available, use long-play modes (60-90 minutes or more), turn the recorder on, and let it run throughout your investigation, whether you remain stationary or walk about the site.

Wear a lapel microphone connected to a small audio recorder carried in your pocket. Operated in the sound-activation mode, this device will also provide you with a means of making audio notes rather than written notes. A headset with a microphone is especially useful with this technique.

Ghost hunters must carefully analyze their audio recordings, and the environment in which they are obtained, to be certain they are not inadvertent recordings of natural or normal sounds. Sound may carry great distances, particularly over bodies of water and when there is fog or low overcast. If a tape recorder is used, a new tape may reduce the chances of artifact. I recommend computer software such as Adobe Audition for editing your EAP recording. With a little practice, you will be able to suppress or eliminate extraneous sounds while enhancing spirit communications.

The American Association for EVP maintains a website for general information and advice: www.AA-EVP.com. Several websites may be accessed to hear examples of EVP. Use a search engine aimed at "EVP" to locate them.

VIDEO RECORDING

Video recorders offer a wide variety of recording features from time-lapse to auto-start/stop, and auto focus. These features enable you to make surveillance-type recordings over many hours while you are off-site. Consult your user's manual for low-light recording guidelines and always use a tripod and long-duration battery packs.

If you plan to attempt video recording, consider using two recorders, at equal distance from a specific object such as a chair. Arrange the recorders at different angles, preferably 90 degrees from each other.

Another approach you might try is to use a wide-angle setting on the first camera to get a broad view of a room, porch, or courtyard. On the second camera, use a close-up setting to capture ghostly apparitions at a door, chair, or window.

You may have more success with sequential, manual, or timer-actuated recordings than with a continuous-run technique. If you try this technique, use recording runs of one to five minutes. Practice using the method that interrupts the automatic setting should you need to manually control the recording process. Always use a tripod that can be moved to a new location in a hurry.

HIGH-TECH EQUIPMENT

You can buy devices such as electromagnetic field detectors, infrared thermometers, barometers, and motion detectors at your local electronics store or over the Internet. Good sources for high-tech ghost hunting equipment are the Society for Paranormal Investigation, the Ghost Hunter Store, and the EMF Safety Superstore.

Inexpensive, battery-operated motion detectors can be placed at several locations within an investigation site. Some of these allow users to select an audio signal or a silent flashing light signal and connect the output to a central monitor. These devices work by measuring optical or acoustical changes in the environment. Therefore, they are most reliable when remote surveillance is performed and investigators are certain that no living beings have entered the site.

Infrared thermometers have been used to search for cold spots that may signal the presence of a ghost. While these devices are widely used and sometimes displayed on paranormal TV shows, they are often used incorrectly. They cannot be used to assess changes in the temperature of an air mass because of its very low density and minimal emission of IR energy. Infrared thermometers may be used to detect the surface temperature of solid objects, liquids, dense gases, and clouds. With a laser to assist aiming, the device can be used to measure the temperature of objects that cannot be reached due to obstructions, such as fences, and hazards, such as bodies of water that cannot be crossed, unsafe structures, or animals.

Night-vision goggles can be useful in low-light situations. These devices enhance the intensity of light within the visual spectrum and augment the resulting image with non-visual sources of electromagnetic radiation such as near-infrared or ultraviolet light. Night-vision devices enable users to see doors and other objects move that you might not otherwise see. The resulting scene appears monochromatic but preserves fine details.

The most advanced and expensive piece of equipment used by ghost hunters is the FLIR imaging device. This acronym stands for *forward-looking infra red.* FLIRs detect thermal energy in the infrared range. The FLIR lens focuses the scene on a vast array of sensors that produce thousands of simultaneous measurements of thermal energy. Software then assembles the thermal measurements into a mosaic or picture that is displayed on a hand-held video screen. In the picture, elements of the scene are colored according to the temperature or level of infrared radiation. The result resembles a coloring-book image in which some elements are blue, indicating colder temperatures, while others are yellow, orange, or red, indicating warmer temperatures.

FLIR systems can see through atmospheric obscurants, such as smoke or fog, and in total darkness. Ghost hunters use them to detect spirits that do not generate an image within the human visual spectrum. Theoretically, when spirits appear on our plane, they draw energy from the environment, creating a cold spot. A FLIR will detect subtle changes in temperature and depict the shape of the cold spot on the video screen. When the shape of the cold spot is humanoid, ghost hunters claim they have evidence that a ghost is present.

Despite the technical sophistication and expense of FLIRs, the images they produce may be misinterpreted. FLIRs may detect sources of heat or cold created by normal processes not noticed by the user. A living being who occupied the scene moments before a FLIR-equipped ghost hunter arrived may leave residual heat in a chair or on a door knob. Finding the scene unoccupied by any living being, the ghost hunter might mistakenly cite the detected thermal anomaly as evidence of ghostly presence.

Electromagnetic field (EMF) detectors are used by paranormal investigators to detect the presence of ghosts in spite of the lack of scientific evidence that EMF and spirit presence are linked. Ghost hunters who use EMF detectors claim that spikes in a local electromagnetic field are created when a ghost transitions onto our plane of existence. These devices, however, often pick up EMF generated by unseen electrical appliances, faulty wiring in an old house, cell phones, walkie-talkies, video recorders, and numerous other sources including solar flares and geomagnetic storms. EMF detectors may be useful if proper controls are established and all possible sources of natural EMF are identified.

Electronic gadgets can be useful and fun, but unless you have a means of creating a record of the instrument's output or storing images or data in a computer, your reports of light anomalies, apparent paranormal motion of objects, changes in the physical characteristics of the environment, or apparitions will not constitute the kind of hard evidence you need to satisfy skeptics. Keep in mind that even expensive instruments may produce erroneous data or signals if they are incorrectly calibrated, misused, or improperly maintained. Also, data can be easily misinterpreted if the user does not understand the technical or operating limitations of the device. The use of expensive high-tech gadgets does not guarantee accurate results nor does it validate a ghost hunt as scientific investigation.

LOW-TECH DEVICES

I've had great success in detecting spirit activity with common household items that comprise a low-tech method of investigating the paranormal. Ghosts often become active when they are irritated by changes in their favored environment. If you tilt a picture hanging on the wall, leave an object in the ghost's rocking chair, or leave a book open, a ghost may straighten the picture, remove the object from his chair, or close the book.

Spirits may be attracted to objects they can manipulate easily. Leave four aces at the top of a deck of cards. A ghost may shuffle them throughout the deck. Ghosts are often attracted to water. A glass left full may later be found empty and the contents wetting the floor. A paper and pencil may be used by a ghost to leave bizarre marks or a legible message. Leave two stacks of coins—ten pennies in each stack—on a stable surface and leave the room for an extended period of time. When you return, the coins may be scattered. If both stacks are scattered, a gust of wind or vibration of the building may account for the change. If one stack remains untouched while the other is scattered, that may be the work of a ghost. I used this technique at the Myrtles Plantation in St. Francisville, Louisiana. I found ten pennies rearranged in a circle around the other stack of coins, which remained standing.

OTHER EQUIPMENT

Various authorities in the field of ghost hunting suggest the following items to help you mark sites, detect paranormal phenomena, and collect evidence of ghostly activity.

White and colored chalk
Compass
Stop watch
Steel tape measure
Magnifying glass
First-aid kit
Thermometer
Metal detector
Graph paper for diagrams
Small mirror

Small bell
Plastic bags for collecting
    evidence
Light-reflecting tape
Matches
Tape for sealing doors
String
A Cross
A Bible
Cell phone

THE PSYCHIC METHOD

The Psychic Method relies upon your intuition, inner vision, or emotional connection with a deceased person, object, place, or point of time in history. You don't have to be a trained psychic to use this approach. All of us have some capacity to tap into unseen dimensions and use some of the psychic tools described in the parapsychology literature and popular books by authors such as Sylvia Browne and Jane Roberts. Your ability to use psychic tools for successful ghost hunting depends upon three factors: your innate ability, receptivity, and sensitivity.

You may have an ability to successfully use psychic tools in a ghost hunt if you are one of those people who can readily identify isolated places within a room that give that chilling feeling that there is something bizarre or paranormal about the spot. The ability to identify these places must include a capacity to sort out your impressions, clear your mind of extraneous thoughts and distractions, and focus your attention on the particular point from which a paranormal impression emanates.

You may have sufficient receptivity to effectively use psychic tools if you feel more intensely connected to a place or past era than others, or often feel mentally transported to another era. Do you often get that curious feeling that some unseen person is standing behind you, watching you, or touching you? When you touch an artifact, such as a weapon, do you get the impression that you have become aware of information about the object or its user? If so, you are receptive to unseen dimensions and likely to have success hunting ghosts with psychic tools. Highly receptive people often visit a place for the first time yet feel they have been there before. This is called ESP, or extrasensory perception, and reflects a high degree of receptivity.

Your receptivity can provide considerable focus to your ghost hunt if you first obtain information about the key elements and historical context of the entity's death. This includes architectural elements of a home, theatre, airplane or ship, and objects such as furniture, clothing, weapons, or any implement or artifact of the specific time period of the entity's death. Touching or handling pertinent artifacts, sitting in the deceased person's chair, or standing within the historic site will enable you to get in touch with the historical moment that is most pertinent to the ghost.

You may have exceptional sensitivity if you get vivid impressions of emotions in specific locations within allegedly haunted places. Do you walk into a historic building and get that eerie feeling that something or someone from the past still lingers there? Do you get a sense of fear, anger, pain, or suffering when you visit historic places or places known to be haunted? If so, you may be sensitive to residual energies from past events, emotions that played out in a particular place or the actions of people who have been gone from the scene for decades. Sensitive people often detect a distant time, or a voice, sound, touch, or texture of another dimension often described as a change in atmosphere.

Your sensitivity will pay off in a ghost hunt if your investigation is aimed at strong paranormal imprints or attachments of spirits. Strong imprints and attachments are indicated by the frequency, duration, and consistency of the paranormal event reported to occur at a particular place. The strongest imprints are created by intense emotions such as fear, rage, jealously, revenge, or loss, especially if they were repetitive over long periods of time prior to death. Strong attachments are created by love for a person, a place, or an object, or they are created by a sense of obligation to provide guidance and protection. Biographical research may reveal this kind of information, particularly if personal letters or diaries are examined. Old newspaper articles, suicide notes, and photographs are useful too.

You may enhance your sensitivity by developing and expressing empathy for the ghost's lingering presence at a haunted site. Empathy can be based on your research which may reveal information about the entity's personal history and probable emotions, motivations, problems, or unfinished business at the time of death. You may also learn that a ghost may be trapped, confused, or have chosen to remain at a site to protect someone or guard something precious. Historical sources like newspaper articles and obituaries, old photographs, or biographies can help you discern the motivations behind a ghost's reluctance to move on. Useful, intimate details might be found in letters, suicide notes, diaries, and wills, too.

Your sensitivity to ghostly environmental imprints and spirit manifestations may also be increased by meditation, the relaxing of one's physical body to eliminate distracting thoughts and tensions and to achieve emotional focus. Meditation allows you to focus your spiritual awareness on a single subject—a place, entity, or historic moment in time. As the subject comes into focus, you can add information obtained from your research such as the type of device used for a suicide or murder, a favored book, a musical instrument, etc. Through this process, you will become aware of unseen dimensions of the world around you, creating a feeling that you have moved through time to a distant era. Meditation gets you in touch with the place, date, and time pertinent to a ghost's imprint or death. It also enables you to disregard personal concerns and distracting thoughts that may interfere with your concentration on the ghost you seek.

Keep in mind that it is possible to be in a meditative state while appearing quite normal. The process is simple and easy to learn. When you arrive at the site of your ghost hunt, find a place a short distance away to meditate. Three essentials for any effective meditation are comfort, quiet, and concentration.

Comfort: Sit or stand in a relaxed position. Take free and even breaths at a slow rate. Do not alter your breathing pattern so much that you feel short of breath, winded, or lightheaded. Close your eyes if that enhances your comfort, or focus on a candle, a tree, or a flower. Do not fall asleep. Proper meditation creates relaxation without decreasing alertness.

Quiet: Meditate in a place away from noises generated by traffic, passersby, radios, slammed doors, and the like. If you are with a group, give each other sufficient personal space. Some people use mantras, repetitive words or phrases, or speak only in their mind in order to facilitate inner calmness. Mantras are useful to induce a focused state of relaxation, but they may disrupt the meditation of a companion if spoken aloud. A majority of ghost hunters do not believe that mantras are necessary in this instance. They point out that ghost hunting is not like a séance as depicted in old movies. It is not necessary to chant special words, call out to the dead, or invite an appearance "from beyond the grave."

Concentration: First, clear your mind of everyday thoughts, worries, and concerns. This is the most difficult part of the process. Many of us don't want to let go of our stressful thoughts. To help you let go of those thoughts, let the thought turn off its light and fade into darkness. After you clear your mind, some thoughts may reappear. Repeat the process. Slowly turn off the light of each thought until you can rest with a completely cleared mind. This might take some practice. Don't wait until you are on the scene of a ghost hunt before you practice this exercise.

Once your mind is clear, focus on your breathing and imagine your entire being as a single point of energy driving the breathing process. Then, open yourself. Think only of the entity you seek. Starting with the ghost's identity (if known), slowly expand your focus to include its personal history, the historical era of the ghost's death or creation of the emotional imprint, the reported nature and appearance of the haunting, and any specific ghostly activity.

Acknowledge each thought as you continue relaxed breathing. Find a thought that is most attractive to you, and then expand your mind to include your present surroundings. Return slowly to your current place and time. Remain quiet for a minute or two before you resume communication with your companions, and then move ahead with the ghost hunt.

PSYCHIC TOOLS

Clairaudience: Impression of sounds generated by paranormal sources may be perceived through clairaudience. The term is derived from the French, meaning "clear hearing." People with this ability may hear the voices of spirits who are trying to communicate, or sounds of events that occurred years or decades earlier. The latter are environmental imprints most often created by intense repetitive emotions or events that had a strong emotional component.

Clairsentience: Some ghosts manifest by creating impressions of physical sensations in receptive people that may include a feeling of being touched and perception of fragrances or odors. The ability to perceive or detect impressions of physical sensations that do not truly exist in real time is called clairsentience. Signature perfumes or the fragrance of favorite flowers can help you identify a ghost. At the world-renowned haunted Myrtles Plantation in Louisiana, the ghost of Sara Woodruff creates the fragrance of her favorite flower, the magnolia. Odors such as cigars, oranges, and hemp are common ghostly manifestations. Sometimes, ghost hunters encounter the noxious odors of rotting meat or burning flesh.

Clairvoyance: Information or impressions may be received from objects or spirits at the present time without the use of "normal" senses. The process is called clairvoyance and usually refers to visual impressions. People who see ghosts are clairvoyant whether the image is life-like or merely a human-shaped fragment of a shadow. Visual information or impressions may include orbs, amorphous clouds, or objects. Since clairvoyance is limited to "real time" events, any visual experience suggests a ghost is present at the moment.

Retrocognition: Perception of visual impressions of events or places from the past is a form of clairvoyance called retrocognition. Psychic Derek Acorah dramatically portrayed his retrocognition ability during ghost investigations in the popular TV show *Most Haunted*. If you watched my TV show *Ghosts of the Queen Mary*, you've seen me perform retrocognition. The most famous case of retrocognition was reported by two teachers, Charlotte Moberly and Eleanor Jourdain, after they visited the Petit Trianon at the Palace of Versailles in France in 1901. Known as the Moberly-Jourdain Incident, the women reportedly witnessed people dressed in seventeenth-century clothing and structures that no longer existed. Their detailed descriptions of the experience, published in their 1911 book, *An Adventure*, matched obscure historical records suggesting the retro-cognitive experience was genuine. Detailed accounts of the Moberly-Jourdain incident can be found online.

Psychometry: Information about an object or one of its users may be obtained by psychically gifted or skilled people through psychometry. First described in 1842 by Joseph R. Buchanan, the process has been used in séances, ghost hunts, and crime-scene investigations. After a few minutes of handling an object, practitioners of psychometry get visual impressions or become aware of information that cannot be the result of logical inference (piecing things together from clues you might have). Ghost hunters can use psychometry to gain information about a spirit's affinity for a chair or a book, or why it moves a particular glass or key. Any object that has reportedly been moved by a ghost should be examined by psychometry. Investigators may get clues about the identity of the ghost or reasons for its haunting activity.

Retrieval of information by psychometry may be possible because of changes in an object's electromagnetic field (EMF) created by users. Repetitive handling of an object by its owner may alter its EMF and leave durable traces of the user's energy, much like a fingerprint, especially if intense emotions were associated with frequent use. A good example is my Civil War cavalry saber that was used in several battles. Psychometrists who handle the saber become aware of fear, rage, and remorse, and perceive the image of a middle-aged Union Army officer.

GROUP ORGANIZATION AND PREPARATION

It is not necessary to believe in spirits or paranormal phenomena in order to see a ghost or experience haunting activities. Indeed, most reports of ghost activities are made by unsuspecting people who never gave the matter much thought. But you should not include people in your group who openly express negative attitudes about these things. If you include skeptics, be sure they agree to maintain an open mind and participate in a positive group attitude.

Keep your group small, limited to four members if possible. Ghosts have been seen by large groups of people but small groups are more easily managed and likely to be of one mind in terms of objectives and methods.

Meet an hour or more prior to starting the ghost hunt at a location away from the site. Review the history of the ghost you seek and the previous reports of ghost activity at the site. Discuss the group's expectations based on known or suspected ghostly activity or specific research goals. Review any available reports of audio phenomena, still or video images, and visual apparitions and decide what methods would be optimal for recording these phenomena during your investigation.

Most importantly, agree to a plan of action if a sighting is made by any member of the group. The first priority for a ghost hunter is to maintain visual or auditory contact without a lot of activity such as making notes. Without breaking contact, do the following: activate recording devices; redirect audio, video, or photographic equipment to focus on the ghost; move yourself to the most advantageous position for listening or viewing the ghostly activity; attract the attention of group members with a code-word, hand signal (for example, touch the top of your head), or any action that signals other hunters so they can pick up your focus of attention.

Should you attempt to interact with the ghost? Do so only if the ghost invites you to speak or move. Often, a ghost hunter's movement or noise frightens the ghost or interferes with the perception of the apparition.

SEARCHING FOR GHOSTS

There are no strict rules or guidelines for successful ghost hunting except *be patient!* Professional ghost hunters sometimes conduct investigations over a period of several days, weeks, even months before achieving contact with a ghost. Others have observed full-body apparitions when they least expected it, while concentrating fully on some other activity. Regardless of the depth of your research or preparation, you need to be patient. The serious ghost hunter will anticipate that several trips to a haunted site may be required before some sign of ghostly activity is observed.

If you are ghost hunting with others, it may be advantageous to station members of your group at various places in the ghost's haunting grounds and use a reliable system to alert others to spirit activity.

In the event that even one member sights a ghost or experiences some evidence of ghostly activity, confirmation by a second person is important in establishing validity and credibility. In the previous section, a hand signal (hand to the top of the head) was recommended as a means of informing others that they should direct their eyes and ears to a site indicated by the person in contact with a ghost. Because of this, all ghost hunters need to keep their companions in sight at all times and be aware of hand signals.

An audio signal can often reduce the need for monitoring other ghost hunters for hand signals. Equally important for a group is to establish a method for calling other hunters who may be some distance away, as when each member patrols a different portion of the site. Tugging on a length of string can be an effective signal if ghost hunters are stationary. So can mechanical devices called "crickets" and flashes from a penlight, i.e., one flash for a cold spot and two flashes for an apparition. Hand-held radios, or walkie-talkies, can also be effective. Some models can send an audio signal or activate flashing lights. Cell phones can be used but the electromagnetic activity may be uninviting to your ghost.

Remaining stationary within a room, gravesite, courtyard, or other confirmed location is often most productive. If a ghost is known to have a favorite chair, bed, or other place within a room, he will appear. Under these conditions, the patient ghost hunter will have a successful hunt. If your ghost is not known to appear at a specific place within a room or at an outdoors area, position yourself to gain the broadest view of the site. A corner of a room is optimal because it allows the ghost unobstructed motion about the place while avoiding the impression of a trap set by uninvited people who occupy his favorite space. If you are outdoors at a gravesite, for instance, position yourself at the base of a tree or in the shadows of a monument to conceal your presence while affording a view of your ghost's grave. If your ghost is a mobile spirit, moving throughout a house, over a bridge, or about a courtyard or graveyard, you may have no choice but to move around the area. Search for a place where you feel a change in the thickness of the air, or a cold spot, or a peculiar odor.

Once you are on site, the above-described meditation may help you focus and maintain empathy for your ghost and enable you to effectively use psychic methods of investigation. Investigate sounds, even common sounds, as the ghost attempts to communicate with you. Make mental notes of the room temperature, air movement, and the sensations of abrupt change in atmosphere as you move about the site. Changes in these factors may indicate the presence of a ghost. Pay attention to your own sensations or perceptions, such as the odd feeling that someone is watching you, standing close by, or touching you. Your ghost may be hunting you!

WHAT TO DO WITH A GHOST

On occasion, professional ghost hunters make contact with a ghost by entering a trance and establishing two-way communications. The ghost hunter's companions hear him or her speak but the ghost's voice can only be heard by the trance communicator. Sylvia Browne's book *Adventures of a Psychic* describes several of these trance communication sessions. Most ghost encounters are brief with little opportunity to engage the entity in conversation. But the ghost may make gestures or acknowledge your presence through eye contact, a touch on the shoulder, sound, or a movement of an object. The ghost hunter must decide whether or not to follow the gestures or direction of a ghost.

Visitors to the Bay Area's historic ships, graveyards, theaters, mansions, or inns feel the touch or tug of a ghost on their arm or shoulder. Spirits of deceased sailors, miners, victims of disasters, or outlaws may be trying to get living souls to notice them, move out of their way, or follow them to some important destination.

Ghosts at Antioch's Rose Hill Cemetery have been so active that more than 100 exorcisms have been performed in an effort to rid visitors of tenacious spirits. Many who have visited this place have run from the old cemetery, frightened by images of miners crushed in cave-ins and a famous spirit known as the white witch. In contrast, a kindly ghost at Mission Dolores cemetery in San Francisco sings to visitors in Spanish. At Oakland's Evergreen Cemetery, spirits that hover near a mass grave of Jonestown victims generate a profound sense of sadness in sensitive visitors.

Phantom sailors aboard the WWII aircraft carrier USS *Hornet,* in Alameda, have been spotted in the chapel, sick bay, the hangar deck, and the captain's bridge, forward anchor chain locker, and the engine room. Some of them beckon to visitors as if they expect startled ghost hunters to lend a hand in running the ship. At San Francisco's Maritime Park, a suicidal woman runs the length of the ferryboat *Eureka* before disappearing. Nearby, crew members of the 1880s square-rigged *Balclutha* generate intense cold spots at places where fatal accidents occurred.

In Clayton, Emeryville, Fairfield, and Fremont, the ghosts of Indian chiefs and shamans have appeared in shopping centers, private homes, parks, vineyards, and inns that stand on Native American burial grounds. The menacing appearance of these tall spirits—sometimes dressed in colorful robes—has left some observers stunned and others scared out of their wits, but there are no reports of physical or psychological injury.

At the several hotels in San Francisco—including the Palace, York, St. Francis, and Queen Anne—guests come face to face with luminaries of the city's fabled past and sometimes feel caught up in wild parties, clandestine meetings, or criminal acts. On Alcatraz Island, the negative energy of former inmates is too much for some visitors. Many cannot enter some of the prison cells, the prison's hospital, or tolerate even a short visit to the guard stations of cell block D. Disembodied screams, running footsteps, the crashing sound of heavy doors slamming shut, and intense sensations of rage have caused some anxious visitors to leave the tour and head for the dock.

The idea of a close experience with a ghost is frightening to most of us. More often, the ghost's activities are directed at getting the intruder to leave a room, house, or a ship. If you sense your ghost wants you to leave, most hunters believe it is best not to push your luck. When you have established the nature of the ghost activity, ascertained that your companions have experienced the activity, taken a few photographs and run your audio recorder for a few minutes, it may be time to leave. An experience with an unfriendly ghost can be disturbing.

Residents of haunted houses and employees of haunted business establishments often accept a ghost's telekinetic or audio activities without concern. It is part of the charm of a place and may add some fun to working in a spooky building.

AFTER THE GHOST HUNT

Turn off all recorders and remove them to a safe place. Some ghost hunters suspect that ghosts can erase tapes and other recording media. Label your tapes and disks with the date, time, and location. Use a code number for each media. Keep a separate record of where the recording was made, date, time, and contents. Place recording media in a waterproof bag with your name, address, telephone number, and a note that guarantees postage in case it is misplaced. Have photographic film developed at a professional color laboratory. Professionals at the lab may help you with special processing. Have copies made of the negatives that contain ghostly images.

All members of the group should meet right after the investigation, away from the site, for debriefing. Each investigator who witnessed ghostly activity or an apparition should make a written or audio statement describing the experience. The form presented in Appendix A should be completed by the group leader. Video and audio recordings made at the site should be reviewed and reconciled with witness statements. Then, plans should be made for a follow-up visit in the near future to the site to confirm the apparition, its nature and form, and the impressions of the initial ghost hunt.

Data about the ghost's location within a site may indicate the optimal conditions for future contact. Things to be aware of include the time of day or night, day of the week, the phase of the moon, the season, and the degree and size of cold spots, as well as the form and density of the apparition. Patience and detailed records can help you to achieve the greatest reward for a ghost hunter, unmistakable proof of ghostly activity.

Chapter 2

North Bay Area

For years, the North Bay area has been known as the quiet part of the Bay Area. Much of the land in this region is devoted to agriculture, primarily wine grapes, and there are no large cities comparable to San Jose, Oakland, or San Francisco. The history of the region is enriched with preserved Spanish Missions, newly discovered Indian burial grounds and remnants of ancient villages, lonely stretches of country roads, secluded beaches, and several old wineries. The I-80 corridor, traversing the northeastern portion of the region, passes through historically significant towns such as Berkeley, Vallejo, and Fairfield. Highway 37 conveys traffic across the northern end of San Francisco Bay and connects with side-roads that lead to Petaluma, Sonoma, and the Napa Valley.

BENICIA ARSENAL CLOCK TOWER

2060 Camel Road
Benicia, CA 94510
707-745-5435
www.beniciahistoricalmuseum.org

Soon after the U.S. government took control of the 345 acres donated by Benicia's founders in 1849, the military importance of the promontory was recognized. Overlooking Carquinez Strait, the site offered high ground and commanding views of boat traffic on San Pablo Bay and the Sacramento River, the main water route to the gold fields and mines of the Sierra foothills. In 1849, construction projects included a barracks, hospital (still standing today), quartermaster's depot, and the arsenal. Designated one of five permanent arsenals in the U.S. in 1852, an ordnance supply depot was established that included a once grand building that is known today as the "Clock Tower."

The crowning achievement of military construction at the arsenal was a massive building known as the fortress. Constructed of locally quarried sandstone, chisel marks of the stone masons are clearly visible all around the building. Arsenal commander Franklin Callender specified that the building should have a tower at each corner to repel attack by foreigners or citizens, but only two towers were completed, one at each end of the building. In 1912, the fortress contained supplies for an army of 30,000 soldiers that included 15 million rounds of ammunition, 34,000 rifles, thousands of small arms, boots, uniforms, and blankets. In April of 1912, all of that was blown into the air by a massive explosion.

It is suspected that an accident while filling shells with black powder or a fire from faulty wiring caused an explosion that blew the building's slate roof and blocks of stone that composed the third floor hundreds of feet from the site. In addition, thousands of cartridges discharged, making any attempt at containing the fire extremely dangerous. When the flames were finally extinguished, the second and third floors lay in rubble on the ground floor, and the east tower was missing.

Within two years, reconstruction of the fortress was completed, but the third floor and the east tower were not rebuilt. The west tower was reconstructed with the addition of a huge clock, and by 1920, the old fortress was known as the clock tower. The huge building was still used to store and prepare munitions, especially during WWII and the Korean War.

Is the old fortress haunted? Most of the locals I spoke to believe that ghosts of soldiers killed in the 1912 explosion walk the second floor. Many people report hearing unexplained noises such as heavy crates being dragged across the floors, the clang of metal shell casings touching, hushed conversations in male voices, and marching boot-clad feet. There are reports of ghost children too. They create cold spots in which sensitives feel a playful energy. Some visitors have reported a malevolent spirit believed to be a soldier. He touches visitors making them feel that they should leave the building. It is likely that this spirit believes civilians should not be present inside a hazardous military facility.

While you are in the area, stop at the Benicia Arsenal Post Cemetery. Opened in 1849 at the end of Hospital Road, the graveyard contains 211 graves that hold the remains of soldiers, a few civilians who were residents at the arsenal, and prisoners of war held at the arsenal during WWII. Most of the wooden grave markers became so worn from wind, rain, and sunlight that the inscriptions were unreadable. When the graveyard was renovated, the old wooden markers were discarded and replaced with marble headstones engraved with the words "Unknown U.S. Soldier." Some restless spirits can be found at graveside. I suspect they are hoping to attract the attention of anyone who can restore the proper name to the grave. Ghost hunters who perform EAP sweeps in the graveyard should entice spirits to manifest by asking for the name they wish to be restored to the headstone.

In 1912, the third floor of this 1852-vintage stone arsenal was destroyed in a massive explosion that killed several soldiers.

THE REDHEADED GHOST

Captain Blyther's Restaurant
123 First Street
Benicia, CA 94510
707-745-4082

Paranormal research groups have visited this landmark restaurant on Benicia's historic First Street in their quest for the ghost of Captain Samuel Blythers. The history of the Blythers family suggests the patriarch or members of his family may haunt the place. In 1879, just a few weeks after the construction of the present building was completed, the captain died in one of the second floor rooms. Years later, his daughter, Julia, married Thomas McDermott in the house. Her husband may have left some environmental imprints of his agony in the place as he recovered from a traumatic amputation of his right leg caused by a railroad car passing over his limb. Blyther's wife, Annie, may have left imprints that sensitives detect as hauntings too. After Sam's death in 1879, she continued to live in the house as a widow, raising three children. She died in the kitchen in 1909.

Environmental imprints of the Blythers family or ghosts of Sam and Annie may be found in this popular restaurant, but staff members and patrons I spoke to believe the most active spirit in the place is that of a red-headed prostitute. After the death of the last Blyther, George, the building was sold and used as a boarding house for a short time before it became a brothel known as the Alamo Rooms. Its location at the foot of First Street, adjacent to the train station and the riverfront docks, made it a convenient location for the kind of men who would patronize such a business. During WWII, the place was one of eleven brothels in Benicia and business was profitable, allowing for renovation of the second floor into eight small rooms. The restaurant's manager told me that each room had a double bed, night stand, a small window, and hooks on the wall for hanging clothing. One room had a "mayor's closet" accessed through a concealed door. It provided the mayor and other town officials a hiding place during police raids in the 1950s.

In 1982, the brothel was gutted and converted to a restaurant.

Soon after the second floor was renovated as a bar, the apparition of a tall, slim, red-headed woman began to appear to staff members and customers. At first, this ghost showed up near closing time, leading most witnesses to dismiss the experience as the effects of fatigue and alcohol. But staff members working during the day noticed that objects were moved in inexplicable ways. Glass, ash trays, chairs, bar stools, and napkins were either lined up in orderly fashion or scattered, depending upon how staff members had left them. Some workers reported feeling as though someone stood close to them or touched them as they worked alone in the building.

Eventually the red-headed ghost appeared so frequently that staff named her Rebecca. Naturally, there is no record available of the brothel's employees or owner, but a psychic who visited the place in 2008, without prior knowledge of its history, told me that she detected the presence of a woman named Reba, a nickname of Rebecca. The

Named for Captain Blyther, this Benicia café harbors the ghost of a woman named Rebecca.

psychic also noted that Reba is happy with the place, especially because the customers are cleaner than her former patrons and she doesn't have to share a bed with them.

YOUNG GHOSTS OF THE OLD HOTEL

Union Hotel
401 First Street
Benicia, CA 94510
707-746-0110
www.unionhotelbenicia.com

The history of this Gold Rush-era hotel includes so many legendary characters, secret tunnels, and stories of bags of gold hidden in the walls that it would be a surprise if the place was not haunted. Constructed in 1854 on Benicia's main street, the Union Hotel provided feather beds and clean sheets to ragged miners who were en route from the gold fields to San Francisco with fortunes in gold dust and nuggets. After years of sleeping in tents, eating rotten food, and suffering from the hot summers and cold winters in the Sierra foothills, these newly rich characters felt as though the Union Hotel were heaven, offering luxuries they had only dreamt of while they panned and picked for gold. Aside from good food and comfortable beds, the hotel also offered strong drink, card games, and female companionship. The hotel also catered to politicians, land developers, card sharks, and con men that preyed upon the gullible miners. It is rumored that some of the miners hid their gold inside the walls of their rooms while they slept or ate their meals. Some of these poor fellows ran into thieves who dragged them into the alleys and shot them, leaving the gold undiscovered.

It is rumored that tunnels ran from the hotel to a nearby bank, enabling some miners to save their fortunes. Cave-ins and ambushes may have left some fellows buried under the streets of old Benicia while tying their spirits to the last place of comfort they knew when they were alive, the Union Hotel. These spirits may be responsible for the disembodied voices that are heard in the hallways late at night. At times, brief bursts of festive conversations fill the halls or elevators, startling guests. The sound gives the impression that a noisy group of people have opened a door and spilled the revelry of their party into the hallway, yet no open doors or living souls are seen.

Early in the morning, lights flicker on the second and third floors and musty odors are detected that have been described as stable straw, mud, and filthy clothing. During periods of renovation, the playful spirits of this old hotel have moved tools to distant locations and made workmen feel as though they were being watched.

The apparitions of two ghosts have been spotted in the hotel by staff members and guests. The transparent but fully formed image of a young man has been seen in the bar and dining room. He has been seen sitting in a chair and walking about in the foyer, giving witnesses the impression he is nervous. Dressed in a white shirt with string tie and a black coat, this fellow is believed to be connected to the female ghost that haunts the upper floors.

The female ghost appears to be in her twenties and is well-dressed, giving the impression that she is a guest of the hotel and not a staff member. This apparition has been seen in several rooms on the second floor and in the corridor. Legend says that she was heartbroken by a failed relationship and, in her grief, hung herself in a second-floor room. I could find no historical references that mention the suicide of a young woman, however.

Visitors to this hotel should keep an eye on doors and mirrors. Witnesses have reported door knobs that turn by invisible hands, doors that swing open and then close, and apparitions that appear in mirrors or are reflected in windows. Some astonished passersby have spotted the forlorn female ghost looking out a second-floor window to the street.

GHOSTS OF BENICIA'S FIRST STREET

First Street
Benicia, CA 94510-3210
707-745-2120 (Chamber of Commerce)

Conceived in 1846 by Robert Semple and Thomas Larkin, Benicia was founded in 1847, making it one of the oldest communities in the Bay Area. With the assistance of the last Mexican commandant of Alta California, General Mariano Vallejo, who provided land at a cheap price, Semple and Larkin turned a humble boatman's landing on the Sacramento River into an important town in little more than two years. These pre-Gold Rush entrepreneurs expressed their gratitude to Vallejo by naming the town after the general's wife, Francisca Benicia Carrillo de Vallejo. Eager to cash-in on wealthy miners returning from the Sierras in 1849, businessmen filled First Street with hotels, shops, bars, and brothels while commercial developers and politicians promoted the town as the economic hub of California Territory. Situated on the major waterway between the gold mines of the Sierras and the port of San Francisco, Benicia quickly became a town populated with wealthy and powerful people who believed the site was ideal for a capitol should California gain acceptance into the Union.

Even before statehood was granted, Benicia's status as a major economic power was greatly overshadowed by San Francisco and Sacramento. Benicia did achieve some political success, though, by serving as California's third state capitol for thirteen months from 1853 to 1854. The Greek Revival building that served as the new state's seat of government was constructed in ninety days of bricks and lumber salvaged from ships that had been abandoned in San Francisco Bay by crews who rushed to the gold fields. The building has been restored and is now open as a museum. The establishment of the U.S. army's arsenal at the eastern border of Benicia in 1849 added enormously to the local economy and status of the town. Some of the town's most interesting historic buildings were constructed for high-ranking officers and merchants who became wealthy by selling goods to the arsenal.

Ghosts of the old Capitol Building appear to be the members of the state legislature who met there between 1853 and 1854. Apparitions are often spotted in the second-floor meeting hall wearing long coats and high hats. These apparitions are most often nearly-transparent and partially formed, sometimes appearing only as a head and shoulders.

Witnesses have reported that the long coats worn by these ghostly politicians range from shiny black to dusty gray. Single entities may be seen sitting in one of the chairs, leaning against the side walls, or standing on the platform at the head of the room. As many as four entities have been spotted standing together against the east wall.

The main thoroughfare through old Benicia is First Street. Sloping downward from the Military Highway to the waterfront, Civil War-era buildings line both sides of First Street and many side streets. Still in use as shops, bars, and restaurants, many of these buildings have a ghost or two. A walking tour takes visitors past the oldest and best documented structures such as Jurgeson's Saloon, at the foot of First Street, to the very haunted, popular Union Hotel, Strum's Store, and the Congregational Church. On side streets, many Victorian homes still stand. Among the most historic are the Frisbie-Walsh House (1850) at 235 L Street, the Riddell-Fish House (1890) on K between Second and Third Streets, the Jefferson Mansion (1861) at 1063 Jefferson Street, the Carr House (1870) at 165 East D Street, Fisher-Hanlon House (1856) at 137 G Street, and the Salt Box House at 145 West D Street. Many of these places are rumored to have ghosts or other paranormal phenomena such as light anomalies and EAP.

Ghostly residents of Benicia's old days still roam the streets of this charming town. One kindly man, who looks to be about sixty years of age, appears in work clothes and stands with his dog at the entrance to alleyways. The man greets passersby in a clear voice and appears completely life-like, as does his dog. Moments after receiving a nod that acknowledges his greeting, the man disappears. Patrons at some of the bars on First Street are familiar with this man but no one knows his name, when he may have died, or his reason for haunting First Street.

Visitors to shops and restaurants on First Street often encounter intense cold spots in the older buildings and a creepy feeling that someone is standing close behind them. Most shop owners can tell you stories of creaking floorboards, swinging doors, and peculiar odors such as cigar smoke, hemp, or oranges that signal the presence of a ghost from Benicia's past.

GHOSTS OF THE COMMANDANT'S MANSION

Old Benicia Arsenal
Benicia, CA 94510-3210
Benicia Historical Museum
707-745-15435
www.beniciahistorcialmuseum.org

In 1859, General Julian McAllister assumed command of the U.S. Army Arsenal at Benicia. Many believe that he remains at his post today. Officially his tour of duty ended in 1866, but after so many years, including the dramatic Civil War years, he seems to have found it impossible to give up his mansion overlooking the arsenal and the waters of Carquinez Straits.

Among the many buildings that General McAllister built during his tenure is the commanding officer's house, officially designated Arsenal building No. 28. Constructed in 1860, this Greek Revival style mansion is certainly not typical of other structures on the arsenal grounds. Clearly, McAllister's vision of a personal residence included elements of Victorian grandeur. The beautiful white building, resembling the White House in many ways, stands on a hill, two stories tall with Doric columns decorating the balustrades that enclose wide verandas. Over the years, the interior has been remodeled several times by succeeding commanding officers, but prominent Victorian architectural features remain throughout the house, preserving the nineteenth-century elegance. The woodwork of the staircase, chair rails in the den, and doorways is original.

In the 1980s, the mansion was converted to a restaurant. Several workers and patrons experienced ghostly activity to the extent that the place became widely known as a haunted house. Most reports described a male figure that appeared hazy and transparent. This ghost was quiet, but his appearances created intense cold spots in the former den that was used as a bar. There are no published reports of detailed sightings, but people associated with the historical preservation may offer more information based on their personal experiences.

In 1989, the mansion was investigated by world-renowned paranormal expert Loyd Auerbach. He was unable to verify the nature and extent of the ghostly activity. During my visits to the mansion, between 1998 and 2002, I spotted the transparent apparition of a short man dressed in an elegant uniform. A white, mutton-chop style beard was clearly apparent, but this apparition appeared without legs. Most of these sightings occurred at the base of the staircase as if the ghost of McAllister were waiting to receive welcomed visitors or standing at an advantageous spot to scrutinize the strangers who entered his house. Whatever his reasons for haunting the place, this ghost is not belligerent.

I also detected the presence of two female entities. Dressed in white Victorian gowns, one of these is an older woman while the other appears to be a teenager. I could not locate information about deaths that may have occurred in this house nor could I obtain pictures or information about McAllister's family. Since the general's tour of duty ended in 1866, it is possible that the teenage daughter and wife of a subsequent commanding officer may have died in the house. The identity of these female spirits would be a good starting point for future paranormal investigations.

Gen. Julian McAllister built this impressive mansion in 1860 as a residence for the commandant of the Benicia Arsenal. His ghost may still haunt the place.

Today, the commandant's mansion stands beautifully restored. The magnificent parquet floors and woodwork looks new and evokes a feeling in visitors that time has turned back to the 1860s. The mansion is used for special events and is opened to the public on selected holidays.

GHOST OF THE REMORSEFUL SOLDIER

Starr Mansion
503 McLane Street
Vallejo, CA 94590
707-645-8164
www.starrmansionbb.com

This 1869-vintage mansion was occupied by two well-known families that left behind spirits. The most active ghost in this magnificent house is that of a Civil War soldier. Other spirits include a young lady who plays the piano in the parlor, a young man who apparently committed suicide in a closet, and a matron who managed this house for many years. These ghosts generate high-quality EAP, move dowsing rods, create light anomalies and cold spots, and fill rooms with their presence, causing unsuspecting visitors to wonder if some unseen being stands close behind them.

The grand mansion was built by Abraham DuBois Starr (1830-1894) in 1869 as a monument to his success as a business man and politician. Starr left Ohio in 1850, crossed the Great Plains and Rocky Mountains, and arrived in California in time to make a fortune selling supplies to gold miners. As the Gold Rush declined, Starr opened a grain mill in Marysville that was later moved to Vallejo. After becoming rich, Starr sold the enterprise that later became General Mills.

In 1870, Starr's brother, James, arrived in Vallejo, still suffering from the emotional stress of having served in the Civil War. James moved into a second floor room—now called the Americana Room—and remained there most of the day, staring at the walls or stars painted on the ceiling, apparently too stressed to leave for a walk around town. At times, his emotional and mental problems overwhelmed him and

The ghosts of tortured souls haunt the Victorian-era Starr Mansion in Vallejo's historic district.

resulted in admission to the state mental hospital in Napa. During my investigation of James's room, I was accompanied by dowsing rod expert Karen Adamski. We received more than thirty responses to questions that revealed James's anguish and his deep remorse for the many lives he extinguished during bloody battles of the Civil War. EAP in this room also revealed a tortured man whose guilt plagued him until his death in 1895.

The ghost of an elderly lady has been spotted in a second floor bedroom, the parlor, and piano room. She is believed to be Mary Anna Teegarden, wife of Abraham Starr. Mary died in 1889 while traveling in Europe, but it is believed that her ghost returned to the mansion in Vallejo where she raised her only child, Ada Deborah Starr.

Born in the mansion, Ada grew up with several cultural advantages over other children in the predominantly blue-collar town. Daily piano lessons were required and may account for the strong residual imprints that sensitives detect when standing next to the antique instrument. Like her mother, Ada died while abroad but dowsing rod and audio investigations suggest her spirit has returned home.

The Starr family left the mansion after the bank panic of 1893, which left Abraham nearly destitute. Relatives resided in the house until 1933 when it was sold to Clarence Rothschild. A Jewish immigrant from Germany, Clarence worked at Marie Island Naval Shipyard as a pipe fitter and supported and moved several relatives into the rooms of the former Starr mansion. Known as a magician and ventriloquist, Clarence performed throughout California until the late 1940s. Paranormal investigation suggests one of his relatives committed suicide in a hall closet on the first floor. EAP recorded at this site and psychic investigation revealed the presence of a spirit still tormented by the stresses that led to the suicide decision or the act itself.

The Starr mansion is now a popular bed-and-breakfast inn. The inn's guests may peruse a large collection of photographs from the Rothschild era that may facilitate paranormal investigation. Period antiques, including Ada Starr's piano, have many residuals attached that add to the excitement of spending a night in the mansion. I highly recommend this B-and-B to ghost hunters who wish to

perform nighttime paranormal investigations while enjoy
time pleasures of the nearby Napa Valley.

GHOST OF 3 WEST

Kaiser Foundation Medical Center
975 Sereno Drive
Vallejo, CA 94589
707-651-2360 (Hospital's Volunteer's Information desk)

The first hospital to occupy this ground was established early in 1940 as a convalescent and rehabilitation center for soldiers and sailors wounded or injured during service in WWII. No public records exist of the number of beds that composed the medical wards nor is there any information about the number of patients who died there. Historic photographs reveal that the buildings were constructed in a style typical of military barracks: two stories high with a central hallway on both floors. After WWII, Solano County took over the facility and converted it to a public hospital. In the late 1940s and throughout the 1950s, the vast majority of patients were male civilian employees at Mare Island Naval Shipyard. In the early 1960s, the county hospital expanded its services and offered care to women and children. During this time, one of Kaiser Permanente's pioneering rehabilitations doctors, Henry Kabot, established a cutting-edge rehabilitation program for patients afflicted with neurological disorders. This opened the way for Kaiser to purchase the property, tear down most of the old WWII-era buildings, and establish a world class rehabilitation center. A large, modern hospital complex was constructed in 1966, but some of the old country buildings remained in use as offices and clinics until 1991 when they were torn down and replaced with modern facilities. Another round of major construction began in 2004, culminating in a new medical center complex that opened early in 2010.

In spite of the major reconstruction that has occurred on this site, ghosts from the WWII-era continue to haunt the place. The ward currently designated "3 West" is believed to occupy space that was

ill or injured military personnel. In this
for months, suffering from wounds that
ections, or crippling neurological injuries.
area has been called the "ghost of 3 West"
a bomber-style leather jacket, this ghost
ng man, standing less than six feet tall,
Many hospital employees have seen this
visual experience is usually very brief. The apparition
is most often spotted moving around a corner or peeking through
a partially open door. To some employees, this ghost has appeared
completely life-like, leading them to conclude that someone is walking
the hallways after visiting hours. When they walk around a corner
in pursuit of the unauthorized visitor, no one is found. This ghost
has been seen most often late in the evening by housekeeping staff
members in areas now used for offices but mostly by housekeeping
staff members late in the evening. He has seldom been seen in midday
hours, although one morning a woman watched in amazement as a
depression formed in a vinyl seat and then returned to a more rounded
shape as if someone sat down briefly, and then stood up.

In addition to appearing as an apparition, this ghost manipulates
light switches and moves doors and small items left on desks. He also
moves carts used by housekeeping staff. Most recently, staff members
reported to me that this ghost has been changing the settings on
clocks. One secretary told me that each day for two weeks, when she
arrived for work, her digital desk clock would be set one hour ahead.

The ghost of 3 West also creates the sensation of a thickened
atmosphere and cold spots. Several staff members have reported a
chilling feeling as if some unseen being was standing behind them as
they worked at a computer.

Electrical problems have plagued 3 West for many years. New
electrical circuits were installed on the floor in an attempt to resolve
power surges, lighting failures, and other phenomena for which no
apparent cause could be found. Some staff members have become so
unnerved by electrical disturbances that they routinely leave lights on
in rooms at their work at night.

Many staff members have reported bizarre experiences to me
that suggest many areas of the medical center are haunted. In the

out-patient physical therapy clinic, the odor of cigar smoke has been detected by two witnesses simultaneously even though smoking is banned on the entire campus. At least two apparitions of patients have been seen in ICU beds. Nurses report that an elderly woman dressed in black has been seen standing at the bedside in ICU room 13. When staff members note her presence, she vanishes.

In the chemotherapy clinic, apparitions of former patients, now deceased, have been seen clearly enough to be identified. In the cardiac rehabilitation center, a block from the medical campus at the corner of Broadway and Sereno Drive, dark humanoid shapes have been seen walking near the office. In the men's restroom, a stall door swings open and then closes slowly. All efforts to debunk this phenomenon have failed to reveal a normal explanation.

VALLEJO NAVAL AND HISTORICAL MUSEUM

734 Marin Street
Vallejo, CA 94590
707-643-0077
www.vallejomuseum.org

Housed in Vallejo's former city hall, ghost hunters might anticipate that this museum is haunted by naval officers and others who played important roles in the Mare Island ship building industry. There are plenty of maritime artifacts from the nineteenth and early twentieth centuries—including a submarine periscope visitors use to check out traffic on the streets of Vallejo—and some may have a ghost attached, but the spirits that haunt this stately building are definitely not sailors.

Built in 1927, the two-story federal-style building was once filled with politicians and civil service employees. On the second floor, glass insets in several doors still display the titles of city employees who occupied the offices. A ghost of a middle-aged man has been seen leaving the city manager's office, turning to his left, walking ten feet, and then vanishing through a closed door marked "private." This apparition appears life-like from the knees upward. His lower legs and feet are not visible. The man wears dark pants, a white shirt with sleeves rolled up to the elbows, and wide ties, and appears to have very thin dark hair. A psychic who attempted to learn something about this ghost got the impression that his name was Fred Laven or Lannon. I could not locate city records from before 1950 that might verify this discovery. The psychic told me that this man had a heart attack in the 1930s while working on the second floor of the city hall.

The ghost of Rose Borgia also appears on the second floor of the museum. Before the city hall was constructed, the Vallejo Canteen occupied the site. In 1922, Rose Borgia was scheduled to sing for the visiting King of Portugal, but legend says that she was kidnapped by the family that owned the canteen and held in the attic for two years before dying there. Some versions of this story tell us that Rose was the king's wife, but this is not true. A resident of Vallejo and a favorite of the Portuguese community, Rose Borgia was a good singer but not good enough to satisfy the cultured audiences of San Francisco.

Having failed to show up for a chance to perform for royalty, Rose makes appearances in the small theater that was once the city council chamber. Sensitives who stand in the center of the room often hear a shrill voice, struggling to perform an aria. Sometimes, Rose cannot gather the energy to sing, but her presence is detected by the scent of gardenia, the flower she always wore in her hair when performing.

MARE ISLAND CEMETERY

Railroad Avenue to Meseda Road
Contact: Navy Yard Association of Mare Island
P.O. Box 2034
Vallejo, CA 94592
707-562-1812
www.mareislandnya.com

On June 13, 1892, fifteen sailors from the USS *Boston* were sent ashore on Mare Island Naval Yard to prepare ammunition. A short time after they entered the magazine, a huge explosion killed them. It is thought that one of the men dropped a shell and the concussion led to the disaster by igniting hundreds of pounds of explosives.

Remains of the sailors were retrieved from the magazine and placed in a mass grave marked by a beautiful marble monument erected by their shipmates. The monument stands today as a focal point in the quiet cemetery and lists the names of all fifteen sailors. The tragedy of their deaths was recently publicized with the news that this cemetery, under the jurisdiction of the Navy's Bureau of Yards and Docks for nearly 150 years, would no longer be maintained by naval personnel. The grave of the *Boston*'s sailors and the graves of many others have since been abandoned to be watched over only by the spirits of those resting below the stately monuments.

Mare Island Naval Cemetery was established by the famous American war hero, Commodore David G. Farragut, who arrived there in September of 1854. Soon after the grounds were marked, the place began to fill up. In 1863, the bodies of eight Russian sailors were buried thousands of miles from their homeland. These brave men lost their lives fighting a fire in San Francisco. Every autumn, representatives of the Russian Orthodox Church conduct a memorial service at the grave site.

Light anomalies hovering around the Russian monument have been captured in still and video photography. Some of these are clearly photographic artifacts while others have variations in tone within them that give the visual impression of a human head.

The island's cemetery is also the final resting place for sailors from England, Canada, Denmark, France, Spain, and Germany, including German prisoners-of-war. Ghost hunters may find the story of Lieutenant Sam Wilson interesting. Sam died while serving with the US Navy's Far East fleet in 1879. Official records indicate he was buried in China. Eight years later, his body was discovered in Building #77 near the dry docks. An official inquiry revealed that Sam had been shipped home with a cargo of obsolete ordnance and left in Building #77 because warehouse workers were unaware that the battered crate contained a body. Sam's widow, who had remarried, purchased a carved tombstone which was set in place during a burial ceremony on August 8, 1887. It is believed that Sam's ghost still haunts the building. Perhaps he is unaware that his body has been discovered and given a proper burial.

Anna Arnold Key Turner, daughter of Francis Scott Key (author of the "Star Spangled Banner"), is buried next to her daughter, Anna Turner, near the USS *Boston* monument. Ghost hunters have obtained some amazing EAP at these graves. Several audio recordings of flutes have been captured together with a female voice humming.

Hundreds of graves fill the tiny 2.4 acre cemetery. Some of them are marked only with a name while others give a fascinating history of the deceased. At many grave sites, sensitives detect imprints of dire emotions and experience the anguish of relatives who visited the graves for years before they too passed on.

The ghosts of this historic cemetery tend to appear at dusk and dawn when subdued light filters through the surrounding trees. Many visitors have seen thin, pale apparitions of amorphous shapes marching or slowly stepping across the grounds. At some graves, large cold spots are easily detected that suggest more than one spirit is present. Ghost hunters have reported the sounds of rattling anchor chains, cannon fire, marching troops, drums, bugles sounding retreat to indicate the end of the day, or "church call" to announce the formation of a funeral escort. The muffled sounds of men shouting orders and whispers in a feminine voice have also been heard.

EMPRESS THEATRE

338 Virginia Street
Vallejo, CA 94590
707-552-2400
www.cinematreasures.org/theater/1632/

It has been said that all old theaters are haunted. I've investigated theaters in such famous cities as Charleston, New Orleans, San Diego, San Francisco, and Seattle and not-so-famous places like Nevada City; Petaluma, California; and Missoula, Montana. I've had paranormal experiences in most of them. Older theaters, such as those that were constructed before 1930, typically show their age but still reveal magnificent and fascinating architectural features. Some of these have been obscured by modernization and seismic retrofit, but most have been recognized for their intrinsic value and beautifully restored. This is certainly true of the Empress Theatre in Vallejo, which stands as the focal point of the revitalized historic district.

Like old ships, theaters attract and hold spirits because of intense, repetitive emotions that may have been experienced by stage performers, musicians, and creative staff that may include directors and writers. Spirits may be bound to a theater because of wonderful experiences they had in life including unanticipated success, great elation after exceptional performances, adoration by the audience, or a steamy affair with another actor. Negative experiences have been found to hold spirits in theaters too. Failure to get a role after months of rehearsals, performances that fall short of the actor's estimation of his abilities, or desire for revenge on a rival actor all account for the disruptive behavior of many theater ghosts. Some ghosts stay in their favorite theater because they love the décor or the excitement of seeing a play or concert produced. When I walk through the old Empress Theatre, I always get the feeling that great performances occurred

After extensive renovation, ghosts have become more active in the Empress Theatre in Vallejo.

there that have kept spirits on stage and members of the audience in their favorite seats.

The Empress Theatre was built in 1911 and staged its first vaudeville production on February 14, 1912. With 940 seats and architectural features that many incorrectly describe as art deco, the place was spectacular. Within a few years, ownership changed hands and the place became known as the Republic Theater. More changes were made in 1929 as vaudeville acts were canceled and talking pictures equipment was installed. On March 30, 1930, a fire gutted the theater, leaving little more than the brick exterior walls and rafters. Despite the economic constraints of the Great Depression, the theater was rebuilt and given such amenities as a neon marquee and in-house restrooms. After WWII, another round of renovation removed the balcony and left the place with 471 seats arranged stadium style. Decorative elements known as Skouras style were restored. These include undulating waves raised across the walls, lush swags, and spectacular ceiling panels. The theater flourished in the 1980s until the Loma Prieta Earthquake of 1989 caused so much damage that the place sat vacant for the next eighteen years. I suspect that this long period of vacancy gave spirits a chance to re-establish themselves and renew their hold on the place.

On entering the tiny lobby, sensitive visitors get the impression that the space is filled with unseen beings, many dressed in pre-WWII fashions. In the auditorium, the modern sound control station, located amid the seats, does not detract from the psychic impression of unseen patrons. I saw the pale apparition of a short, stocky man sitting in the front row with a sheaf of paper in his hand that could have been a script.

While walking near the stage, I picked up on sound remnants that were reminiscent of a musical. On my audio recorder, I discovered brief bursts of sound created by piano, violin, and drums, yet no musicians were present during that visit.

The Empress reopened in the spring of 2008 and now offers screenings of vintage movies and live musical performances. The best way to investigate this place is to attend a performance or movie and then discuss your interest with a staff member. Several EAP can be captured within a short visit if you can get permission to enter the auditorium when no one else is in the building.

CHILDREN OF THE EVIL SERPENT

Children of the Good Servant Orphanage
Hiddenbrook Parkway
Vallejo, CA 94591-6436

For decades, myths and ghost stories have circulated throughout the eastern San Francisco Bay Area about an orphanage near Vallejo that housed incorrigible, emotionally disturbed children in the late nineteenth and early twentieth centuries. Many stories mention that the name of the place was modified from Children of the Good Servant to Children of the Evil Serpent because the headmaster and his assistants perpetrated unspeakable child abuse. Allegedly, children were sexually abused, burned, kept in solitary confinement, starved, denied clothing or shoes, raped, and murdered. Some of these unfortunate kids were sent to the orphanage as part of the Appalachian Experiment with Children, of which I can find no credible information, because they were considered beyond salvation. Others were sent there because of physical deformities or severe learning problems. Wikipedia claims that the heinous abuse was the worst "ever recorded in American history." The trouble is that a thorough search of local historical records revealed no mention of the orphanage or heinous crimes committed in the area. My review of topographic maps created as early as 1940 showed no structural remnants or place names that give credence to the Evil Serpent legend. Added to that, I reviewed State of California records dating from 1891 that list private institutions supported, in part, by state aid and found no mention of the Good Servant orphanage. Other orphanages in the area were listed, including Vallejo's Good Templars' Orphan's Home.

Following vague reports that the Evil Serpent orphanage consisted of a collection of "buildings that was once a farm" located at the end of a "desolate, abandoned road" in the area believed to be the site of an upscale housing development and a golf course, local ghost hunters have searched for the place without success. On old maps, the area is labeled "Page Flat" and comprises a valley located about a half mile from St. John's Mine.

Targets of local investigations have been the roads and public grounds of Hiddenbrook, a small community of homes inspired by artist Robert Kincade that surrounds a golf course. Some ghost hunters have roamed the golf course with divining rods, EMF detectors, and audio recorders, but no credible reports of spirit activity have surfaced. Nonetheless, there are numerous reports on the Internet and in correspondence directed to me that describe encounters with apparitions of battered or deformed children who appear alongside the manicured roads of this community, inside private homes, on the fairways of the golf course, and near remnants of the old McIntyre Ranch.

In my research, I encountered information about a nearby orphanage that aroused suspicions of a connection with the Evil Serpent story. From 1870 to the 1930s, the Good Templars' Orphan's Home in Vallejo provided a home, education, training in trades such as agriculture and construction, and religious instruction. It is possible that incorrigible children at that institution were sent to outlying ranches, such as the McIntyre Ranch, to work off their aggression or learn menial jobs. This may have fostered an urban legend that persists to this day. Even if an orphanage did not exist in the Hiddenbrook area, I concede that it is possible that children sent from the Good Templar's home to ranches as punishment might have suffered the abuse described in various Internet reports.

Some writers mention that the horrible abuse perpetrated at the Good Servant orphanage was such an embarrassment to the city of Vallejo and Solano County that all records of the institution were destroyed. I find this impossible to believe. Maps, state funding records, crime reports, oral history records, personal diaries, or published exposes would have preserved some credible evidence that such an evil place once existed. No information from these sources can be found, however.

So, we are left only with an intriguing urban legend and a few credible reports of apparitions that fit the principals of the legend. My visits to this location have not produced impressions of spirit activity. Construction of the Hiddenbrook community appears to have erased any landmarks or remnants of buildings that might have housed children as well as any environmental imprints that may have been created by the heinous abuse that allegedly occurred there. Added to that, the community is not a place that ghost hunters can investigate without attracting unwanted attention. Ghost hunters might start at McIntyre Ranch Park at the end of St. John's Mine Road or the end of Alder Creek Road.

EAP OF TRAGEDIES AND MOURNING

Rockville Cemetery and Stone Church
4219 Suisun Valley Road
Fairfield, CA 94534-3104
707-864-2421
www.rockvillecemetery.org

In 1852, settlers in the Suisun Valley region held church services on the banks of a creek and performed baptisms in the deep pools under shady oaks. By 1856, local settlers had raised enough money to build a simple but beautiful church using stone quarried from surrounding hills, hence the name Rockville. The church and adjacent cemetery were established on 5 acres donated by Landy and Sarah Alford. One of its first clergy was the Reverend Orcenith Fisher, known as the "Son of Thunder" because the stone walls of the church amplified his strong voice.

As expected, the Stone Church was the site of some sad events over the years. In 1863, the congregation was split by the Civil War with northern sympathizers leaving to worship elsewhere. A stone plaque, still visible, was erected by southern sympathizers marking the church as "Methodist Episcopal Church South." Today the Rockville Stone Church is a pioneer monument and also a place of worship. Funerals and other events that evoked intense emotions from participants have left some amazing paranormal imprints at the doorways and at the altar.

One of the most tragic funerals to be staged in the church was for the Alfords' three-year old daughter, Sarah. Her carved stone marker, now heavily eroded by the passage of time, is a focal point of the cemetery and still lends a tragic air to the place. Nearby, a stone monument marks the final resting place of little Sarah's parents, Sarah and Landy. Orbs have been captured at these grave sites that vary from

The Stone Church of Rockville has been the scene of Civil War unrest and countless funerals.

tiny spots of light to large ovals that almost cover the entire frame.

Perhaps the most tragic collection of graves is that of the James family, whose final resting place is located about 100 feet north of the church. John (1816-1906) and Mary (1832-1909) had several children who died at a very young age. This unimaginable tragedy was made even more horrific by the loss of four children in the same year, 1876. William died on June 10 at age ten. His brother, David, died fifteen days later at age twelve. In August, Jenny died on the sixth at age twelve. Five days later, her fourteen-year-old sister Mary died. At the family plot, sensitive visitors detect the intense imprint of the tragedy including inconsolable anguish and fear. EAP at this site have included a female voice humming, a child's voice speaking unintelligible words, and a male voice that says, "Committed to God."

Also interned in this historic graveyard is Granville P. Swift, a member of the Bear Flag Revolt that took place in Sonoma in 1846. Swift died on April 21, 1875, a week short of his fifty-forth birthday, when he fell from his horse while prospecting in the nearby Suisun hills. His partial apparition has been spotted astride a horse standing

Paranormal audio phenomena are frequently recorded at the James family plot in Rockville Cemetery.

near the wall of granite that arises at the back of the cemetery. At times, this apparition appears to blend with light filtering through the tall trees near his grave.

Ghost hunters who performed EAP sweeps in the graveyard should be aware that the tall trees are populated by a community of turkey vultures who create bizarre sounds resembling screams and cries.

GHOSTS IN THE TRAINS

Cordelia Junction Antique Mall
4560 Central Way
Fairfield, CA 94534
707-864-1244

This landmark store at Cordelia Junction houses one of the largest collections of antiques in the Bay Area. With 19,000 square feet of floor space and thousands of objects from all over the western U.S., there is plenty of room for ghosts. Passersby on busy I-80 can't help but notice the eclectic architecture of concrete slab construction typical of warehouses and the large collection of passenger and freight railroad cars imbedded in the walls. These brightly painted cars are antiques too, left over from the heyday of rail travel and once used as dining rooms for a restaurant called Victoria Station that occupied the building in the 1970s.

Staff members at this massive consignment store have experienced paranormal activity for years, but increasingly bizarre and frequent events culminated in a phone call to me in December of 2008. Intrigued by reports of paranormal experiences by staff and customers that included surveillance video of unexplained movement of objects, I visited the place several times with colleagues Jackie Ganiy, Darlene Dwyer, and Sally Aquino. We performed an extensive EAP sweep of several areas within the store and a psychic investigation of spirits attached to several antiques.

Staff members showed me a surveillance video that served as a basis for my investigation of the Antique Mall. The video shows a plastic action figure of a soldier, complete with a tiny rifle held at his shoulder, sitting on a shelf seven feet above the floor. From this stable position, the figure moved slowly over the edge of the shelf and fell to the floor, where its internal, battery-powered motor came to life and created a crawling motion and the sound of the rifle firing. The figure crawled on the floor for two minutes before the motor shut off. The video does not reveal any light anomalies or sounds that might explain this phenomenon. It appears as though an invisible being pulled the toy off the shelf, turned on the switch, and played with the little soldier for a few minutes before leaving.

My investigation of the toy and the site of the bizarre activity failed to detect the presence of ghosts, but one staff member told me that she has seen a thin cloud of light move up and down this aisle near the soldier's usual resting place.

At the other side of the building, the surveillance camera has caught the image of a woman wearing a long dress described by staff as Victorian. This apparition appears next to a large collection of china. In a nearby railroad car decked out in 1950s paraphernalia with a checker-board floor, the apparition of a man appears after an object from the collection is purchased.

In the east end of the mall, I encountered a mahogany dresser that interested me. My EAP and psychic investigation of this piece revealed that it was once owned by a woman named Edith who kept important papers and a gun in the upper, middle drawer. I got the impression Edith was so strongly attached to these papers that she could not leave the dresser. When I opened the drawers, however, I found nothing in them.

Nearby, a railroad dining car is populated by two ghosts. One is a man who worked in the car as a porter. His name was Earl or Merle. He is tall and thin, dressed in dark pants and a white jacket. The other ghost is a woman who responds to ghost hunters by creating audio phenomena on a recording. This woman hums and sings and speaks in phrases of two to four words. Photographs taken in the car did not reveal any light anomalies.

Staff members told me about several customers who came to the cashier's desk to report bizarre sensations such as an unseen being standing very close or a sound of someone whispering in their ear. A number of times women have rushed from the restroom in a panic because of a frightening sound emanating from the ceiling. I investigated this room and found that the ceiling vibrated and a ventilation grate "popped" whenever the door to the adjacent men's room was opened. Apparently, suction created in the common ventilation system caused the creepy sounds, not a ghost. Ordinarily, these sounds would be dismissed as uninteresting, but many people who visit this fascinating mall and spend time browsing among the huge collection of antiques experience eerie feelings simply because of the ambience created by old dishes, furniture, jewelry, toys, and clothing. It is well-known that antique stores are among the most haunted places because many ghosts can't let go of their cherished possessions. For some, a chair or piece of jewelry may be their only link with the life they once knew. Beyond the presence of ghosts, antiques often contain imprints of former users or owners. Resembling recordings of emotions, sounds, and even odors, these paranormal imprints can be detected by sensitive people who might have never even given ghosts any thought.

GHOSTS OF THE GREENWOODS

Greenwood Mansion
Napa Valley Airport Business Park
Airport Road and Highway 29
American Canyon, CA 94558

On the evening of February 9, 1891, Captain John Q. Greenwood worked in his yard mending a fence. Two well-dressed men, William Roe and Carl Schmidt, approached on foot asking for food. Something about their demeanor troubled the captain, and so he refused their request and ordered them off his property. Enraged, the two men attacked Greenwood and forced him into the kitchen where they poured sedative down his throat, tied him to a chair, and then administered chloroform. When Greenwood's wife returned from visiting neighbors, she found the men ransacking her kitchen and her husband unconscious.

Lucinda attempted to flee but the thieves dragged her upstairs to a bedroom, tied her hands and feet, and drugged her. Roe and Schmidt then searched the house for valuables but found only a little money and some jewelry. Before leaving, Roe strangled Lucinda as she lay on the bed.

In 1891, the Greenwood Mansion was the scene of a brutal home invasion that resulted in the death of Lucinda Greenwood.

Roe and Schmidt headed for the nearest bar in Napa and spent a good portion of their stolen money on drinks. It is believed that they made casual inquiries about Captain Greenwood and were told that he kept a large amount of cash hidden on his ranch. Thinking they might have a chance to increase the payoff of their crime, they returned to the Greenwood house. They found John Greenwood at his wife's feet completely distraught with her death. Roe dragged him into the hallway on the second floor and shot him in the head three times. Although Lucinda had been dead for at least two hours, he shot her in the head as well.

Hours after the murderers left the ranch, John regained consciousness and staggered to a neighbor's. Sheriff George S. McKenzie was alerted, but a man-hunt turned up nothing. John Greenwood underwent surgery and made a miraculous but slow recovery.

Carl Schmidt was apprehended in May of 1892 after drinking too much in a Colorado bar and confessing his crime to an off-duty detective. He was convicted of armed robbery, sentenced to life in prison, and incarcerated on "cranks row" in San Quentin. William Roe was not caught until September 1896 when he confessed to a saloon keeper, W. B Shaug, in San Fernando near Los Angeles. He was tried and convicted and sentenced to die by hanging. On January 15, 1897, at 11:00 a.m., Roe was executed by the Napa sheriff in front of an invitation-only crowd of about 200. This hanging, the last public execution in California, was staged at courthouse square, now bordered by Coombs Street, Third and Second Streets, and Main Street in the city of Napa.

After John Greenwood recovered from his head wounds, he returned to his house and tried to live a normal life. Eventually, his physical wounds healed, but he never recovered emotionally. It is said that he never again entered the second floor bedroom where Lucinda died. In constant mourning for his wife, he moved her little garden wagon into a room on the first floor and slept in it each night until he died years later.

Today, the Greenwood mansion is used for administrative offices for the Napa Airport Business Park. Several cold spots have been detected in the upstairs hallway and the first floor room that was once the kitchen. One sensitive visitor encountered a muted moaning on the second floor. The pale apparition of a woman has been seen on the second floor too. This apparition floats down the hallway and then enters a room believed to be Lucinda's bedroom.

John Greenwood lived in this house for nearly ten years after that horrific night of February 9, 1891. The emotional imprint created by the initial attack, second attack, and long, intense period of mourning for Lucinda is strong and easily detected by sensitive visitors.

GHOSTS OF THE OLD SOSCOL HOUSE

Villa Romano Restaurant
1011 Soscol Ferry Road (off Highway 29)
Napa, CA 94558
707-252-4533
www.villaromanorestaurant.com

In 1855, Elijah True and his wife, Elizabeth, built a large two-story inn and named it after a nearby Patwin Indian village called Soscol.

For decades, the Soscol House served as a transportation hub for stage coaches and wagons that brought passengers from nearby towns to the Napa River ferry. The place was also a popular hang-out for gamblers, prostitutes, whiskey salesmen, and sometimes outlaws. The night of February 9, 1891, William Roe and Carl Schmidt stopped here for drinks after murdering Lucinda Greenwood and wounding her husband, John. Some of the unsavory characters from the building's early past still roam the second floor.

One night, a kitchen worker, who was the last to leave the building, got into his car only to find it wouldn't start. Wondering what to do, he looked back at the building, thinking he might go inside and call for help. The man was puzzled when he noticed that the first floor lights were out but those on the second floor burned brightly. He recalled turning off all the lights when he closed the building. As he continued looking at the second floor, he was shocked to see the silhouettes of people moving across the windows. The sight frightened the man so much that he refused to re-enter the building.

The Villa Romano Restaurant offers modern Napa Valley cuisine while harboring ghosts from the nineteenth century.

Some of the people who work at the Villa Romano Restaurant have had some interesting experiences. On the second floor, lights in the two banquet rooms sometimes go on and off without explanation. Water runs in the restroom and doors are heard slamming without movement. People sitting at the bar on the first floor sometimes hear screams, shouts, and moans echo down the staircase from the second floor.

Human-shaped shadows or apparitions are sometimes seen on the second-floor balcony that wraps around the north and west side of the building. These may be the ghosts of prostitutes taking a break in the cool wine country air. Visitors to the balcony and other spaces on the second floor often feel an unseen presence, as if two or three people are standing close by.

The Villa Romano Restaurant has occupied the Soscol House for about fifteen years. During that time, the owners have meticulously restored the place, giving it the feel of an upscale wine country bistro while retaining important elements of its history. In the bar, a collection of photographs adorns the wall giving visitors a chance to see the building's founders, Elijah and Elizabeth True, and the inn's manager in the 1860s, Serena Madland Anderson. Ghost hunters should look for apparitions of these people upstairs.

PHANTOM BOOT STEPS AND COLD SPOTS

Petaluma Adobe State Historic Park
3325 Old Adobe Road
Petaluma, CA 94954
707-762-4871
www.parks.ca.gov/default.asp?page-id=474/

On the east side of Petaluma, General Vallejo's huge adobe hacienda stands on a hillside surrounded by fields that were once part of his huge empire. The hacienda is quiet and serene and slowly decaying as it nears the end of its second century. With the exception of grazing goats and hawks soaring overhead, the place appears abandoned except for the park ranger who offers anecdotes about the

Vallejo family and the Indians who toiled on the sprawling rancho. When asked about ghostly activity, the ranger scoffs and denies that ghosts walk the old adobe building or nearby grounds where huts once housed ranch hands and their families. Pressed a little, he admits that some visitors have mentioned seeing or hearing some strange things on the second floor of the hacienda. When I visited General Vallejo's adobe hacienda, I encountered paranormal activity in two locations.

The restored, two-story, 8,000-square-foot building was constructed in the mid-1830s and served as the hub of Vallejo's 66,000-acre rancho. On these grounds he grazed 3,000 sheep, 10,000 head of cattle, and hundreds of horses. The hacienda was designed to serve as an industrial center, housing shops for manufacturing shoes, belts, clothing, tools, furniture, and tanning hides. Some of the ground-floor rooms were used for storage of tallow and grain before it was shipped to San Francisco where it was placed on ships bound for the American east coast. The second floor was used to house artisans and rancho foremen and their families. The west wing also contained an

Built in the 1830s, this grand rancho was the hub of General Vallejo's empire in the Mexican Province of Alta California.

apartment used by General Vallejo when he visited the rancho. Often, the general traveled from his home in Sonoma to Petaluma to meet important visitors such as merchants and visiting dignitaries.

Most of the rancho's laborers, herdsmen, and staff for the large out-door kitchen lived in a community of shanties and huts that once stood along the creek that separates the parking area from the hacienda. Nothing remains of these structures, but psychically sensitive visitors or those using dowsing rods can identify hot spots of energy. These hot spots probably indicate unmarked graves. On a warm spring morning, I encountered an ice-cold column of air approximately six feet in diameter and four feet high on the south side of the creek. Two other cold spots were found nearby.

On the second floor of the hacienda, ghost hunters have detected the disembodied sound of heavy boots striking the redwood planks of the wide verandas. Sitting on a bench outside Vallejo's apartment with my head against an old adobe wall, I heard the sound of multiple foot-strikes around a corner, as if two people were walking the veranda. I peeked around the corner, but I saw no one and the sound quickly faded. The only other person at the hacienda that morning was the ranger whom I spotted seated on a bench in the broad court-yard smoking a cigarette. As I roamed about the second floor, the muted sound of footsteps was also heard coming from inside Vallejo's apartment. The sounds varied from those expected, heavy boots to a lighter, hollow sound made by the high-heels of a woman's shoe.

Vallejo's hacienda flourished for only ten years before the Bear Flag Revolt of 1846 reduced Vallejo's power as commandante-general of California and ushered into the region numerous squatters who over-ran the property. Many of the rancho's skilled workers and artisans left during the Gold Rush of 1849-50, creating a labor shortage. By 1857, Vallejo found that the 100 square-mile rancho was no longer manageable. Large parcels were sold to Yankees returning from the gold mines of the Sierra, and the general retired to Sonoma.

MYSTERIOUS GHOSTS OF THE OLD OPERA HOUSE

Phoenix Theatre
201 Washington Street
Petaluma, CA 94952
707-762-3565
www.thephoenixtheatre.com

Many of the young people who frequent the Phoenix Theatre teen center will talk about the strange things that they or their friends have experienced in the balcony, backstage, and in the restrooms. Some attribute these experiences to ghosts that are said to roam the entire building. Others are too scared to admit that their favorite hang-out is haunted. If you talk to staff members, you may hear a firm denial that anything paranormal or supernatural goes on in the historic building. A look into the history of the large building on Washington Street, however, reveals some fascinating stories that point to the possibility of ghosts, hauntings, or a poltergeist.

The imposing structure was constructed in 1905 by Josie F. Hill, who named the place the Hill Opera House. A few classic operas might have been staged there in addition to performances by some of the biggest names of the era such as Lily Langtree, Enrico Caruso, and the mysterious Harry Houdini. By 1915, the place had deteriorated into a second-rate vaudeville house that presented performers who could not get work in San Francisco.

Perhaps anticipating the advent of talking movies, Hill's opera house was nearly destroyed by a fire in 1924. Insurance money funded the restoration and enabled Hill to reopen in 1925 as the California Theatre.

On August 5, 1957, a second fire destroyed the roof and a false ceiling. The Tocchini family took over the property, rebuilt the roof and remodeled the interior, and then reopened as the Showcase Theatre. In 1982, a new owner took over and named the place Phoenix Theatre after the legendary bird that arose from its ashes to live again. The 1989 Loma Prieta earthquake caused significant damage to the building that required yet another round of renovations. When the place reopened, it took on the role of community center for Petaluma's teens. Local hero Tom Gaffey opened the doors after school, giving adolescents a safe place to play games, socialize, do homework and receive tutoring, or simply hang-out as an alternative to street activities. Under Gaffey's supervision, several theatre and performing arts programs were started that gave young people an opportunity to learn about concert production and theatre management, acquire musical skills, and take dance classes. In recent years the Phoenix has survived thanks to appearances by some big-name entertainers that include Hilary Duff, Huey Lewis and the News, Metallica, the Ramones, Neville Brothers, Jimmie Vaughan, and Devo.

Two devastating fires and a major earthquake that nearly ended the life of the Phoenix may have created the non-living entities that haunt the place. The nature of the ghostly activity that occurs at various locations suggests more than one spirit person haunts the old theatre. Locals who have spent a lot of time inside the building will tell you that weird, unexplained things happen there. When pressed for details, one patron in his thirties who attended Phoenix events over a twenty-year period described the apparition of an angry man—old, with long hair, ashen skin tone, sunken eyes, and bad teeth—often seen in the mirror of the men's restroom. Many people who have been alone in this room leave quickly because of intense anxiety or fear that something bad was about to happen.

So many people have reported frightening experiences in the balcony that this part of the theatre is kept locked except for special events. A Phoenix regular told me that strange odors reminiscent of rotting flesh have been detected in the balcony.

There are reports of objects being moved, sometimes taking flight off a shelf or table. Loud tapping noises that seem to come from the walls and the sound of slamming doors are often heard too. These paranormal phenomena may be poltergeist activity.

GHOSTS OF THE CHINESE FISHERMEN

China Camp Regional Park
Exit Highway 101 onto North San Pedro Road
San Rafael, CA 94901-2520
415-456-0766

During the 1860s, thousands of Chinese laborers were imported to

California to build the Union Pacific Railroad, construct mines and tunnels, and work in industries such as brick manufacture and mining. After a few years of working dangerous jobs under harsh conditions, Chinese who had worked as fishermen in China abandoned their occupations and established thirty shrimping villages around the San Francisco Bay. At McNear's Point in modern-day Marin County, the village was initially composed of renegade fishermen who had escaped from contracts that would have kept them working for decades. Their dwellings were so crude that the place became known as China Camp. Early success brought modest wealth that enabled the fishermen to establish families. At its height, China Camp was home for 77 fishermen who supported more than 500 people. In the early days of the shrimp industry, few laws regulated business. In 1901, 1905, and 1911, laws were enacted that made Chinese fishing methods illegal or severely limited the tonnage that could be taken from the bay. As a result, many fishermen operated outside the law.

Earlier illegal activities of shrimp fishermen served as a basis for several stories by famed local author, Jack London. In his *Tales of the Fish Patrol* and the classic short stories "Yellow Handkerchief" and "Yellow and White," London describes his exploits against the

Preserved remnants of a Chinese fishing village that once flourished on the shores of San Francisco Bay harbor ghosts from the nineteenth century.

China Camp has been the scene of several ghost sightings that include a Chinese fishing boat.

fishermen of China Camp as a member of the fish patrol (forerunner of the state fish and game wardens). Early in the twentieth century, encounters between Chinese fishermen and law enforcement officers were often violent. Some shrimpers were shot or drowned. Other tragedies that befell this community included fires that almost destroyed the village and the great earthquake of 1906.

Some of the residents of old China Camp who lost their lives over a century ago still occupy the place. While sitting on the quiet beach, visitors have heard Chinese spoken in muffled tones. This audio phenomenon has been captured on tape and other recording media by ghost hunters. At places where the remains of shacks are found, cold spots occur and light anomalies show up in photographs.

Buildings currently standing at the camp are reproductions, but they were constructed from boards and timbers found at the site that were once part of the Chinese community. Consequently, sensitives who visit the shacks and pier get bizarre impressions that include the sound of chimes, flutes and drums, odors of rotting fish, and the shuffle of feet on the ground. One of the best sightings at China Camp was a vision of a Chinese fishing boat that appeared a short distance offshore. The boat was estimated to be 40 feet long with a single large sail typical of Chinese junks. Six to eight men were seen on deck as the boat glided into the shallows with its sail slack. Upon coming to a stop, the boat vanished.

MISSION SAN RAPHAEL

1104 Fifth Avenue
San Raphael, CA 94901-2502
415-456-8141

In 1817, the fathers of Mission Dolores in San Francisco directed Father Luis Gil to establish an "*assistencia*" or sanitarium on the northern shores of San Francisco Bay. With hundreds of sick Indians on their hands, the mission fathers realized that sunshine, dryer air, and infrequent fog would provide a healthier environment for Indians weakened by poor nutrition, the cold damp climate of the central Bay Area, and diseases imported by Spanish soldiers and others. On December 1871, Father Gil opened his *assistencia*, but the place soon gained independence from Mission Dolores and was raised to full mission status under the patronage of San Rafael Archangel, the angel of bodily healing. Many Indians who went there from other missions were restored to good health by the merciful care of Father Gil and the abundance of fresh produce from nearby farms. Others were too far gone and died soon after arriving on mission grounds.

In 1821, the mission was a thriving community under the new leadership of Father Amoros. More than 1,000 Indians lived at the mission in 1828, and the number of animals exceeded 5,000, including 454 horses. The idyllic location, abundance of food and water, and isolation from Spanish soldiers quartered in San Francisco created a peaceful settlement, but the mission was not without great sorrows. While many Indians regained in good health there, hundreds died. In 1825, one death occurred every five days. In 1838, a smallpox epidemic killed hundreds. All of these unfortunate natives were buried in the mission graveyard, which is now covered by a parking lot.

More deaths occurred from armed conflicts between renegade

Indians and mission neophytes backed by Mexican soldiers. Attacks occurred in 1824 and 1832 that left several church neophytes dead on the mission's steps and twenty-one pagan Indians killed. In 1826, Indians named Marin and Quentin terrorized the mission with frequent skirmishes. They were eventually captured and immortalized by the use of their names: Marin County and San Quentin Prison.

By the mid-1830s, peace returned to the mission as the process of secularization spread throughout the chain of California missions. In 1837, General Vallejo became administrator of the mission buildings and lands and dispersed the Indians to work on ranches. Mission San Rafael was torn down by Americans in 1861 and Saint Rafael's church was built on the old mission grounds. The footprint of the new church overlapped the foundation of the old Spanish mission. A replica of the Spanish mission was erected in 1949, slightly removed from the original location.

The partial apparition of a hooded figure, no doubt that of Father Gil, is often seen walking through the walls of the newer mission church as he passes down what might have been an aisle or hallway of the original mission. In spite of his frequent appearance in the

Ghostly candles have been spotted floating inside this old mission.

replica mission, this ghost seems unaware of the walls of the newer structure. He walks as if he sees only the 1817 church. At times, only a candle moves down the path of the former aisle as if it is carried by an invisible entity. The muted sounds of sick Indians gasping for a few final breaths have been heard at the steps of the new St. Rafael church and at the adjacent upper playground. Historical research reveals that these steps sit on the spot where the mission chapel once stood. The upper playground was the site of the mission's hospital. No doubt many Indians died at this location after suffering for months with incurable illnesses. EAP investigations at these locations are often highly productive.

FALKIRK CULTURAL CENTER

1408 Mission Avenue
San Rafael, CA 94901
415-485-3328
www.falkirkculturalcenter.org

The last time I visited Falkirk Mansion—now called Falkirk Cultural Center—I had paranormal experiences that I did not anticipate. I suspected that the ghost of the mansion's builder and first resident, Ella Nichols Parks, would be detected roaming about the first floor foyer and grand stair that leads to the front doors, but I did not expect to learn about an angry butler or a spiritual descendent of Alice Dollar Hayden, who was born in the house in 1917.

Falkirk was not built by the wealthy business man who gave the place its Scottish name. The massive Victorian mansion was constructed in 1888 by Ella Nichols Parks, who was a Gold Rush baby, the eighteenth-century version of the post-WWII baby boomers. Ella was born in Vermont in 1847. In 1850, news of easy riches in the gold diggings of California aroused the wanderlust in her parents, who packed up the little girl and booked passage on a ship to Panama. There, they trekked overland and found a ship waiting on the Pacific coast that took them to San Francisco. It is not clear how Ella's parents

The ghost of Ella Nichols may still haunt Falkirk Mansion in San Rafael.

made their fortune, but their wealth was sufficient to gain entry to the Bay Area's upper class society. Before her twenty-fifth birthday, Ella married Traenor Parks and found herself firmly established in Marin County society. The death of her husband in 1882 left her widowed and wealthy and longing to get out of the house she had shared with her husband. With limitless resources, Ella hired renowned architect Linton Day to build a huge mansion for the family she would never produce.

Soon after Ella's death in 1905, another Gold Rush baby, Captain Robert Dollar, purchased the estate, renovated it, and gave it the name of his native village in Scotland. The Dollar family, rich from timber and shipping businesses, lived in the house until 1972 when the old place was in such a state of decay that it was scheduled for demolition. Fortunately, local citizens created a foundation which saved the mansion, renovated it, and opened it to the public as the Falkirk Cultural Center. Generations of Dollars have left their mark on the place, but it is the ghost of Ella Parks that makes this amazing house such a fantastic experience for ghost hunters.

The history of Falkirk that doubtless includes the birth of babies and death of its aged members in the upstairs bedrooms, its prominent position perched on a hill overlooking a valley now filled with the town of San Rafael, and numerous architectural remnants of the eighteenth century will arouse the interest of ghost hunters. Many will visit Falkirk looking for Robert Dollar, the dirt-poor immigrant infant who rose to great wealth, or members of his family. But the most active ghosts here are Ella Parks and an angry butler.

Since the 1980s, the Falkirk mansion has been known as a haunted house. Remnants of the Victorian garden, dark windows, weathered paint, and the appearance of an abandoned house gave the place a spooky ambience. After renovations and rebirth as a community center, it became clear that Ella Parks was haunting the house she built. In 1995, an administrator who was working late one night documented her spirit encounter, which included the apparition of Ella walking about the second floor landing, passing through the front door, and then descending the stair to the driveway. Being familiar with the likeness of Ella Parks from historic photographs, there was no doubt that the apparition was that of the mansion's first owner. Since the mid-1990s, local ghost hunters have encountered Ella's ghost on the front stair and on the second floor of the house.

Throughout the home, original door knobs and amazing woodwork offers practitioners of psychometry a chance to feel the vibes of the home's occupants. My daughter, Sarah, and I both felt an electric sensation when we touched several door knobs. On the back stairway, we perceived the laughter and giggling of children as they descended the stairs.

Sarah entered a main floor restroom to wash her hands but could not open the door. Responding to her cries for help, I approached the door and detected a thickened atmosphere as if some unseen person were standing between me and the door. I tried the door knob and found that it opened easily. When asked what happened, Sarah told me that an angry butler had locked her in the room. Throughout our visit to Falkirk, Sarah detected the presence of an old, angry fellow who did not like children. She explained that he did not like the children running down the back stairs or laughing and talking in loud voices, because the stair way was close to the kitchen where he worked most of the time.

The most amazing aspect of my last visit to Falkirk was Sarah's reaction to the place. She had never been to Falkirk, yet she immediately recognized the place and insisted that she once lived there. Moving about the huge mansion, Sarah seemed familiar with each room and recalled running down the back stairway with other children, laughing and talking so loudly that she incurred the wraith of the angry butler who did not like her. During our extensive visit to Falkirk, Sarah's reactions and familiarity aroused my suspicions that she had a past life in the mansion, perhaps as Alice Dollar Hayden (1917-1997), daughter of Harold and Agnes Dollar. That investigation is on-going.

Ghost hunters may get some amazing EAP on the back stairway, in the main parlor, and in the dining room where the Dollar family gathered every Sunday.

Falkirk is open to the public from 10:00 a.m. to 1:00 p.m., Wednesday through Saturday.

ANGEL ISLAND

Angel Island State Park
415-435-3544
Ferry boat service from: Vallejo (707-643-3770)
Alameda (510-769-5500)
San Francisco (415-929-1543)
Tours via tram: 925-426-3058
www.angelisland.com

This beautiful island, with the prophetic name, is haunted, but it was not named for those good spirits that inhabit the many ruins of Civil War-era military facilities or the immigration station. Spanish explorer Juan Ayala entered San Francisco Bay on August 5, 1775, and anchored his tiny ship, the *San Carlos*, in a sheltered cove. Sensing the tranquility of the place, Ayala named the island *La Isla de Nuestra Senoras de Los Angeles* (Our Lady of the Angels Island). The *San Carlos* spent a month at anchor in the cove that now bears Ayala's name, but it is often called Hospital Cove.

On Angel Island, Hospital Cove was once a detention center for Asian immigrants whose experiences created strong imprints that account for bizarre audio phenomena.

The narrow channel that separates Angel Island from the nearest landing on the mainland is called Raccoon Strait in honor of the H.M.S. *Raccoon*, a British sloop of war that arrived in San Francisco Bay in 1814. Leaking badly and in desperate need of repair, the crew was unable to beach the disabled vessel near the Presidio, and so they drifted into the strait and beached in Ayala Cove.

The island was property of the Mexican government until the Bear Flag revolt of 1846, when it came under American control. Within a few years, modest military outposts were constructed on the island to protect the port of San Francisco. With the outbreak of the Civil War, fears of a Confederate attack on the Pacific Coast prompted the construction of extensive Union Army facilities including thirteen gun emplacements. By 1863, Camp Reynolds housed 500 officers and men and their families. In 1864, a hospital was constructed in Ayala Cove.

At Camp Reynolds, a long row of officers' houses still stands facing a parade ground that slopes to the Bay. The house closest to the Bay was the home of the commanding officer and his family. The ghost of an elderly woman dressed in dark clothing is often seen on the porch of this house. She sits in a rocking chair staring at the parade ground, watching intently as if troops are on display. This apparition is seen in daylight hours, but she fades when approached by ghost hunters.

Other ghosts appear at many of the civilian and military ruins scattered around the island. The first murder on Angel Island occurred at Hospital Cove (now called Ayala Cover) in 1854 when two men argued over ownership of a boat. Eddie Fiefirst attempted to dismantle a boat that he jointly owned with Captain Edward Payne. After the initial clash, both dashed away from the beach to retrieve their guns and, apparently, starting firing at each other from some distance away. The exchange of shots continued as they neared each other until Payne was mortally wounded. The captain's ghost still roams Hospital Cove near the waterline and shows up when small boats are beached.

In 1858, two friends, U.S. Commissioner George Pen Johnston and State Senator William I. Ferguson, dueled at Quarry point. In front of one thousand witnesses, these men traded several shots before each was wounded. Johnston survived, but Ferguson suffered for days with an infection before dying. Legends surrounding the duel say that

On Angel Island, Camp Reynolds still houses the ghosts of soldiers and some family members who appear in broad daylight.

Johnston stayed by Ferguson's side for days, begging forgiveness, but the dying man refused to speak to him. Now, a brooding ghost wanders the plateau above Quarry point, harboring resentment and anger toward his former friend.

One of the most tragic events to take place on the island was the murder of Emma Spohrs on May 23, 1872. At the age of fifteen years, Emma was the belle of the island. On the evening of her death, Emma attended a dinner and dance staged to honor Company H, scheduled to depart the island within a few days. She was escorted by her father but followed about by an unwelcome admirer, Sgt. Fritz Kimmel. According to witness accounts, Emma ignored Kimmel's advances all evening. About midnight, he walked to her left side, placed a gun at her temple, and pulled the trigger. Within moments, he turned the gun on himself and fired. Emma was buried at the Camp Reynolds cemetery in grave number 45. For some inexplicable reason, Kimmel was buried in grave number 46. Most of the graves—including those of Emma and Kimmel—were removed to the mainland in 1947. Bizarre light anomalies and other creepy experiences reported by visitors suggest some graves were left behind.

The hall at Camp Reynolds where the Spohr-Kimmel tragedy occurred stands in ruins on a bluff overlooking the main camp. It is a brick building of Civil War vintage. The place is not open to visitors, but sensitive ghost hunters exploring the exterior of the site have experienced strange auditory phenomena that may be paranormal remnants of the fateful party of May 23, 1872.

Most of the active ghosts and fascinating paranormal phenomena on Angel Island can be found at the Immigration Center known as the North Garrison. Located one mile east of Ayala Cove and often referred to as the "Ellis Island of the West," the center was opened in 1910 to control the flow of Chinese into the U.S. Since the Chinese Exclusion Act of 1882, Chinese and other Asians were unwelcome and entry into the country was allowed only if immigrants could produce proof that they were related to U.S. citizens. Thus, the immigration center became a processing facility at which documents were reviewed and personal interviews conducted, with the help of a team of interpreters under the watchful eye of soldiers, to determine if an applicant had a legal right to immigration. Between 1910 and 1940, 175,000 Chinese were examined at the center. Some were detained for a little as three days while others stayed as much as two years. Housed in barracks, many homesick, frustrated, angry immigrants scratched poems and other graffiti on the walls. During restoration of the facility, great care was taken to preserve some of these inscriptions. Some of them reflect the anguish of separation from family and shame from denigration to the status of cattle. Contemporary interpreters of the Chinese experience also report that many of those incarcerated at the center were fearful of being turned away and sent back to the poverty they experienced in China.

The intense repetitive emotions experienced by detainees have left several imprints in the barracks. Some of these were created during the smallpox epidemic and other periods when illnesses swept through the facility. Decades of neglect and years of restoration have not erased these paranormal records of voices in conversation, humming, singing, sobbing, screaming, and moaning. Ghost hunters who perform EAP at the barracks and elsewhere on the immigration center's grounds should remember that most detainees did not speak English. Some sensitives pick up the peculiar odors of people living in close quarters and Chinese herbs.

Apparitions of Chinese dressed in their traditional clothing have been spotted walking the halls of the barracks. Witnesses report that these apparitions are nearly life-like but appear for only a few seconds. They are often preceded by the sound of cloth slippers sliding on the wood floor.

Some of the paranormal activity reported at the immigration center was created by the experiences of 19,000 Japanese "picture brides," who were processed on the island between 1910 and 1920, and several hundred prisoners of war incarcerated during WWII. Prisoners from Japan and Germany were held for several months before internship at camps in the interior of the U.S.

I have always felt that the creepiest place on the island is the collection of buildings that once composed Fort McDowell, known as the East Garrison. Most of them look as though they have been bombed, but their appearance stems from years of decay by the salt-laden air. I've walked through these ruins and noted misty apparitions, bizarre auditory phenomena, and unexplainable cold spots. If you enter these structures, be careful. Some areas have unseen hazards.

Angel Island is currently a state park, accessible only by ferryboat from San Francisco, Vallejo, and Sausalito. The best way to explore the island's numerous ruins and historical points of interest is by bicycle. The eight-mile perimeter road is an easy ride for occasional cyclists. A small bookstore at Hospital Cove offers maps, guidebooks, and brief histories of island events.

OTHER PLACES TO SEARCH FOR GHOSTS:

INDIAN BURIAL SITE

Tower Market
4155 Rockville Road
Fairfield, CA 94533

For decades, the intersection of Suisun Valley Road and Rockville Road has been known as Rockville Corners. The little community of farms and homes on a few acres sits on ground that once supported a large Indian village. Some of my friends who live in the area tell me that they often find arrow heads, spear points, and other artifacts of the Patwin tribe. Occasionally, a bone turns up that is found to be human. In 2008, the gas station and convenience market at this intersection began an ambitious reconstruction project to expand the facility. When an old parking lot was torn up and trenches dug for a foundation, several Indian graves were found. Construction was halted for several months while archeologists and tribe representatives removed the remains for reburial elsewhere. Naturally, many people assumed that some bodies would be left behind. Some paranormal investigations anticipated that the desecration of so many graves and the failure to locate all the remains would result in spiritual activity in the new store. None of the customers or staff I spoke to would admit to paranormal experiences, but I found the interior of the store to be quite strange. It has a sterile, antiseptic atmosphere that seems unaffected by the cool breezes and sunshine outside the buildings. Each time I've entered the store, I've noticed that the four images on the large surveillance TV screen are distorted by static. A clerk told me that the TV always has a "hazy picture." Music that emanates from the store's loud-speakers is also full of static. When I walked to the back aisles and attempted to capture EAP, I heard a static "hiss" on playback but no other sounds could be labeled paranormal. I suspect restless Indian spirits haunt this place.

TIBURON RAILROAD FERRY DEPOT MUSEUM

1920 Paradise Drive
Tiburon, CA 94920-1954
415-435-0875

Built in 1884 as the terminus of the Northern Pacific Railroad, the Tiburon depot also included a dock for San Francisco ferryboats. The first floor of the depot was used for business offices while the second floor was constructed as a home for the stationmaster and his family. The current restoration was based on the recollections of Florence Bent Palmer, daughter of the last stationmaster, William Bent. The ghost of a man dressed in a train conductor's uniform has been spotted in the tiny laundry room of the second-floor home. The uniform described by witnesses may have been that of one of the stationmasters or a conductor who may have arrived at Tiburon ill and later died. Docents have no information about deaths in the building or details of the ghost sightings that may lead to identification of the spirit.

ST. PETER'S CHAPEL

800 Walnut Avenue
Mare Island
Vallejo, CA 94592
707-557-1538

Opened in 1901 to serve the growing community of ship builders comprised of U.S. Navy personnel and civilian contractors, this

St. Peter's Chapel on Vallejo's Mare Island served the naval community since 1912 as a venue for special events including hundreds of funerals.

little chapel has been the venue of countless weddings, funerals, and memorial services. Its sixteen Tiffany stained-glass windows (the largest collection in any single building in the U.S.) cast a dazzling display of light over the pews, giving the place a surreal ambience. People have told me how quiet the place seems, yet when I've attended services there, I've heard several voices speaking simultaneously in a whisper. Access is limited to special events, but ghost hunters who gain legitimate entry should try to capture EAP here.

Chapter 3

San Francisco Peninsula

Separating the Bay from the Pacific Ocean, the San Francisco Peninsula extends northward from a cluster of Silicon Valley towns, notably Mountain View and Palo Alto, to the magical city-by-the-bay, San Francisco. A wide variety of ghost-hunting sites can be found in the quaint, small towns of the peninsula, ocean-side towns, and rocky promontories washed by the Pacific Ocean. San Francisco itself may be one of the most haunted cities in the U.S. More than 200 years of history have left adobe buildings, hundreds of Victorian mansions, and fascinating bars, restaurants, schools and colleges, ships, bridges, libraries, and graveyards that offer unparalleled opportunities for experiencing paranormal activity.

GOLDEN GATE BRIDGE

San Francisco, CA 94129
415-921-5858

On August 5, 1775, Juan de Ayala became the first European to sail through the narrow entrance to San Francisco Bay that would later be known as the Golden Gate. For the next seventy-five years, the 1.25 mile wide channel remained an elusive target for ships' navigators, resulting in many wrecks. Soon after the Americans took California from the Mexicans in 1846, travel across the Golden Gate between San Francisco and settlements in Marin County by small boats and rafts became frequent but proved dangerous as swift tides and strong winds caused many drownings. In the early part of the twentieth century, ferry boats carried large numbers of passengers between Sausalito, Tiburon, San Rafael, and San Francisco. Sometime in the late 1920s, the idea that a bridge could span the gap was introduced.

The Golden Gate Bridge project began in 1932 with construction of two huge towers that stood about 1.1 miles apart. During construction of the foundations for these towers, at least three workers fell into the flowing wet cement, to be buried alive and forever entombed in the base of the Golden Gate Bridge.

Soon after the bridge opened, it became a popular place for committing suicide. Since 1936, over 1,200 people have hopped the railing and thrown themselves to death. It is widely believed that the actual number of suicides is much greater. The drop from mid-span to the water's surface is 286 feet. From that height, the velocity upon impact is so great that the effect on a human body is the same as hitting concrete. Ghost hunters who seek spirits on the Golden Gate should view a documentary film by Eric Steel entitled *The Bridge*. In 2004, Steel's cameras captured the images of nineteen people as they jumped to their deaths from the span.

FORT POINT

Long Avenue at Marine Drive
San Francisco, CA 94129
(415) 556-1693
www.nps.gov

Standing in the shadow of the Golden Gate Bridge, this lonely remnant of a distant historical period possesses an intense ghostly atmosphere. Cold, dark, brick corridors, bastions, and casemates still fitted with massive cannon offer quick passage to another time, putting the sensitive visitor in touch with spirits who still stand guard on the ramparts or practice gunnery.

The first fort on this site was a crude adobe and log facility constructed by Spanish soldiers in 1794. By 1821, the tiny fort had fallen into disrepair from neglect and the harsh San Francisco climate.

This decaying out-post served little purpose until 1846 when it became a military objective of the Bear Flag revolt. Kit Carson led a group of Americans across the Golden Gate and up the sandy slope to attack the poorly manned fort. Later, the strategic importance of the site was recognized by the U.S. Army, especially with the onset of the Gold Rush in 1849 and the massive influx of foreign ships into the Bay Area.

Construction of the present fort was begun in 1853 and completed in 1861 with the assistance of army engineer Robert E. Lee. The largest masonry fort west of the Mississippi River, Fort Point has been called the "Gibraltar of the West" and one of the most perfect models of masonry in America. Together with gun emplacements on Alcatraz and at Fort Lime Point near the present town of Sausalito, Fort Point was America's primary means of defending San Francisco and Northern California from foreign encroachment. Despite its extensive armament, Fort Point never fired a gun in battle. Instead, the lonely fort slipped into disrepair and decay by the turn of the century. Fortuitous circumstances saved the fort from destruction when the Golden Gate Bridge was constructed in the 1930s. After extensive renovation, the essence of an era has been revived.

As visitors to Fort Point pass down the dark, deserted corridors, the sounds of soldiers living on the very frontier of America, far from home, mix with the roar of surf surging against the outer walls. Many soldiers came to this desolate place with a sense of apprehension over the harshness of life and duty at the Fort and a longing to return to civilized America. Some lost their dreams amid the tumultuous history of the opening of the West and never returned to the East or Midwest. A few of these lost soldiers still stand guard at Fort Point on the Golden Gate. One of them, Pvt. James Aitchison, died at the fort on January 5, 1965, of a mysterious cause. His ghost is said to walk the barracks of the second floor. Other ghosts of soldiers who died during the Bubonic plague epidemic of 1900 walk these rooms too. During the four years of plague infestation, hundreds of soldiers were quarantined in the fort and an unknown number died there.

Outside the walls of the fort, sensitives often detect the tortured souls of passengers who died on February 21, 1901, when the SS *City of Rio de Janeiro* crashed into the rocks. Reportedly, panic swept the decks as passengers fought for the inadequate supply of life jackets and seats in leaky life boats. Witnesses reported that most of the life boats, launched less than 100 yards from shore, sank, spilling passengers into the icy water. Less than thirty minutes after striking the rocks, 129 passengers and crew died in the waters off Fort Point while only 85 survived. Many who made it ashore clung to the rocks as waves washed over them. Their screams for help can be heard by sensitives and sometimes captured on audio recorders.

GHOSTS OF THE OLDEST HOUSE IN SAN FRANCISCO

Officer's Club of the Presidio
50 Moraga Avenue
San Francisco, CA 94129
E-mail: events@presidiotrust.gov
415-561-5444

Founded on March 28, 1776, by Colonel Juan de Anza of the Spanish Army, the Presidio of San Francisco covers 2,200 acres of historic ground at the edge of the bay. The first structures consisted of a crude perimeter wall made of adobe, brush, and wood that enclosed several small buildings. Standing 14 feet high, the wall composed a square that measured 200 yards on each side. Barracks, officers' quarters, storehouses, and kitchens were topped with thatched roofs and attached to the perimeter wall. When the English Captain George Vancouver visited the Presidio in 1792, he described the square as "resembling a pound for cattle." In his memoirs, he noted the Presidio was so badly constructed and fortified that it was "incapable of making resistance against a foreign invasion."

Captain Vancouver also visited the commandant's house which is known today as the Presidio's officer's club. He noted that the floor was "native soil raised about three feet from its original level, without being boarded, paved, or even reduced to an even surface." Vancouver mentioned that the lack of windows and other basic elements made the place "in winter, or rainy season, at the best, very uncomfortable."

In 1820, Spain relinquished the province of Alta California to Mexico and the Presidio became a key element in limiting Russian

Built in the 1770s, the Officer's Club of the Presidio of San Francisco is the oldest house in the city.

colonization of the northern part of the territory. In 1846, Mexico lost Alta California to the U. S. and the American flag was raised over the Presidio by Lieutenant John C. Fremont. For the next 148 years, the Presidio supported American military operations by serving as a training facility for infantry and aviators, a post for a variety of intelligence services, and as a vital acute care and rehabilitation center for wounded and injured military personnel. Several U.S. generals, including William Sherman, Winfield Scott, and John Pershing, made their headquarters at the Presidio. In the aftermath of the 1906 earthquake, thousands of people sought shelter at the Presidio. Soldiers established tent cities and housed displaced families for a year while homes were rebuilt.

From 1862 to 1994, the former commandant's house served as the officer's club. In addition to social gatherings, the front parlor in which Captain Vancouver was received in 1792 served as a viewing room where caskets of men killed overseas were displayed while the deceased were honored.

After inactivation of the Sixth Army in 1994 and transfer of the Presidio to the National Park Service, the officer's club was converted to a visitor's center and facility for special events such as banquets and weddings. Soon after renovation was completed, stories of ghostly activity began to circulate. The intensity and frequency of activity was so impressive that in 2007 The Atlantic Paranormal Society (TAPS) traveled from their offices in Rhode Island to investigate the oldest house in San Francisco.

TAPS based their investigation on reports made by two high-ranking officers who had experienced dramatic ghostly activity in the former viewing room, now a lounge, and the Moraga Room. Their reports included the unexplained odor of cigar smoke, fragrance of flowers, tapping sounds emanating from the fireplace, and the apparition of a woman dressed in a Spanish style dress of the early nineteenth century.

The TAPS investigation debunked the floral scent and odor of cigar smoke. The former was attributed to cleaning supplies in a nearby closet while the latter was believed to be the result of smoke-saturated wood that had been exposed during various renovations. TAPS could not explain, however, why the odor was detected in isolated cells and not throughout a large area adjacent to the wood.

TAPS video cameras caught the apparition of a woman walking through the Moraga Room. When I viewed the video, the image appeared to be that of a woman wearing a mantilla or headpiece to which a veil was attached. Some TAPS members dismissed the apparition as a shadow but they could not explain its source. People who work in the officer's club have told me they've seen the shadow many times, usually late in the afternoon when the great room is empty. Since females were forbidden to enter the social areas of the officer's club throughout most of the Presidio's American period, it is likely that this apparition is the ghost of a member of the Spanish or Mexican commandant's family, perhaps a lady who dressed in her finest gown for the reception of the great English Captain Vancouver in 1792.

While visiting the Presidio, ghost hunters should explore the former Letterman Arm Hospital (now the Thoreau Center for Sustainability), the impressive red brick barracks of Montgomery Street, and the San Francisco National Cemetery. On Mason Street, ghost hunters

Dating from the late 1850s, Barracks Row on the Presidio of San Francisco is haunted by the ghosts of soldiers who served in many of America's wars.

will find Building 640, a 1928 vintage aircraft hangar that housed the Military Intelligence Service Language School in 1941. Several gun emplacements standing on the west and north perimeters of the Presidio remind visitors that military leaders once considered San Francisco Bay vulnerable to attack by Japanese naval forces.

GHOSTS OF THE SAILORS

Balclutha
San Francisco Maritime National Historical Park
2905 Hyde Street
San Francisco, CA 94109
415-447-5000
www.nps.gov

This beautiful square-rigged tall ship was built in Glasgow, Scotland,

The tall ship Balclutha *never leaves her dock, but a ghostly crew still works in the rigging and below decks.*

and launched in 1886. She is over 300 feet in length and stands with three masts rising 145 feet above the deck. She served many years by hauling coal from England to San Francisco. On the return voyage to England, she carried grain from the San Joaquin Valley loaded at San Francisco wharves. These 10,000-mile voyages took her through tropical heat, freezing cold, many storms, and the treacherous Cape Horn, which she rounded seventeen times in a thirteen year period.

As with many sailing vessels of her day, men died on board. Health care was non-existent and the splinting of broken bones and stitching of lacerations was often left to the cook or sail maker. Several sailors died of chronic illnesses such as diabetes and lung disease while others succumbed to hard labor. Virtually every sailor who died on board was buried at sea. The early log books of the *Balclutha* are not available to determine how many at-sea burials took place, but records from similar ships suggest at least five deaths per year. Whatever the number of deaths that occurred on the *Balclutha*, it appears that several decided to stay aboard after their bodies were committed to the deep.

This huge sailing vessel is a spooky ship, especially below decks when no one is around. Visitors have been so surprised by eerie sounds that they've made reports to docents that must be described as paranormal. Below decks, odd sounds are heard that include the muted moaning of sailors struggling through their final minutes of life. Unexplained sounds also include coughing, whistling, flute, drums, and the shuffling of boot-clad feet on the deck. Sometimes, visitors feel the cold presence of someone standing behind them or cold spots near the crew's quarters. An intense cold spot is often detected near the foremast on the starboard side of the ship. This may be the spot where a sailor landed after falling from the tall mast during a gale off Cape Horn.

While ghost hunters visit the *Balclutha*, they should take note of the vessel's characteristics including the shape of the hull, sweep of the decks, and position of yardarms on the mast. Familiarity with these features may enable ghost hunters to spot ghost ships floating on San Francisco Bay that resemble the *Balclutha*. On foggy days, astonished visitors to the waterfront have been amazed at the sight of a square-rigged tall ship gliding out of the mist only to disappear again. Some have called the police or Coast Guard to report that the *Balclutha* has slipped her moorings and drifted into the shipping lanes on the bay. Panicked callers are assured that the great ship is safely moored. What these people saw is one of several ghost ships from the nineteenth century that still sail the bay. The most famous sighting occurred September 15, 1942, when the destroyer U.S.S. *Kennison* entered the fog-bound bay. Fresh from combat in the Pacific, the ship's look-out Howard H. Brisbane called the bridge to report an old sailing vessel with two masts that came into sight as the fog lifted. Brisbane entered his report in the *Kennison*'s log which included mention of two masts, an unpainted hull, and ragged sails. Several crew members came on deck to get a look at the old ship as the *Kennison* maneuvered to avoid collision. As the two vessels passed each other, the sailing ship disappeared in a fog.

This sighting is considered one of the most valid ever made because the *Kennison*'s crew were fresh from combat and their skills in observing other vessels were considered highly developed and not prone to error. Added to that, at least thirty men on board the destroyer witnessed the older vessel.

GHOSTS OF THE PRISONERS

Alcatraz Island
San Francisco, CA 94123
Ranger Station
(415) 561-4900
Ferry Tickets/Reservations, (415) 981-7625
www.nps.gov

Sitting 1.5 miles from San Francisco's world-famous Fisherman's Wharf, Alcatraz Island, which is named for the huge flocks of pelicans that populated it, is always included on top-ten lists of America's most haunted places. Known for its federal prison and the infamous characters who were incarcerated there, the island has a long history of paranormal activity spanning centuries. Several paranormal research groups have performed investigations of the prison. In September of 2009, celebrity ghost hunters Barry and Brad Klinge transported their *Everyday Paranormal* team and vast collection of equipment to the island and performed an extensive investigation that was broadcast on their TV show, *Ghost Lab*. Two months later, an investigative group called Sonoma SPIRIT, led by Jackie Ganiy, was the first to spend an entire night on the island. The prison's ghosts have been described by Peter James and channeled by world-renowned psychic Sylvia Browne. Ghost hunters Loyd Auerbach, Michael Kouri, and Richard Senate have published detailed reports of their experiences with the ghosts of Alcatraz. With rare exceptions, access to the island is restricted to scheduled tours guided by docents working for the U.S. National Park Service.

Surrounded by dangerous currents, Alcatraz remained undeveloped during the Spanish and Mexican occupation of northern California. Indian legends that told of evil spirits dwelling in caves in the island may have hindered development. After the American annexation of California in 1846, the importance of the island to bay navigation led to construction of a lighthouse. During the Gold Rush years (1848-1858), a tremendous influx of immigrants and visitations by ships under foreign flags prompted the installation of a military facility on the island. From 1853 to 1858, the Army Corps of Engineers installed 105 cannon on the island and constructed barracks and other facilities. During the Civil War years, the military presence on the island was increased to protect the bay from Confederate sympathizers and privateers sailing outside the Golden Gate. The fort's guns were never fired in battle, but Confederate prisoners were imprisoned in the basement of the guardhouse throughout the Civil War.

By 1867, the threat of foreign encroachment was ended and Alcatraz was converted to a military prison and disciplinary barracks. Inmates were army deserters and Hopi Indians, but the population remained less than 100 until the Spanish-American War of 1898, when as many as 450 prisoners were crowded into tiny cells. After the San Francisco earthquake of 1906, hundreds of civilian prisoners were incarcerated on the island. A large cell block, the "Citadel," was constructed in 1912 followed in 1920 by an additional three-story cell block. By 1933, the military had evacuated the island and transferred ownership to the Federal Bureau of Prisons. In August of 1934, the first federal prisoners arrived on the island, beginning a twenty-nine year period that fostered a reputation as an inescapable prison while earning the moniker, "the Rock."

Paranormal activity on Alcatraz is the result of Native American evil spirits, imprints and hauntings resulting from military and civilian prisoners, and numerous sailors, fishermen, and swimmers who lost their lives in the treacherous swirling currents surrounding the island. At the water's edge, six prisoners were shot and killed during escape attempts. Three others drowned after slipping into the icy water. Hundreds of paranormal imprints or painful and intense emotional experiences were created by prisoners who were tortured in cells called the "strip cells" in D-Block. In these cells, prisoners were stripped naked and enclosed in total darkness with only a toilet, a sink, and a mattress that was removed during the day. Deprived of contact with others, including the guards, and exposed to very cold temperatures, many prisoners succumbed to the stress and became mentally unstable.

Several Alcatraz inmates achieved fame before their incarceration. Al Capone (1899-1947) served a little more than four years at Alcatraz before developing symptoms of tertiary syphilis for which he was transferred to Terminal Island in Los Angeles. Other notables include George "Machine Gun" Kelly (1895-1954) and his partner Harvey

The prison on Alcatraz Island is believed to be one of the most haunted places in America.

Bailey (1887-1979), Alvin "Creepy Karpis" Karpowicz (1907-1979), and leader of the 1946 Alcatraz prisoner revolt, Joseph Cretzer (1911-1946). Others became known because of unique talents developed during imprisonment. Foremost of these was Robert Stroud (1890-1963), also known as the birdman of Alcatraz. During his incarceration, Stroud became a self-taught expert in ornithology. He was portrayed by actor Burt Lancaster in the movie *The Birdman of Alcatraz.*

Aside from documented prisoner deaths resulting from gunshot wounds inflicted by guards, fatal stabbings during fights among inmates, and drownings that occurred during escape attempts, an unknown number of suicides and natural deaths occurred on Alcatraz that have most certainly added to the spirit population.

Long before the prison closed in 1963, ghost stories circulated among the guards and their families. In February of 2008, I interviewed a woman who lived on the island for fifteen years, leaving at the age of eighteen. Her father worked as a guard and her mother performed part-time secretarial work for the warden. Throughout the federal prison's twenty-nine years, guards reported unexplained eerie screams, metal doors slamming shut, footsteps, cannon fire, gun shots, moans, cries, sobbing, voices whispering, foul odors, and scratching

The exercise yard at Alcatraz Prison was the site of riots and inmate violence.

sounds. These unexplained phenomena were encountered throughout the cell blocks and in the laundry, hospital, shops, mess hall, and even the warden's house. Apparitions were also reported. In 1940, guards attending the warden's Christmas party observed a ghostly image appear wearing a gray suit, cap, and mutton-chop sideburns. The apparition, which resembled a Confederate prisoner held on the island during the Civil War, persisted for several minutes. Moments after it vanished, the room became very cold. Unfortunately, the warden's house now stands in ruins, precluding investigation of this ghost.

In the hospital, disembodied sounds of prisoners in agony echo through the rooms. Cries, moans, sobs, and screams are commonly experienced by tourists and docents. Aside from these audio phenomena, sensitive visitors have detected the presence of a kindly man who is eager for conversation. This entity may be Robert Stroud, the "Birdman," who lived in the hospital eleven years before being transferred to the Medical Center for Federal Prisoners in Springfield, Missouri, where he died in 1963. Guards used to play checkers with Stroud, who often carried on long conversations about his studies of birds.

The laundry room in Cell block C has the ghost of a murderer. According to prison records, Abie "the Butcher" Maldowitz was killed by two other prisoners. In 1992, psychic Sylvia Browne toured the laundry with former Alcatraz inmate Leon Thompson. Sylvia discovered a ghost she described as tall and thin with beady eyes.

Cell block D is the site of the most frequent and intense paranormal activity on the island. It was designed to be the "treatment unit" with various degrees of restrictions, isolation, and deprivation. D Block prisoners were not allowed to have meals in the mess hall, use the exercise yard, or work in the shops. The boredom and depression of the sufferers has left audio and emotional imprints in virtually all of the cells.

Six cells in D Block were modified as punishment cells. Known as the "strip cells," these cells were used for the most incorrigible prisoners. With only a toilet, sink, dim light, and a mattress that was removed from the cell throughout the day, many prisoners in the strip cells went crazy. One of them screamed incessantly throughout most of the night until a bizarre silence filled his cell. In the morning, he was found dead from strangulation with his face frozen in extreme fright.

Visitors who enter the strip cells often experience such frightening impressions that they cannot stay more than a minute. Guards used to tell of beady, evil eyes that appeared in the darkness of empty cells and of ghosts of dead prisoners who lined up with the living for roll count in the morning.

Although access to Alcatraz is limited to daylight tours conducted by docents, ghost hunters will have many opportunities to conduct EAP sweeps, snap pictures inside prison cells, and check EMF meters. Ghosts seems to be everywhere on Alcatraz, affirming the prison's place on everyone's top-ten list of haunted places in America.

HOTEL FOR GHOSTS

San Remo Hotel
2237 Mason Street
San Francisco, CA 94133
415-776-8688
www.sanremohotel.com

Considered by many to be one of San Francisco's finest boutique hotels, the San Remo Hotel is also one of the city's most historic and most haunted buildings. Built in the days following the 1906 earthquake by Bank of America founder A. P. Gianini, the hotel provided housing to many people left homeless by the catastrophic event and fire that followed. Christened the New California Hotel by Gianini, the 62-room, Italianate Victorian structure stood as a beacon of hope and renewal for many as they rebuilt their homes and businesses. By 1909, much of the city had been rebuilt and the clientele of the hotel changed to sailors, fishermen, journalists, writers, and artists who offered their paintings as payment for their rooms. Cheap accommodations located only a few blocks from the city's north beach and wharves assured a steady flow of customers, some of whom still reside there as spirits.

By 1922, North Beach was a robust Italian community that attracted long-time residents from other communities and immigrants fresh off the boat. The changing character of North Beach prompted owners to change the hotel's name to the San Remo Hotel, after a picturesque town on the Gulf of Genoa, Italy. Today, the San Remo Hotel stands as an icon of the fabled North Beach community, offering guests an old world ambiance, Victorian heirloom furnishings, and the Fior d' Italia restaurant founded in 1886.

It is unknown how many people died in the hotel, but historical documents confirm that two murders and one suicide occurred there. Much of the paranormal activity in the place has been investigated by members of the San Francisco Ghost Society. These paranormal investigators have identified several ghosts and countless residual hauntings, or imprints that account for reports by guests that the place is full of spirits.

Built after the 1906 earthquake as a refuge for the homeless, the San Remo Hotel remains a home for several ghosts.

In room 33, the ghost of a woman known as the "painted lady" moves objects left on the bed, whispers to guests, and creates cold spots. Her name is lost to history, but she is known to be a long-term resident of the hotel, residing there many years after retiring as the madam of a brothel in the Haight-Asbury district. People who have seen her apparition report that her face appears heavily made-up, as if she had resorted to make-up to regain a youthful appearance.

In 1970, a man committed suicide in room 42 by shooting himself in the head. This tragic event has left intense residuals or imprints that sensitives describe as depression, loneliness, tension, and misery. Some guests have reported a male voice in this room. Speaking only two or three words that are intelligible but make no sense, he moves about as if he is pacing the floor. Guests often report hearing knocking on the door. Upon opening the door and gazing into the hallway, no one is seen. Astute guests report that the knocking sound emanates from a position low on the door, as if a child is in the hallway seeking entry to the room.

During a 1911 wedding reception in the dining room of the San Remo Hotel, a tragic double murder occurred that created ghosts who still haunt the place.

A lot of ghostly activity at the San Remo occurs in the hallways. On the first floor, the apparition of a sailor appears pacing about as if he is looking for someone. Witnesses report that he is dressed in a navy or merchant marine uniform. On the second and third floors, the apparition of a girl, aged ten or twelve years, appears in a night gown and barefoot. Her laughter is heard as she moves about, stopping in front of some of the doors to knock on them. The face of this ghost has been spotted in the central air shaft, looking over the railing to the floor below. This ghost may be one of the children who likely died in the hotel in the months following the 1906 earthquake when tainted water caused hundreds of deaths, particularly among very young children.

On the second floor, at the bookcase, the ghost of a young woman appears with long, dark hair and a white blouse. Holding a book, she moves about, creating the sound of floor boards creaking and intense cold spots. Many ghost hunters who visit this location find orbs in their photographs.

A double murder occurred in 1911 in the restaurant of the old New California Hotel that has left intense residuals and a ghost believed to be that of the murderer. During a wedding reception staged in the area now occupied by the Fior d'Italia restaurant, a former lover of the bride showed up. Enraged with the loss of his love to another man, the party crasher began fighting with guests as the bride tried to calm him and usher him from the restaurant. As the man neared the door, he turned, rushed back into the restaurant, pulled a gun, and shot two men seated at a table. The two victims were rushed to the hospital where they died while friends of the bride captured the murderer. The perpetrator, known by local ghost hunters and hotel staff members as Jack, died in prison. Apparently, his ghost has returned to the hotel and appears as a dark shadow that walks across the Fior d'Italia restaurant. Witnesses describe him as a short man with slicked back, black hair.

The best way to experience the ghosts of the San Remo Hotel is to stay two nights in room 33 or 42. Leave audio and video recorders running in your room while you roam about the hallways or dine in the restaurant. The active ghosts of this landmark hotel will amaze you.

GRACE CATHEDRAL

1100 California St
San Francisco, CA 94108
(415) 749-6304
E-mail: theshop@gracecatherdral.org

Churches are often good locations for conducting paranormal investigations. Spirits of former parishioners and clergy are often found in adjacent cemeteries or, less frequently, at the altar or pulpit. At Grace Cathedral in San Francisco, ghost hunters may visit a number of locations known for paranormal activity, including an encounter with former Bishop James A. Pike (1913-1969).

Located on Nob Hill, Grace Cathedral was built after the great fire of 1906 swept through the district. Center of the Episcopal Diocese of California, the cathedral has become a destination for church members from throughout the world and has also become well-known for its liberal policies of welcoming people who follow non-traditional lifestyles. The massive cathedral is also well-known for several distinctive architectural features. Aside from a vast collection of stained glass windows measuring more than 7,000 square feet, the cathedral has medieval furnishings, an AIDS Chapel altarpiece, a replica of Ghiberti's massive doors called *Gates of Paradise*, and two labyrinths. The labyrinths are based on the labyrinth of *Cathedral Notre-Dame de Chartres* in France. Walkers report that meditating in the passage gives them a sense of purgation, illumination, union with God, and other mystical and paranormal experiences. Ghost hunters who have walked through the out-doors labyrinth have told me that, for weeks after the experience, they feel more sensitive or aware of spiritual entities.

It has been reported that the ghost of former bishop James Pike haunts the cathedral. Ordained in 1946 after many years as a professed agnostic, lawyer, and officer serving in naval intelligence during WWII, Pike became the outspoken bishop of Grace Cathedral in 1958. In 1966, he was relieved of his duties because his views and actions were in conflict with church doctrine.

In his last days as bishop, Pike reported intense poltergeist events within the cathedral which he attributed to his son Jimmy's recent suicide from a drug-overdose in New York City.

Pike openly reported that books flew off shelves and vanished, clothing was ejected from closets, and numerous signs appeared within his home and the cathedral that spelled out the hour of Jimmy's death, 8:19. According to newspaper accounts, Pike staged public investigations and séances aimed at contacting Jimmy at a time when most people did not believe in ghosts or even consider the possibility of communication with the dead. In September of 1967, a televised séance conducted by medium Arthur Ford earned Pike an unflattering reputation that worsened until his death in an Israeli desert in 1969. A fascinating account of Pike's attempt to contact his son is contained in his book, *The Other Side*.

Visitors at Grace Cathedral have reported seeing Pike's ghost wander among the pews, hover around the pulpit, and even stand at various locations on the front stairs. The reason for Pike's spiritual presence in the cathedral is unknown. He died in Israel and was buried in a Protestant cemetery in Jaffa. Perhaps he believes that the spiritual power of the grand cathedral he loved may yet enable him to contact his son.

Grace Cathedral faces Huntington Park, a gathering spot for participants in San Francisco's Vampire Tour. The park is the former site of the Huntington mansion which was destroyed by the fire that followed the 1906 earthquake. Across the park, the Flood mansion withstood the conflagration and still stands as the home of the Pacific Union Club.

GHOST OF RUNAWAY BRIDE

California Street between Powel and Jones Streets
San Francisco, CA 94108

In 1876, James and Bedellia Sommerton were members of the upper crust of San Francisco society. Ever mindful of the challenges of sustaining a high social status and economic gain, they arranged for their charming daughter, Flora, to marry a gentleman whose family was solidly entrenched in the city's financial ruling class. Unfortunately, the man was much older than the teenaged Flora and, according to ghost tour historian Jim Fassbinder, the man was lacking in the usual attributes that a young lady would desire. Aside from all of that, Flora hardly knew the man. She was aware that marriage would provide her family with many advantages, including a higher social status and significant financial gains, and so, for a while, she went along with her mother's grand plans for a lavish wedding.

On the eve of the wedding, however, while trying on the extravagant white gown that was destined to be the talk of San Francisco, Flora realized she could not go through with the ceremony. Quickly taking stock of her situation, she realized she had only one course open to her.

She dashed out of her Pacific Heights mansion, ran down California Street, and disappeared. When her family discovered her missing, the police were called and the neighborhood filled with officers who searched every street and alley while Flora's parents waited at home, anticipating the delivery of a ransom note. Within twenty-four hours, a large reward was offered and the search for Flora was widened to include the waterfront and train station.

A claim for the reward was not made until 1926 when Flora was found dead in Butte, Montana, in a house rumored to be a bordello. Flora, perhaps having anticipated her death, was found wearing the elegant wedding gown she had worn when she made her escape from San Francisco in 1876. Her body was brought home and buried in the family plot in Colma.

More than a century later, the apparition of Flora Sommerton has been seen by hundreds of astonished people as she repeats her get-a-way dash on California Street. She has appeared as a nearly amorphous white cloud and fully life-like. Some witnesses claim they have been pushed aside as the frightened, angry bride makes a dash for freedom.

Skeptics participating in Fassbinder's San Francisco ghost tour have spotted the young bride's apparition and had to reconsider their opinion of the paranormal phenomenon. I witnessed Flora Sommerton on two occasions. Both times she first appeared as a humanoid white cloud within which I could make out a head, draped with a bride's veil, and an arm and torso. This ghost usually appears to be walking in the street, but she has been reported floating over the sidewalk too.

ATHERTON MANSION

1900 California Street
San Francisco, CA 94109
415-391-2000

The history of this landmark house in San Francisco's Pacific Heights district has all the elements needed to create strong environmental imprints that have persisted for more than a century. Imprints are created when living persons experience intense emotions, in a specific location, that are repetitive. Emotions that produce the strongest imprints are fear, jealously, anger, hatred, and anxiety. Disdain and condemnation also lead to strong imprints. According to the history of the first family to inhabit this Atherton House, two domineering women and one meek fellow experienced many of these emotions often. Residual imprints may be responsible for some of the paranormal activity reported to occur within its walls. Some activity may be attributed to imprints created by a subsequent owner who lived in the place with fifty cats. A ghost may haunt the great house as well, creating enough scary experiences for residents to justify inclusion of the Atherton House on San Francisco's foremost ghost tour.

The grand mansion was built in 1881 with money earned by Faxon D. Atherton (1834-1872). A native of Massachusetts, Faxon settled in Valparaiso, Chile, and made a fortune in the hide and tallow industry before moving on to San Francisco. Before leaving Chile, he married Dominga de Goni. The family settled in rural San Mateo country on land that eventually became the city of Atherton. Upon Faxon's death, the domineering Dominga took charge of his financial enterprises and moved to San Francisco. After increasing the family fortune and delighting in the power it brought her, she built the Atherton House that stands at the corner of Octavia and California Streets. She raised her son, George, in this house but crushed his will by controlling every aspect of his life. By the time George achieved adulthood, he was meek and lacked ambition. It is likely that he suffered severe anxiety and viewed his life as a miserable existence. In spite of that, he married a woman who was just as domineering as his mother. George's wife, the noted author Gertrude Horn, may have been trying to get a share of the Atherton wealth, but Dominga embraced her. The two strong-willed women waged a war of the sexes against poor George, who was out-numbered and out-matched by their intellect and temper.

In 1887, an escape route became available to George. During a grand party staged to honor visiting Chilean naval officers, George accepted an invitation to sail to Chile. Fearful of making a move without his mother's approval, however, George wavered at the last minute. Eager for a few months without her disappointing husband, Gertrude literally pushed him out the door and George sailed away. The voyage was short-lasting, however. After a few days at sea, he became ill with a kidney disorder and died. The ship's captain kindly preserved George's body in a cast of rum and transferred it to a passing ship bound for San Francisco.

When the cask arrived at the Atherton House, it was assumed to be a gift and placed in the basement. Weeks later, a butler opened it to fill a pitcher only to discover the pickled body of George Atherton. Upon hearing of the grisly discovery, Gertrude is reported to have said, "I had an uneasy feeling that George would haunt me if he could." This suggests Gertrude knew how miserable she had made her husband and

Now a private residence, the Atherton House was the scene of a grisly discovery when a man's body was found in a keg of rum.

that she anticipated reprisals if he ever managed to find the strength. As a ghost, George apparently found the strength. For decades after his death, residents of the house reported strong gusts of wind that roared through the place without explanation. Many have reported knocks on the wall, a frightening atmosphere in the basement, room temperatures that swing from very cold to very hot and back to cold, disembodied footsteps, light anomalies, and an angry presence believed to be George Atherton. Participants in Jim Fassbinder's ghost tour have spotted an eerie face in a window that flashes in and out of view.

Psychics who have visited the house report as many as four spirits roaming the rooms. Sylvia Browne encountered one female that kept insisting "This is my dwelling." Sylvia reported that the spirit was possessive of the house, volatile, full of energy, short, and buxom. It is known that Dominga Atherton was only five feet tall and weighed 200 pounds. A native of Chile, she was also known for a fiery Latin temper.

Psychics have also encountered a spirit believed to be Gertrude

Horn Atherton. Gertrude's spirit may, indeed, be in the house but, at the very least, imprints of her anger, disappointment in George, hatred of the marital trap into which she had fallen, and energy from conflicts with Dominga fill many rooms.

Psychics have also discovered the spirit of Carrie Rousseau. In 1923, Carrie purchased the house and renovated it into several apartments. Keeping the main floor for herself, Carrie moved in and accumulated fifty cats. The felines lived primarily in the former Atherton banquet hall. Carrie died in 1974 at the age of 93. Her body was discovered surrounded by starving cats.

GHOST OF THE VOODOO LADY

Site of the Bell Mansion
1661 Octavia Street
San Francisco, CA 94109

The ghost of a short black woman has been spotted lurking among a stand of giant eucalyptus and nearby shrubbery at the corner of Octavia and Bush Streets in San Francisco. Known as the ghost of Mammy Pleasant and sporting a colorful headdress once typical of southern female slaves, this spirit haunts the trees she planted that front Octavia Street on which she built a thirty-room mansion sometime in the 1860s. So many bizarre events occurred at the mansion that the place became known as the "Bell House of Mystery." The eponym was taken from Thomas Bell, a front man for Mammy Pleasant's numerous and nefarious financial adventures, who may have died by her hand.

Known widely for running houses of prostitution, manipulating Bell and other bankers, extorting, blackmailing, and using voodoo to extract information from vulnerable people, revisionist historians have rewritten Mammy Pleasant's history using fragments of her diaries and a few pages of other "lost accounts" written by her contemporaries. Revised history presents Mary Ellen Pleasant as an impoverished female who was born in the South, escaped slavery, and worked her way west. The new story describes Mary Ellen as a self-made millionaire who helped shape the social fabric of late nineteenth-century San Francisco by succeeding in business at a time when black women were denied access to financial markets, altering racial stereotypes, and providing sanctuary to others who had escaped the degradation of slavery, indentured servitude, and abuse. Some writers have called her the "the Mother of Civil Rights in California," a generous community benefactor, and the most influential female in San Francisco civic affairs in the 1880s. In spite of all that, the arcane legend of Mammy Pleasant persists largely because she was rather like a Robin Hood: she did a tremendous amount of good for her community largely through illegal means. Added to that, many still believe that Mary Ellen did, indeed, push Thomas Bell off the balcony of her house, killing him to keep him from divulging her secrets.

Mary Ellen Pleasant (1814-1904) arrived in San Francisco from New Orleans in the early 1850s. It is known that her mother was a free black woman and her father was a Cherokee Indian. She had one blue eye and very high cheek-bones that gave her a distinct appearance among the local black population. Without question, she practiced a kind of voodoo magic and blackmail that she learned from the high priestess of voodoo, Marie Laveau of New Orleans. Mary Ellen used both devices as a means of gaining control over several wealthy people in the city, including Thomas Bell, an investment banker. Once in control of the man, she established herself in his mansion as the housekeeper, overseeing several servants and exerting considerable control over Bell's personal life. It is said that she coerced him into marrying one of her blackmail victims who had become Bell's mistress. That relationship proved to be a wild one. When the new bride tried to run away with jewels and other valuables, she was arrested. Mammy Pleasant interceded with the police and managed to have the woman returned to the household without civil punishment. This act has been interpreted as once of kindness and forgiveness but, in reality, Pleasant merely sought to insure that the woman could not talk further with police or newspaper reporters about Bell's activities and the control Pleasant had exerted over him.

Legend tells of Bell and Mammy Pleasant amassing a fortune that exceeded $30 million by practicing voodoo among some of the city's wealthy people. They worked well together until October

16, 1892, when Bell fell from a third floor balcony after a fierce argument. Mammy's red scarf was found with his body but no charges were brought against the seventy-eight-year-old woman. Mammy continued to dominate the widow Bell's household until 1896 when she was finally forced out of the mansion without money or any of the other fruits of her nefarious business.

As a homeless person, Mary Ellen took up residence in a grove of trees near the mansion. From this sanctuary, the demented woman attempted to work her voodoo magic, without success, on people who would walk by the place. Mary Ellen died a penniless street person at the age of ninety on January 11, 1904. In spite of the many good things she did for the poor of San Francisco, there were many who rejoiced at this event.

For decades after her death, residents of the Pacific Heights neighborhood perpetuated the rumors of evil and bizarre events that took place at the Bell mansion, and the place became known as a haunted house, haunted not only by Mary Ellen but the ghost of Thomas Bell as well. The place survived the 1906 earthquake but in 1920 was destroyed by fire. Soon after the ashes were cleared away, people started reporting the apparition of Mammy Pleasant, lurking in the trees. Many people in San Francisco swear that she is there to this day. She emerges from hiding, trying to work her old magic on unsuspecting passersby.

Mary Ellen Pleasant is buried in Tulocay Cemetery in Napa. As a penniless, ninety-year-old homeless person, it seems odd that she managed to have her corpse removed from the city and buried in a town that, at the time, was a sleepy backwater to vibrant San Francisco. Despite her years as a destitute street person, the Oakland Tribune reported that the assets of the deceased Mary Ellen Pleasant were valued at nearly $150,000.

GHOSTS OF MISS MARY AND THE GIRLS

Queen Anne Hotel
1590 Sutter Street
San Francisco, CA 94109
(415) 441-2828
www.queenanne.com

This landmark hotel stands as an icon of the paranormal in San Francisco's celebrated Pacific Heights district. Aside from the prison on Alcatraz Island, the Queen Anne Hotel may be the best-known haunted place in the city. Featured on numerous television shows, visited by more than fifty paranormal investigation groups, and serving as the home of Jim Fassbinder's Haunted San Francisco Tour, the Victorian building has not only captured several ghosts from the city's past but also retains the beautifully eerie atmosphere of the 1890s.

In 1888, architects Schulze and Meeker designed the structure to serve as a boarding school. Builder John T. Grant started construction in 1889 with funds provided by Comstock silver baron James G. Fair (1831-1894). Fair's interest in a boarding school for girls is hard to fathom, but clues may be found in his personal life. After becoming one of the richest investors in Nevada's silver mines, Fair married Theresa Rooney in 1861. Twenty-two years later, she divorced him on grounds of "habitual adultery." After a single term as a U.S. Senator, Fair return to San Francisco and became socially prominent as one of the wealthiest bachelors in the Bay Area. There is speculation that the fifty-five-year-old man became infatuated with a young school teacher, Miss Mary Lake. Having no funds of her own, it seems obvious that Mary prevailed upon multi-millionaire Fair for a few thousand dollars to help her create a young lady's finishing school. This was a personal favor since the boarding school could not possibly be viewed as a reasonable business venture for a man worth $40 million in 1888 dollars.

Miss Mary Lake opened her "private boarding and day school for girls" on February 15, 1890. The school offered young women a basic education equivalent to a high school and finishing classes that groomed them for entry into the higher strata of San Francisco

Built in 1889, the stately Queen Anne Hotel is one of the most haunted buildings in the San Francisco Bay area.

society. A faculty of seventeen teachers managed the curriculum for as many as seventy students. Some of the faculty, including Miss Mary, resided on the fourth floor of the school. Mary used room 410 as an office and private apartment.

The school became a quick success largely due to Miss Mary's skill as an educator and administrator, and also because of the elegant parlors and dining rooms, well-equipped classrooms, and several architectural innovations including a trunk lift, an infirmary, and numerous bathrooms paid for by Fair's money. James Fair died in 1894 but the school continued operation until 1898.

Miss Mary's ghost haunts her former room, and perhaps several other parts of the former school, but I could not trace Mary's history after 1902. She is listed in the San Francisco City Directory of Businesses in 1890 and the telephone directory of 1892, but I could not find any notice of additional businesses after 1902, notice of her death, or burial information. The census of 1880 lists only two women named Mary Lake in the city of San Francisco. One was born in Ireland in 1846 and the other in New York in 1850. One of them, Mary O. Lake, was listed as "unmarried" but accompanied by a daughter. It is tempting to speculate that the daughter was progeny of James Fair, hence his ready support of Mary's school. It is interesting to note that, after his death, several women came forward claiming they had been secretly married to Fair.

Much of the paranormal activity detected in the Queen Anne Hotel has been attributed to Mary Lake. Spirits of teachers who boarded at the Mary Lake School and students may be active as well. Intense environmental imprints and trapped spirits may have been created by subsequent tenants. A year after the school closed, members of the secret Cosmos Club purchased the building and staged their mysterious rituals there for twelve years. The Episcopal Diocese then assumed ownership and opened the Girls Friendly Society Lodge, a home for young working women until 1936. By 1970, the building was so badly dilapidated that it was nearly uninhabitable. Renovations that included conversion to a hotel that was started in 1980 and completed in 1995 awakened spirits of former residents.

Paranormal activity has been detected on every floor of the hotel. Guests and staff have experienced isolated cold spots, tapping sounds on walls and doors, unexplained breezes, doors that open and close, the swishing sound of long skirts, the touch of invisible hands, and the unsettling sensation of being watched. Ghost hunters have captured orbs and other light anomalies in photographs. Some of these have a humanoid form. Audio phenomena have also been captured on recording media. These sounds include the laughter of young girls and the voice of an older woman saying "well!" Many witnesses claim to have seen apparitions of women in long skirts and high-collar blouses walking the halls and appearing in mirrors. In room 310, guests have complained to staff that they felt as though unseen hands tried to push them out of bed.

In Miss Lake's former suite—room 410—ghost hunters have captured some impressive EAP and witnessed the movement of small objects placed on a table. Male guests sleeping alone have reported that they awoke in the morning and found that someone had tucked the blankets around them. The benevolent Miss Lake does not seem to mind people staying in her room, but she does not hesitate to remind guests that she is in charge.

SPIRITS OF THE SILENT CEMETERY

Neptune Society Columbarium
1 Loraine Court
San Francisco, CA 94118
415-752-7891
www.neptune-society.com

Built in 1898, this stately structure is a blend of Roman, Baroque, and English architectural designs. Once owned by the Odd Fellows Association, the structure was the central feature of a cemetery that once covered 167 acres on San Francisco's Lone Mountain. The original cemetery on this site opened on May 30, 1854. In 1902, at the height of the Bubonic Plague epidemic, the county Board of Supervisors passed an ordinance that forbade additional burials within city limits. It was believed that fresh corpses prolonged the epidemic, and, in a feeble attempt to stem the spread of disease, future burials were prohibited. Fear of contamination of ground water prompted further measures that ultimately required removal of old graves to a new cemetery in Colma. The transfer of bodies took decades and was not completed until 1923. A photograph in the Columbarium office reveals thousands of headstones that once covered Lone Mountain. Today, most of the former cemetery is a residential neighborhood. There has been considerable speculation that many unclaimed graves and human remains still rest under private homes.

The Columbarium's stunning Neo-Classical architecture, stained glass windows, and quiet ambience within create a perfect resting place for the remains of more than 8,000 people. Some of the deceased were prominent figures in the city's tumultuous past, including members of famous families such as the Stanfords, Folgers, and Magnins. Among its ordinary residents are the remains of a little girl named Viola Von Staden. Viola, and the Columbarium, survived the earthquake of 1906. In the days and months that followed, much of the city burned and the people suffered in many ways. Clean drinking water, unspoiled food, and adequate shelter were in short supply and unavailable in many parts of the city. Little Viola drank water from a polluted well near her home and became ill. She died at the age of seven in 1907, in her bedroom. Her ashes are kept in a brass urn in a niche also occupied by the ashes of Anna Von Staden (1867-1958) and Christina Von Staden.

Little Viola seems to like the Columbarium, for her apparition has spoken to the caretaker, Emmitt Watson. In 1997, while Emmitt stood on a ladder performing routine maintenance, he heard a little girl speaking. Thinking that a visitor was heading his way, he descended the ladder and found a little girl standing in front of the Von Staden niche. As he walked toward her, she disappeared. At the time, Emmitt did not recognize her as Viola Von Staden. Later, when he mentioned the episode to her descendents, they produced a photograph of Viola. Emmitt recognized the child in the photograph as the very same one he had seen in the Columbarium in 1997. In 2009, Emmitt and I discussed his sighting of Viola's ghost as we walked around the Columbarium. With a vivid memory, he recounted every detail including the tone of her voice. He hasn't

The Neptune Society Columbarium is one of the few burial sites remaining in the city of San Francisco.

seen the little girl for more than ten years but he feels her presence, always close to the niche that contains the ashes of her mother, Anna, and older sister, Christina.

Other niches in the Columbarium contain the remains of some of the city's quirky citizens whose sense of humor dictated rather bizarre burial arrangements. Barbara Fernando's ashes lie in two 150-year-old tobacco canisters. Antique Martini shakers adorn the niche of Norman White, while the ashes of the man below him sit beside a bottle of Johnny Walker Red and a shot glass.

Visitors are free to roam the three tiers of the Columbarium. Ghost hunters often perform EAP sweeps, hoping to capture sounds of some of the deceased or environmental imprints created decades ago by the living who stopped by to mourn.

LADY OF THE LAKE

Stow Lake
50 Lake Street
Golden Gate Park
San Francisco, CA
415-752-0347

Legend tells of a forlorn woman who walks the shores of Stow Lake at night searching for the bodies of her children. She roams Strawberry Hill, a tiny island, and the bridges that connect it to the mainland of Golden Gate Park. Witnesses claim she has appeared floating over the surface of the water and on the many roads surrounding the lake. At times, the woman approaches visitors as if she seeks their help. After making an appearance, however, the apparition disappears. The apparition has been described as transparent or opaque, with powdery white skin, a soiled white dress, and invisible from the knees downward. She makes eye contact with witnesses and spreads her arms as if she is begging for help.

The story of the ghost woman of Stow Lake first appeared in a San Francisco literary magazine, the *Overland Monthly*, in 1901. It recounts the sad tale of a woman whose children often played at the shores of Stow Lake in the early 1890s. When the children failed to come home for dinner one day, she went to search for them but never found them. Heartbroken, she returned to the lake every day, for many years, until she died. A variation of this story appears in Internet sources. The period is sometimes stated to be the 1880s and the number of children varies from one to three. Some writers state that the woman was enjoying a rowboat cruise on the lake when her baby fell overboard. The woman jumped into the lake to save the baby, but both drowned.

Many people have dismissed reports of the Stow Lake ghost because the legend appears to be a reiteration of a Hispanic story entitled "La Llorna" (the crying woman). I encountered this legend at Black Lake near San Luis Obispo, California, and other locations throughout the southwest. In some variations, the woman kills her children and then spends eternity searching for them. In the case of the Stow Lake ghost, however, credible paranormal investigators have reported to me that they've captured EAP/EVP of a woman sobbing and photographic records of unexplained light anomalies on Strawberry Hill and the south bridge. Several pages of postings can be found on the Internet. Many of those accounts are stereotypical ghost stories. The large number of sightings reported over the past 100 years, however, has given credence to the legend and kept Stow Lake on the list of potential hot spots for ghost hunters.

WESTIN ST. FRANCIS HOTEL

335 Powell Street
San Francisco, CA 94102-1804
415-397-7000
www.westinstfrancis.com

This grand hotel, built in 1904, has been the scene of wild parties and tragic deaths that may have contributed to some of the spirits said to walk its halls. After the 1906 earthquake, the two original towers remained standing but the hotel was gutted by fire, leaving frightened guests stranded across the street in Union Square.

Apparitions of former guests and staff members have been spotted in many parts of the hotel, but room 1221 is the most haunted location. On September 5, 1921, silent screen star Fatty Arbuckle celebrated completion of a movie by staging a wild party that flowed through several rooms including 1221. Alcohol flowed so freely that several people later testified they passed out or witnessed others lose consciousness. As a result of this wild affair, Virginia Rappe died. Arbuckle was accused of playing a role in her death, but he was later acquitted. On October 23, 1950, in the same ill-fated room 1221, famed vaudeville performer Al Jolson sat with friends at a table, playing cards. While shuffling a deck, he said, "Boys, I'm going," and collapsed and died. Séances have been staged in the room in an effort to conjure Jolson's spirit or get in touch with Virginia Rappe. I have no record of results of these séances, but several staff members told me they believe room 1221 is full of ghosts. I stayed in the room one night and experienced a continuous cacophony of whispered voices that seemed to emanate from the walls. Interestingly, none of them were captured by my audio recorder.

GHOSTS OF THE SURVIVORS

Lotta's Fountain
Market Street at Geary and Kearny Streets
San Francisco, CA 94108

Standing on busy Market Street, Lotta's Fountain is an icon of nineteenth-century San Francisco history that is unnoticed and unappreciated by the thousands of people who pass by each day. In fact, the fountain and its role in the city's history are virtually ignored except on April 18. On that date—the anniversary of the great earthquake of 1906—survivors gather at 5:12 a.m. to commemorate the moment. Accompanied by civic officials, history buffs, and descendants of people who experienced this cataclysmic event, only a few survivors are able to attend, but their presence reminds residents of the Bay Area that the "big one" is yet to come.

Installed on Market Street in 1875, Lotta's Fountain became a meeting place for thousands of homeless people after the 1906 earthquake.

The fountain was a gift to the city from Lotta Crabtree (1847-1924), the first child star in the U.S. Arriving in the Gold Rush country in 1853, six-year-old Lotta started her career entertaining miners by singing and dancing. An instant hit, she was paid in gold nuggets, eventually accumulating an estate worth $4 million. By 1856, Lotta and her family had moved from the rough mining camps of the Sierra to San Francisco. In 1859, she was dubbed "Miss Lotta, the San Francisco favorite." By 1863, Lotta was ready to expand her notoriety and cash-in on her fame. Heading east with her own theatrical company, she played in theaters in major U.S. cities before embarking on a European tour. Always fond of San Francisco, Lotta dedicated an elaborate sculptured fountain on September 9, 1875, as a token of appreciation of the adulation the people held for her.

Servicing pedestrians and horses alike, the fountain did not become a vital element of the city's infrastructure until April 19, 1906. On that date, Lotta's fountain stood amid the rubble of a once great city as one of the few recognizable landmarks that could serve as a meeting place. Word passed throughout devastated neighborhoods that scattered families would reunite at Lotta's Fountain. For weeks, desperate people loitered about the fountain, waiting for lost family members or information about the status of their neighborhoods. At Christmas in 1910, a celebration of the city's reconstruction was staged at Lotta's Fountain. The San Francisco Chronicle reported that more than 250,000 people gathered around the fountain to hear Italian soprano Luisa Tetrazzini fill the street with "songs the angels sing."

During the century that followed, Lotta's Fountain continued to serve as a beacon for the lost. So many desperate and earnest people have left emotional imprints on the fountain that sensitives easily detect them. There may not be ghosts there, but the iconic fountain is a mass of paranormal imprints that are often discovered through EAP and EMF investigations.

GHOSTS OF THE FRIGHTENED GIRLS

Cameron House
920 Sacramento St.
San Francisco, CA 94108-2015
(415) 781-0408
www.cameronhouse.org

Evidence of ghostly activity within the Cameron House may not be sufficient to satisfy seasoned paranormal investigators, but there are plenty of environmental imprints there that generate bizarre experiences. Reports posted on the Internet suggest that the place is haunted by the ghosts of female Chinese slaves killed in police raids. Other reports describe fires set by angry mobs and shootings that resulted in fatalities. My research indicates these reports are untrue. However, the history of this building and the intense emotional energy expended by those who sought refuge there is sufficient to create durable environmental imprints that appear to many as ghostly activity. It is possible that ghosts do haunt the place. One of them may be Donaldina Cameron (1869-1968), a social reformer who spent forty years serving the local Chinese community. The ghosts of some of the girls and young women who sought refuge there may rest in the rooms where they succumbed to illnesses or the harsh treatment they had received as slaves or indentured servants in San Francisco's Chinatown in the latter half of the nineteenth century.

The four-story brick building that stands on Sacramento Street was constructed in the late 1860s by the Presbyterian Church and opened in 1874 as the Occidental Mission Home for Girls. Head mistress Maggie Culbertson operated the home as a refuge for Chinese and Japanese girls and women who had been smuggled into the country or admitted by falsified documents presented by Asian men who claimed to be relatives. Once inside the country, older females, usually aged fifteen to twenty, were put to work as prostitutes. They were treated so harshly that most died before the age of twenty-five. Girls were sold for household slaves called *mui tsai*. Many of them were kept in locked rooms and, as they grew older, suffered sexual abuse by their owners.

Maggie Culbertson often joined with police and staged raids on

Cameron House in San Francisco's Chinatown was the scene of several tragic events, including a fire that may account for the ghosts of young Chinese women seen there.

homes and businesses where the abuses were so bad that reports had been leaked to doctors or city officials. The rescued girls were taken to the mission house and given medical care. Although some died in the house, most thrived in the loving environment and learned domestic skills that enabled them to find legitimate jobs or husbands.

In 1895, Maggie hired Donaldina Cameron as a sewing teacher. Donaldina participated in many raids and quickly became enamored with the Chinese girls she rescued. Soon after Maggie Culbertson's death in 1897, Donaldina became the new head mistress of the mission. Deeply appalled at the continuing slave trade in Chinatown, she stepped up the frequency of raids and became known as a master in finding girls hidden in locked basements or behind false walls. Men who operated the slave trade called her *fahn quai* (white devil) while the girls she rescued called her *lo mo* (old mother). Often these raids were violent operations in which police knocked down doors with sledge hammers and accosted girls' keepers with guns drawn.

The staircase of the Cameron House was the scene of intense emotional events during the 1906 earthquake.

On April 18, 1906, the mission home was rocked by the great San Francisco earthquake and, later in the day, ravaged by the fire that would eventually consume 25,000 structures in the city. After the 5:12 a.m. shock, Donaldina evacuated the girls to the Presbyterian Church on Van Ness Avenue. She then made her way across lines of soldiers who had established marshal law and returned to the mission home to gather legal papers that allowed the girls to stay in the U.S. under her guardianship. While stuffing papers into a canvas bag, a soldier stood at a window pleading with her to run from the building as nearby structures were dynamited to stop the advance of flames up the hill.

By 1908, the mission home had been rebuilt. Donaldina continued her work fighting for oppressed immigrant girls and women in San Francisco and other cities until her retirement in 1934. Her work was supported by police, social workers, and other city officials, but she alone is credited with crushing the Chinese slave trade in the U.S. and rescuing and educating more than 3,000 women and girls. In 1942, the mission house on Sacramento Street where she worked for forty years was re-named the Donaldina Cameron House.

After spending forty years and an incomprehensible amount of energy saving sick and abused Chinese girls, it would be hard to imagine that Donaldina's ghost would not haunt the mission house on Sacramento Street. Historical records affirm that she not only was dedicated to her job but also became a surrogate mother to hundreds of girls who had been kidnapped from their homes in China. After her death, it would seem impossible for her spirit to leave the place where so much torment and suffering was eased by her love. Indeed, photographs that hang on the walls of corridors reveal blurred, white figures in the background that some have interpreted as evidence of Donaldina's presence. People who work in the building told me they frequently feel a female presence standing close by and sometimes hear a woman's voice humming.

After the 1906 earthquake, the mission home was reconstructed with secret passageways that ran throughout the basement and joined at a single door that allowed egress to the alley. The exterior door was concealed by shrubs and provided an escape route that was used when angry Tong leaders stormed through the mission house demanding that Donaldina hand-over their "property." When these raids occurred, the girls cowered behind heavy locked doors awaiting the signal that the danger had passed. On rare occasions, they scurried through the dark passage-ways and escaped to the street. Unfortunately, in 1911, the heavy doors and narrow passage-ways prevented many girls from escaping flames that flashed through the basement after ignition of coal dust. Several were killed by suffocation. Red and gold charms remain over the doorways of the crypts where the girls died. These charms were placed to protect the spirits of the girls that remain in the mission house.

SAN FRANCISCO ART INSTITUTE

800 Chestnut Street
San Francisco, CA 94133-2206
415-771-7020
www.sfai.edu

The austere Spanish Revival tower that rises over Chestnut Street and the campus of the San Francisco Art Institute looks like a spooky place. In fact, it is well known for ghostly activity that has frightened students, custodians, and workers who renovated the tower. Most of the paranormal activity encountered at this place has been attributed to the spirits of people whose bodies remain buried under the campus of this prestigious art school.

From 1848 to 1853, the patch of ground on which the campus sits was used as a cemetery. Fewer than 100 graves were located there, but as the city grew, the graveyard became an impediment. In the 1870s, the graves were removed to Yerba Buena Cemetery that once

The San Francisco Art Institute was constructed over an old graveyard causing spirits to wander the tower stairs.

occupied ground now covered by the Main Public Library of San Francisco. No records of the grave removal process were kept and this has led to speculation that many graves were left behind. Grave markers made of wood may have been so badly worn by the climate, washed away by winter rains, or gathered for firewood by careless neighbors, leaving many graves unnoticed by workers assigned to the removal project. Consequently, many ghost hunters and historians believe bodies remain in unidentified graves under the art institute.

Following the 1906 earthquake, the ground at 800 Chestnut Street was used as a temporary cemetery to accommodate bodies of the victims of the great fire that followed the trembler. It is not known when those bodies were removed, but records show that tons of rubble were dumped at this location in the early days of rebuilding the city. By 1926, much of this history was forgotten as the new San Francisco Art Institute opened with a landmark tower.

The first reports of ghostly activity at the school appeared in 1946. A student working as a night watchman used the tower as living quarters. He noted disembodied footsteps on the stairs, doors that opened and closed without explanation, and the sound of heavy breathing. Over the next fifty years these sounds were encountered by many who visited the tower. In 1968, renovation of the tower proved especially difficult because several workmen quit after frightening experiences. It has been reported that some of those encounters resulting in serious injuries as objects fell on the workers.

Several psychics have spent the night in the tower and reported visions of a derelict graveyard and the corpses buried beneath the school. In 1998, citing concerns for seismic safety, the tower was closed. Many believe the tower was closed because paranormal activity had become frequent and intense.

HOTEL UNION SQUARE

114 Powell Street
San Francisco, CA 94102
415-391-3000

The Hotel Union Square, widely known as one of San Francisco's most innovative boutique hotels, may be haunted by the ghost of playwright Lillian Hellman (1905-1984). Fronting busy Powell Street, the clang of street car bells and din of pedestrian traffic sometimes creeps through the hotel's front doors. But once inside, visitors get the impression that the place has a palpable historical legacy. Aside from stories of ghosts from the Prohibition-era (1920-1933) speakeasy that operated in the basement and subterranean tunnels that lead to Ellis Street, the hotel may be haunted by two of America's most intriguing writers.

Lillian Hellman lived in the hotel off and on for thirty years while she carried on an affair with mystery writer Dashiell Hammett (1894-1961), who is best known for his novel *The Maltese Falcon* which became a hit movie starring Humphrey Bogart. Hammett occupied a suite on the second floor.

In the 1930s, while working as a detective for the Pinkerton Agency quartered in the Flood Building on Market Street, Hammett became acquainted with Hellman. Sharing similar political views that favored communism and anti-fascist movements, the two headstrong characters shared a suite at the hotel and often engaged in alcohol-fueled fights. In spite of their conflicts, the unlikely pair remained romantically involved for decades and Hammett used Hellman as a model for one of his most endearing characters, Nora Charles, of the 1934 novel *The Thin Man* and the 1950s TV series.

Although Hammett and Hellman died elsewhere (she in Massachusetts; he in New York City), some hotel staff members and local ghost hunters believe both writers haunt the place. A female apparition appears to guests in room 207. One male guest complained to the desk clerk that the apparition was "too friendly." Apparently, the man observed a negligee-clad female walk out of the bathroom and cross his room to the bed several times, keeping him awake all night. He had the distinct impression that the ghost wanted to climb into bed with him. That behavior is consistent with Hellman's reputation as an alcoholic who engaged in affairs with young men. In fact, it is said that the night before she died at the age of seventy-nine, she tried to entice a twenty-five-year-old man to spend the night with her. This brazen ghost also likes to move objects in room 207. Brushes, shoes, books, and other small objects may be found mysteriously relocated to odd places.

The Hotel Union Square honors the memory of Dashiell Hammett by offering a suite fitted out with artifacts from the writer's life. An old fashioned typewriter, a suitcase filled with Hammett mysteries, black and white photos of Hammett and his daughters, and other memorabilia give the impression that the writer has recently left the room and that he may return soon. The suite is popular with literary buffs while ghost hunters have gathered reports of unexplained odors such as cigarette smoke and liquor.

GHOST OF PIANO PLAYER

Hotel Vertigo
940 Sutter Street
San Francisco, CA 94109
(415) 885-2859

Movie buffs frequent this hotel because it played a prominent role in Alfred Hitchcock's classic film, *Vertigo* (1958). Paranormal investigators and ghost hunters know about the hotel because of ghostly activity that has been reported there for decades.

Opened in 1922 as the Glen Royal Hotel, the place changed hands in 1926 and became the Empire Hotel. The new owners transformed the place from a quiet hotel to a popular venue for San Francisco's young socialites by adding a cabaret known as the Plush Room. In spite of Prohibition, the Plush Room served alcoholic beverages and quickly gained a reputation as one of the Bay Area's hottest speakeasies. While the roaring '20s dance band took breaks, a young man referred to as Lester by the hotel staff kept the crowd warm by playing the piano. One night in 1931, Lester mounted the stage wearing a top hat and long coat. Instead of his usual set of three songs, Lester continued playing while the band waited for him to give up the stage. Finally, with collar unfastened and sweat dripping from his face, Lester played his last notes, then collapsed onto the piano and died.

Many years after this tragic event, a psychic held a séance in the Plush Room that was witnessed by more than twenty people, including skeptics. Second-hand reports indicate that the psychic made contact with the piano player and learned that his name was Joseph O'Reilly. An extensive review of San Francisco city directories from 1910 to 1930 turned up only one Joseph O'Reilly, who was listed as a teamster. Some historians have speculated that Lester had a chronic disease and, knowing he was about to die, chose to die while doing what he loved most. Perhaps that is why Lester's ghost was seen for decades, walking the area that was once the Plush Room and some of the hallways in the hotel. When I visited the hotel in December of 2009, the former Plush Room was undergoing extensive renovation. Stripped to the studs with the ceiling removed, construction supplies and tools covered the floor hiding obvious remnants of the once-famous nightclub. I found the spot where the stage once stood, however, but I did not detect spirit activity. I suspect that after renovation, the ghost of Lester will reappear to see if the new Plush Room will include a piano and the atmosphere of a speakeasy that made his life so exciting.

The manager of the Vertigo Hotel told me that the ghost of a woman has been spotted on the sixth floor. Dressed in a long white gown, she walks the halls. This ghost is not menacing, but maids refuse to work alone on the floor.

There is inaccurate information on the Internet that claims the Plush Room was in the basement of the hotel. It was, in fact, located on the ground floor to the left of the hotel's desk. Reports of underground passageways are true, but these have been sealed for decades and probably pre-date the 1922 opening of the Glen Royal Hotel.

CURRAN THEATER

445 Geary Street
San Francisco, CA 94102
415-551-2000

Theaters are most often haunted by the spirits of performers, musicians, directors, producers, and even stage hands who fell in love with an actress. At the Curran Theater in San Francisco, the most active ghost is that of a young man who worked in the ticket booth. On the night of November 29, 1933, twenty-five-year-old Hewlett

The ghost of a murder victim is still on duty selling tickets at the Curran Theater.

Tarr stood in the Curran's ticket booth after the last ticket had been sold for the night's performance of *Show Boat*. Producer Howard Lang and the show's manager, Lee Parvin, stood a few feet behind him, engaged in quiet conversation. As Tarr stood at his tiny desk gazing at the theater's entrance for late arrivals, Eddie Anderson stepped up to the window, shoved a gun through the six-inch-high opening and fired directly at Tarr.

According to Lang and Parvin, a sharp crack echoed from the glass of the ticket booth and then Tarr cried, "What was that? I've been shot. My God! I've been shot!" Hewlett fell through the booth's door and down a few steps and died.

Anderson ran from the Curran Theater and then robbed the Koffee Kup restaurant at 18th and Geary of $60. Weeks later, he wounded a police officer as he held up the Bank of America at Geary and Jones Street. After his capture, he claimed his $14 per week job was insufficient to satisfy his new girlfriend, Lorene. He insisted he never intended to kill Tarr, only to scare him by thrusting the gun in his direction to extort two tickets to the play. This meager defense failed and Anderson was convicted of murder in December of 1933 and then hanged at San Quentin prison on February 15, 1935. His body is buried on San Quentin's "Boot Hill."

According to several employees of the Curran Theater, Hewlett Tarr is still on the job. His image has been seen in the large mirror near the theater's entrance and at the spot where he died. Dressed in 1930s-era clothing, he appears calm and pleased to see crowds of people enjoying the theater.

Tess Collins, who managed the Curran Theater for twenty years, has heard hundreds of reports from employees and patrons who have encountered a handsome young man dressed in "old clothing" with slicked back hair.

One psychic who investigated this 1922-vintage theater reported that she found more than 300 spirits in the place. Nearly all of these were identified as patrons of the theater who would not let death separate them from a good musical. It is certain that 300 people have not died within the theater. So, this must be a case in which spirits take up residence in a favorite place after they have died.

SPIRITS OF THE STONES

Buena Vista Park
498 Buena Vista Avenue East
San Francisco, CA
415-551-5111

Located in the famed Haight-Asbury district of San Francisco, Buena Vista Park is an urban oasis that contains more than a lush forested landscape. Officially the oldest park in the city, the grounds were dedicated in 1867 and named Hill Park. The place remained a barren, sandy hill until 1892 when landscape architect John McLaren forested its steep slopes and installed pedestrian walks, scenic outlooks, retaining walls, and drainage ditches. After the 1906 earthquake, the expansive views served as observation points for police and military personnel charged with maintaining marshal law. The towering summit was also a gathering place for displaced families.

In 1930, the park was renovated by the Works Progress Administration. New retaining walls and drain gutters were installed using surplus granite and marble obtained from the city's Lone Mountain Cemeteries. During removal of more than 28,000 graves, many bodies were unclaimed by relatives. Consequently, removal of unclaimed graves was done without care for the deceased. Thousands of headstones were damaged, creating tons of stone that were subsequently used for myriad building projects around the city.

Some of the graveyard rubble was used to construct the seawall at Aquatic Park and the Marina Green. Crushed concrete was used to create the bedding for the Great Highway at Ocean Beach. Tons of broken headstones were hauled to Buena Vista Park and used in the 1930 renovation project.

Vigilant visitors to Buena Vista Park notice fragments of engraved stone lining the draining gutters and embedded in retaining walls. Much of the engraving on these stones is legible. Aside from the spooky feeling that there is something that is not right about breaking, extracting, and reusing headstones in this way, many people feel that spirits from the removed graves now loiter in Buena Vista Park, clinging to remnants of what was supposed to be their final resting place.

Every time I've walked the steep paths of Buena Vista, I've felt an eerie presence, heard disembodied voices speak in hushed tones, and spotted transparent clouds hovering over large pieces of headstones. Several visitors have published Internet accounts of similar experiences, including light anomalies in photographs.

MISSION DOLORES

3321 Sixteenth Street
San Francisco, CA 94114
415-621-8203
www.missiondolores.org

For no apparent reason, this Spanish mission is off the radar screens of most ghost hunters. It is not mentioned in most books about haunted places, and celebrity ghost hunters who have filmed their TV

Built in 1776, Mission Dolores is aptly named for the many tragedies that occurred there and the tortured souls whose bodies fill its tiny graveyard.

shows in San Francisco have skipped this historic and scenic place. Docents guide tourists through the tiny graveyard and the church, but there isn't enough traffic or hype to give this place the appearance of a tourist destination. Almost hidden by a high-density residential neighborhood, the old mission is dwarfed by the neighboring church and its tall steeple which have stood since the 1870s. Some of the city's most ardent ghost hunters, however, know that the mission and its graveyard can be full of spirits at times, creating unforgettable paranormal experiences.

On June 29, 1776, the Mission San Francisco de Asis was founded on high ground that sloped eastwardly to San Francisco Bay. Strictly a religious establishment for Franciscan priests and Indian converts, the mission was miles from the Spanish military contingent located at the Presidio near the Golden Gate. Within a few years, a civilian settlement named Yerba Buena—forerunner of the city of San Francisco—took shape at the edge of the bay. Due to the isolation of the mission and the region's perennial overcast skies, cool climate, and damp grounds, the place became known as Mission Dolores or church of sorrows.

The three settlements remained somewhat separate until the Gold Rush of 1848. From 1800 to 1848, the population of Yerba Buena remained less than 850. By December of 1849, it exceeded 25,000. Prior to this population explosion, the tiny cemetery next to the mission had become crowded with mission staff, a few priests, and about 5,000 Ohlone and Miwok Indians who had become members of the mission's community. By 1854, the city of San Francisco expanded to the mission's walls and began to contribute new internees to the graveyard.

Among the most famous people buried in the tiny plot are first Mexican governor of California Luis Antonio Arguello (1774-1830), first commandant of the Presidio Don Joseph de Moraga, boxer Yankee John L. Sullivan, and one of the most notorious couples in the city's history—Arabella "Belle" Ryan and Charles Cora. Cora was arrested November 15, 1855, for the murder of U.S. Marshall Williams Richardson. While awaiting trial, he had the misfortune to be jailed with City Supervisor James Casey who, on May 14, 1856, shot and killed newspaper editor James King of William. This killing so enraged the community that vigilantes stormed the jailed, dragged both men into the street, and staged brief trials. Finding both guilty of murder, Cora was allowed a few moments to marry his mistress, Belle, before he and Casey were hung from a second floor window as a crowd of one thousand looked on.

It is not known how a murderer such as Cora could have been admitted to the Mission Dolores cemetery, but rumors circulated that his wife, Belle Cora, bribed church officials with an outrageous sum and struck a deal for a grave that she and her lover could share upon her death. Today, the final resting place of these two notorious figures is one of the most visited graves in the mission's cemetery. The grave of murderer James Casey, aged twenty-seven years at the time of his hanging, is nearby.

With a tiny graveyard packed with thousands of dead people, it is no wonder that paranormal activity occurs at the Mission Dolores. Visitors have noticed intense cold spots and places where electrical sensations flow over their bodies. At these spots, many people also feel suddenly nauseated, dizzy, lightheaded, or fearful: all symptoms of enhanced electromagnetic fields. Casual visitors have reported strange experiences to docents that include a disembodied voice whispering in Spanish, chanting inside the church, and unexplained shadows. Ghost hunters have captured audio recordings of a male voice speaking Spanish and the sound of drums and flutes.

FREDDIE'S GHOST

Kohl Mansion
2750 Adeline Drive
Burlingame, CA 94010
650-762-1136

Paranormal activity at the Kohl Mansion demonstrates two aspects of a haunting that are unusual. First, the ghost that haunts this huge house died elsewhere. Ghosts seldom travel, but, in this case, the spirit made the 80-mile journey from his death site in Monterey to a favored place, his grand home on the San Francisco Peninsula. Second, ghostly activity generally declines with passing decades, but the ghost of the Kohl mansion has become more active.

The ghost that is most active in this grand house is believed to be that of the very tragic Freddie Kohl. Born in 1863, Charles Frederick Kohl was the son of Captain William Kohl, owner of the prestigious and highly successful Alaska Commercial Company. Little Freddie grew up riding polo ponies and enjoying yachting parties on the bay. Upon his father's death in 1893, Freddie inherited one of the largest fortunes in California. Seemingly careless and fabulously wealthy, Freddie partied and traveled until October 7, 1903, when he succumbed to the charms of Elizabeth "Bessie" Godie of Washington, D.C. A talented singer, Bessie was also raised amid great wealth and was eager to snag one of the few bachelors of her day who could advance her social station. Although a willing participant, the marriage didn't satisfy Freddie. In 1911, while traveling in Europe with Bessie and his mother, Freddie started an affair with a French maid, Adele Verge. Displaying tantrums that bordered on psychoses, Adele created many problems after the family returned to the United States. Freddie tried to get rid of her by offering to pay her way back to France, but the unstable woman only grew angry and filed suit against the Kohl family. Depressed and nervous about the situation, Freddie was relieved when a judge dismissed the suit. On leaving the courtroom, however, the enraged Adele pulled a gun and shot Freddie in the chest. The wound proved not to be fatal, but the scar on his chest and persistent pain reminded him of a miserable episode that eventually consumed him. Years later, upon learning that Adele had re-entered the U. S. and was heading to California, Freddie checked into the Del Monte Hotel in Monterey, spent the night, had breakfast in his room, and then shot himself in the head. All troubles ended for Freddie on November 23, 1921, but suspicions remain that this was not a suicide. In spite of the discovery that Freddie held the .38 caliber pistol in his hand, many have speculated that Adele found him in Monterey and killed him as he enjoyed a sumptuous breakfast.

Whatever the basis of Freddie's death, he seems to enjoy the home he built in 1914. Soon after his death, ghostly activity was detected in the house. After it was sold to the Sisters of Mercy as a nunnery in 1925, the place gained a reputation as a haunted house. In fact, activity was so bizarre and frequent that a Catholic priest was called in to perform an exorcism. Apparently this ceremony and several masses staged in the great hall directed at cleansing the place of disruptive spirits failed, because the Sisters of Mercy left the place in 1931.

Today, the place is an event center specializing in weddings and grand receptions. Freddie's ghost seems to like the events staged in his home because he is not disruptive nor does he attempt to frighten people away. After a tragic yet privileged life, Freddie shows up in virtually every room of the house. Witnesses report that he appears to be an old man, sometimes gazing out the second floor windows. He also floats across the great hall and through the dining room. Many people have reported the sound of disembodied footsteps made by a person walking with a limp. It is known that late in his life, Freddie developed arthritis of the hip from a riding accident that occurred when he was twenty years old. These bizarre footsteps are frequently heard in Freddie's former billiard room on the second floor. Over the years, people who work in the house have reported white powder appearing on the floor and inside shoes.

GHOST OF THE BLUE LADY

Moss Beach Distillery
140 Beach Way
Moss Beach, CA 94038
650-728-5596
www.mossbeachdistillery.com

Several publications and TV shows have placed the Moss Beach Distillery among America's top-ten haunted places. Since the 1970s, many famous paranormal investigators have visited this place and described its ghosts. Psychics have channeled the victims of criminal activity and picked up on remnants of torrid emotions and tragic deaths. Paranormal experts such as Sylvia Browne, Loyd Auerbach, Richard Senate, Stache Margaret Murray, Neva Turnock, Annette Martin, and Japanese psychic Aiko Gibo have affirmed that the place is haunted.

In the summer of 2008, the investigation team from TAPS (the Atlantic Paranormal Society) visited the Moss Beach Distillery. Entering the famous haunted restaurant with high expectations, TAPS investigators astounded the paranormal community when they discovered several electronic devices that mimicked paranormal activity. Among these "paranormal recreation" devices were a radio-controlled motor that caused a ceiling lamp to swing, audio devices that created disembodied voices and other sounds, and a projector that created the blue-tinged face of a woman in a restroom mirror. Many viewers of the TAPS TV show, *Ghost Hunters*, who were familiar with the considerable technical expertise of these investigators, were amazed that the restaurant's management would use these devices to trick seasoned ghost hunters into concluding the Moss Beach Distillery was haunted. Even without the devices, the long-standing reputation of the place, and its very active ghosts, would have likely resulted in a TAPS conclusion that the building is, indeed, haunted.

The decision of the restaurant's management to install devices to simulate paranormal activity severely damaged the decades-old reputation of the restaurant. Many people now wonder if the highly publicized ghost stories about the distillery ever had any credence. I can tell you that I've had many encounters with paranormal phenomena at this location that match up with reports made in the 1970s, '80s, and '90s. Most of my experiences occurred before the lower level was remodeled and paranormal recreation devices were installed. So, is this place truly haunted? My experience points to the conclusion that ghosts and hauntings, or environmental imprints, may be discovered throughout the building.

At least three ghosts haunt the Moss Beach Distillery. Historical research and investigations by gifted psychics have identified two women and a man who may have been involved in a lover's triangle. They were part of the corrupt society that hung out in the 1920s and 30s at Frank Torres's speakeasy known as Frank's Roadhouse. Located on a cliff overlooking a secluded part of the San Mateo coast, Frank's place was perfect for Canadian bootleggers who landed boats on the beach and dragged kegs of whiskey up the cliff for storage in the roadhouse basement. Some of this contraband was sold on the site to silent-movie stars, politicians, and others from the San Francisco Bay Area who came for a weekend of partying at a time when the sale of alcoholic beverages was illegal. The place also attracted a lot of

Home to at least three ghosts, the Moss Beach Distillery in Half Moon Bay has been named one of the most haunted places on the California coast.

dangerous characters whose clandestine activities included murder.

With the repeal of Prohibition in 1933, business at Frank's Roadhouse increased with the sale of legal drinks and development of a fine restaurant. A hotel located across the street accommodated guests who chose to include sex in their wild weekends on the coast. It is known that one of these encounters ended with a murder.

The most famous ghost at the Moss Beach Distillery is called the Blue Lady. Legend says that she had an affair with the roadhouse piano player, John Contina, a swarthy romantic who used his musical talent to attract women to his room. The true history and identity of the Blue Lady is uncertain, but research, particularly channeling performed by renowned psychic Sylvia Brown, points to three possibilities. On November 13, 1919, Mary Ellen Morley, who was married and had a young son, died in a horrific automobile accident on the coast highway, a few hundred yards from a small bar and brothel that preceded the construction of Frank's Roadhouse. Another possible identity is Anna Philbrick, a jilted lover of Contina who may have been responsible for his murder.

Psychic Annette Martin believes the Blue Lady is the ghost of Elizabeth Clair Donovan. During channeling, this spirit insisted that her nickname, Cayte, be used. Cayte reported that she moved from the midwest to San Francisco with an abusive husband who often beat her. Breaking away from him, she found comfort with the romantic John Contina. Eventually, her husband discovered her whereabouts, confronted her inside the roadhouse or on the beach, and killed her.

It is likely that Contina met his death on the beach at the hands of his other girlfriend, Anna Philbrick.

According to the legend, Contina's most amorous and public relationship was with a woman who showed up almost every night dressed in a blue chiffon dress. Psychics who have contacted this spirit report that the lady loves the color blue but sometimes dresses in a contemporary basic black cocktail dress. This ghost also expressed her happiness that Frank's is still in business and filled with people who like having spirits around.

For nearly four decades, reports of paranormal activity have been made by surprised and unbiased guests, employees, paranormal investigators, and TV production teams. This list of ghostly activity is too long to include in this book. Reports include moving objects such as swinging ceiling lights, glasses moving on the bar, bottles moving off the shelf, chairs and boxes sliding across the floor, and doors opening and closing by unseen hands. One astonished guest reported a table knife turning by itself. Calling for the attention of nearby guests and a waiter, several people confirmed that the objects moved by unseen forces. On several occasions, heavy bar stools have flipped over.

Several reports of objects becoming airborne have been made too. Employees Byron Whipp and Patty McKeller witnessed a stack of bill folders move horizontally off a shelf to the center of a wait station, and then drop to the floor. Former owner Pat Andrews sat in her office, astonished, as a checkbook rose from her desk and floated around the room as if an invisible being were carrying it.

Ghosts of the Moss Beach Distillery like to play with electrical devices. At times, the restaurant's thermostats have reprogrammed with nonsensical start and stop times. TVs and lights turn on and off, sometimes in the middle of important local football games. The restaurant's phone system is a frequent target for ghosts. At times, repeated calls are answered only to find that the caller refuses to speak. Orders for wine that were not made by patrons have showed up on the bar's computer. One night, all transaction dates showed up with the year "1927" instead of the current year.

These antics are fascinating, but most paranormal enthusiasts who visit the distillery want to see a ghost. Many have not been disappointed. Children as young as four years old have spoken of seeing a Blue Lady standing in the bar, restaurant, and lobby. Boys have run from the restroom to report a lady "in the wrong room." Children in the neighborhood used to speak of a Blue Lady who chased them away from the steep cliff adjacent to the restaurant. People walking the beach below the distillery have reported seeing the Blue Lady, a woman dressed in black, a man covered with bloody wounds (probably John Contina), and a rough-looking fellow in seaman's clothes with a gun in his hand who was likely one of the bootleggers from Canada who landed contraband whiskey on the beach.

Paranormal investigator Loyd Auerbach had an unusual encounter with the Blue Lady in the bar. While noting spikes on his EMF meter, Auerbach felt the female spirit pass through his body. This event was witnessed by three psychics who detected the passage of the spirit through living flesh. Auerbach reported that sharing his space with a ghost "felt pretty good."

Numerous séances conducted at the distillery have established connections with spirits who related their reasons for haunting the place. The piano player, John Contina, is still looking for women, including the lady who killed him on the beach. The Blue Lady loves the place and feels comfortable with renovations and the crowds of modern patrons. In spite of doubts cast by the TAPS discoveries of devices that "recreate" paranormal activity, the place remains spiritually active. When I stopped in for coffee late in the afternoon on November 14, 2008, the place was jammed with customers. Business at the bar suddenly slowed and patrons became edgy as bartenders announced the computer system had failed to accept charges from the bar. One long-time employee leaned toward me and whispered, "Must be those spooks you're looking for."

GHOSTS OF THE COLEMAN MANSION

Peninsula School
920 Peninsula Way
Menlo Park, CA 94025-2300
(650) 325-1584
www.pensinulaschool.org

The grand mansion James Coleman built in the early 1880s for his new bride, Carmelita Nuttall Coleman, is still a spectacular place although it shows its age. In 1925, when the massive building was renovated and became the Peninsula School, its Victorian elegance was concealed by blackboards and poster boards and was worn further over the decades by hoards of students. Soon after the school opened, stories began to circulate about ghostly activity noticed by custodial staff working at night and teachers who remained at their desks long after noisy, energetic students had left the building. Rather than diminishing with the passage of time, the ghost of this old mansion appears to have become more active in recent years and attracts the attention of local ghost hunters and paranormal investigators.

The ghost that haunts the Peninsula School is said to be Carmelita Coleman. Her ghostly presence is peculiar because she never lived in the house. It is likely, however, that Carmelita visited the place several times during its construction, perhaps to see some of her ideas and specifications take form. As it neared completion in 1885, she must have been thrilled with the prospect of moving into such a magnificent house with her husband, James.

Until the mansion was ready for occupancy, James and Carmelita lived in a hotel suite in San Francisco. Several writers have reported that, late one night, James arrived home after a long business trip and dropped his valise at the foot of the bed. Being a dutiful wife, Carmelita rose from bed and started to unpack her husband's clothes while he readied for bed. Unfortunately, James forgot to unload the pistol he kept in his valise. As Carmelita moved James's clothes, she accidentally discharged the pistol, killing herself instantly.

Stricken with grief for years, it is said that James never entered the grand house. That's unfortunate, because if he had moved into the place, he may have encountered the ghost of his dead bride.

Custodians have reported hearing footsteps and doors closing and seeing a green mist at several locations within the mansion. The apparition of a woman surrounded by a pale green mist was witnessed by teachers Jose Starr and Monique Caine while they spent the night inside the school with twenty children. By their accounts, all the children saw this apparition too. When asked to draw a picture of their sighting, all of the children chose green crayons to draw a female wearing a long gown. In the years that followed that exciting night, many students at the school reported encounters with the green woman. School officials have downplayed these reports, claiming that stories about hauntings are merely fabrications and that their perpetuation may frighten students. Many teachers dismiss that assertion and enjoy the fact that their school is haunted by a benevolent ghost.

When I last visited the old Coleman mansion, I had an experience that convinced me that a spiritual entity haunts the place. At 10:00 a.m. on a Sunday morning, the place was virtually deserted. As I walked the wide veranda, meditating on Carmelita Coleman, I stopped and stood facing a side door. Peering through the glass, I saw a dark mist appear on the other side. The mist moved toward me, and then disappeared as it passed through the door inches from my body. A moment later, I became aware of a bizarre sensation. I felt as though a female entity occupied the space in which I stood; it was as if the spirit passed through me very slowly, taking several seconds to do so.

In 1990, psychic Macelle Brown conducted a séance in the mansion that was witnessed by fifty people. While attempting to channel Carmelita, the spirit of her father, Robert Kennedy Nuttall, M.D., began to speak through the medium. He claimed the grand mansion was built with his money and implied that young Coleman may have murdered Carmelita. As the séance continued, spirits speaking through the medium suggested James and Carmelita were not happily married. The young wife may have had an affair that aroused James's temper, leading to murder. There is no historical information to support this scenario, but my research revealed some interesting facts that modify the Coleman story as it is told in paranormal literature.

It has been implied that James built the grand mansion with his money. However, in 1880, James was only twenty-six years old and struggling to gain a foothold in California politics by working for politically powerful people. In 1880, he ran for a menial office, a seat on the State Agricultural Board, but garnered only one vote. It is likely that the mansion was, indeed, built with money supplied by Carmelita's father since it is unlikely that young James could pay the $100,000 cost of construction. This confirms the information perceived by psychic Macelle Brown. In 1883, James won a seat in the California State Assembly where he served from 1883 to 1887.

Some writers list 1880 or 1881 as the years in which Carmelita died. I searched old San Francisco records and found that she was buried in Lone Mountain Cemetery in 1885 at the age of twenty-four years. Her body was placed in a vault with her father, Robert Nuttall (1815-1881). Apparently surviving family members did not hold James accountable for the tragedy that took Carmelita's life, because he, too, was interred in the vault after his death on April 13, 1919.

OTHER PLACES TO SEARCH FOR GHOSTS:

THE PALACE HOTEL

2 New Montgomery Street
San Francisco, CA 94105
415-512-1111

This magnificent world-class hotel ought to be called the Phoenix Hotel. Built in 1875 as a rival to the best hotels in Europe, the massive structure burned in the great fire that swept through the area after the 1906 earthquake. A newer structure literally rose from the ashes of the old hotel and reopened in 1909. The grand court, which served as a carriage depot in the original hotel, was converted to a Garden Court and used as a restaurant. Today, it retains the opulence and charm of the old hotel and some audio imprints of horses and the carriages they pulled. Several notables have died at this hotel, including King Kalakaua of Hawaii in 1891 and President Warren J. Harding on

The Garden Court Restaurant of the Palace Hotel was once filled with carriages serving the guests of this landmark hotel.

August 2, 1923. Many other guests have died there but refuse to vacant their rooms. Apparitions and disembodied voices have been experienced by guests and staff members in several rooms and corridors. Ghost hunters should understand that the only viable way of investigating paranormal activity at this location is to patronize the restaurant or rent a room for the night.

FLOOD BUILDING

Management Office
870 Market Street at Powell Street
San Francisco, CA 94102-2907
415-982-3298

Known as a "flatiron" structure due to its triangular shape, the Flood Building may be haunted by some of its former tenants or spirits that died on the site when a preceding structure burned. Built in 1902 by James L. Flood (1857-1926), son and heir of the Comstock silver baron, James C. Flood (1826-1888), the building sits on the former site of the Baldwin Hotel. Named for its owner, Lucky Baldwin (1828-1909), the hotel burned in 1898, killing several people including women and children who sought refuge in the swimming pool. Security guards have reported hearing their screams as they patrolled the hallways at night. Throughout the building, tenants and visitors have experienced unexplained sounds, including whispered voices, and the sensation that unseen beings are standing close by.

The Flood Building survived the 1906 earthquake and fire due to innovative construction that included double-strength steel frames and inter-laced brick walls covered with Colusa sandstone. Some paranormal investigators have speculated that the extensive steel frame and other metal features of the building may account for the persistent paranormal activity. Aside from the victims of the Baldwin Hotel, the site may be haunted by spirits whose bodies were buried there in a small cemetery between 1849 and 1853.

SUTRO BATHS

The Cliff House
1090 Point Lobos
San Francisco, CA 94121
415-386-3330

Once the most elaborate public swimming facility in the world, Sutro Baths is now nothing more than a fascinating ruin chronically dampened with salt spray from the pounding surf of Seal Rocks. Built in 1894 by engineering genius Adolph Sutro, the baths opened on March 14, 1896, and operated for decades until the structure burned in 1966. The baths were massive in size and included six salt water pools of different temperatures and one fresh water pool. During high tides, the water in the salt water pools was replaced in one hour. A giant turbine, once housed in a hole still visible in the cliffs, was used to re-circulate the water during low tides. Today, concrete foundations remain as a tantalizing monument of a once fabulous recreation and social facility. Plenty of people drowned in the pools. Their ghosts are joined by spirits of fishermen who were swept from the rocks by rogue waves and of victims of the many shipwrecks that occurred nearby. Ghostly voices have been heard rising from the tunnel that once housed the turbine. Screams, shouts, and sobbing have been heard in several locations in the ruins. The pale white apparition of a woman has been spotted from observation platforms at the Cliff House as she walks the seawall.

ROSSOTTI'S ALPINE INN BEER GARDEN

3915 Alpine Road
Portola Valley, CA
650-854-4004

This rustic bar was opened in 1853 as a rest stop for travelers on the stage coach. Horses were changed and overnight accommodations were offered to weary travelers. Today, the Rossotti's Alpine Inn is a popular weekend destination for mountain bike riders, motor-cyclists, and others arriving from the nearby Silicon Valley and Stanford University communities. Generally, the affluent clientele comes seeking a calming experience in the wooded Portola Valley. The Alpine Inn offers the best burgers in the area and very cold beer. Adjacent to the bar is an outdoor area for barbeques and alfresco drinking. It is here that the wispy image of a bearded gentleman is sometimes seen. He appears to be dressed as a horse wrangler with heavy boots, a cowboy hat, and a bandana tied around his neck. There is no specific information about the history of the Alpine Inn that might identify this ghost. He may have been an employee of the stage coach line, having met his death while handling horses that were kept here. In the rough and tumble days of the 1850s and '60s, he might have been the victim of a barroom fight, or an outlaw awaiting the departure of the stagecoach.

SUICIDE TRACKS

Caltrain tracks
between East Meadow Drive and El Verano Avenue
Palo Alto, CA

In the space of seven months, five students at Palo Alto's Gunn High School were killed on these tracks. In every case, these deaths are believed to be suicides. The first death occurred May 5, 2008, when a seventeen-year-old boy was struck by a south-bound train. Just four weeks later, a seventeen-year-old girl died in nearly the same spot. In August, another girl died after being struck by the train's engine at 10:45 p.m. These terrible deaths were followed by another in October of 2008 and a fifth suicide in January of 2009. These tragic events all occurred at night on tracks traveled by south-bound trains. The high frequency of suicides at this location has attracted the attention of local paranormal investigators, some of whom speculate that an evil spirit in the area was involved. Any investigation of this phenomenon should be careful not to speculate publicly and to be mindful of local families who still grieve the loss of loved ones.

In 2008, sixteen pedestrians died on Caltrain tracks. Thirteen of those deaths were ruled suicide. Any paranormal investigation in this area should be conducted with the utmost caution. Commuter trains travel at high speed and may not be heard by persons whose attention is focused elsewhere. I recommend a look-out who would sound a warning when trains approach.

Chapter 4

South Bay Area

In the mid-1970s, the South Bay Area was composed of relatively small towns and ubiquitous orchards and vineyards. The peaceful country was dotted with old farmhouses and other buildings that captured the lingering presence of long-past historical eras. The explosive growth of the Silicon Valley industries nearly wiped out the small-town character of many communities as cities paved over open ground and built new structures on historic sites. As the pace of modern development accelerated, many towns recognized the value of the local historic legacy captured in the vintage buildings left standing. A wave of re-discovery and preservation saved hundreds of charming buildings dating from the nineteenth century and revealed ghostly activity that had lain dormant for decades.

GHOST OF THE LONELY PREACHER

130 East El Camino Real
Sunnyvale, CA 94087
408-432-0331

From the outside, Toys-R-Us in Sunnyvale appears to be too busy, too well-lit, and too modern to be haunted, but it is the home of a stubborn ghost who refuses to move onward to the ultimate destination of all spirits. Inside, the store is often a whirlwind of activity, yet employees and shoppers have reported ghostly activity. Stuffed animals flying from the shelves, wall mountings moving, a variety of sounds including footsteps and wood chopping, faucets in the restrooms running and then stopping, and cold spots are all part of the daily activity. Employees arrive for work in the morning only to find merchandise piled on the floors or re-stacked in peculiar shapes. Ghostly activity has been experienced at almost any time throughout the day and night, suggesting that this ghost is always vigilant or protective of something.

Psychic research has revealed that the Toys-R-Us ghost is likely that of John Johnson, also known as Yonny. Yonny was a gold rush forty-niner who settled in the Santa Clara region in the late 1850s. He became a minister of a small local church and, without a home of his own, roomed with farming families that occupied the land on which the city of Sunnyvale now sits. Psychic Sylvia Browne discovered that Yonny was in love with the daughter of a wealthy, prominent judge and businessman, Martin Murphy. Since his poor circumstances made the marriage he desired impossible, Yonny spent his days longing for the beautiful Beth (Elizabeth Yuba Murphy) while he labored on the farm and preached in his church.

Beth married another man in 1863 and the loss of his great love sent Yonny into a state of depression. Even years after Beth's death in 1875, Yonny remained a bachelor and a loner. It is said that while he chopped wood one day, his thoughts wandered to his unrequited love and he injured himself. Severing an artery in his leg, he bled to death somewhere on the land now occupied by Toys-R-Us.

Yonny has been seen by Sylvia Browne and his image has been captured on film. Communications with him have clarified his reasons for haunting this Sunnyvale site. According to Browne, Yonny is waiting for his love, the beautiful Beth, to pass by and notice him. Even when informed that he and Beth are dead, he insists that he must stay on the farm and await her interest. Beyond that, Yonny feels a need to "look after things." He is perplexed by the modern store and the ways of modern people and believes he must do something to prevent the future from intruding on his time period of the 1880s.

Yonny has manifested his presence throughout the large store, but the best places to experience his ghost are on the aisles lined with shelves of stuffed animals, especially the teddy bear section where he rearranges the toys, and in the restrooms where he turns water on and off. Psychics and ghost hunters have also searched the toy store for the ghost of Martin Murphy (1830-1884). Some believe Murphy's spirit has remained on his land more than a century after his death to make certain his daughter is protected from the wood-chopping preacher who had no home of his own.

GHOSTS OF THE TWO CHRISTINES

Rengstorff House
3070 North Shoreline Blvd.
Mountain View, CA 94043-1341
650-903-6392
www.r-house.org

The ghost of Mrs. Christine Rengstorff or the ghost of her daughter Christine haunts the second floor of this 1867 mansion on the southern shores of San Francisco Bay. While viewing the mansion's exterior, visitors have spotted the image of a woman in a second floor window. She appears to be slim with long dark hair. When questioned, witnesses have been unable to clarify whether she is teenaged or middle-aged. Inside the house, visitors and staff members have heard disembodied crying, thumping on walls, footsteps, and breathing. Ghost hunters who tour the place with audio recorders have captured some fascinating EAP, including words spoken in German.

The classic, two-story Italianate mansion was built in 1867 by German immigrant Henry Rengstorff. Arriving from Germany in 1850 with hopes of amassing a fortune in the California Gold Rush, twenty-one-year-old Henry stepped off a ship onto a San Francisco dock during a powerful storm. Because of the bad weather and the realization that snow and ice would soon engulf the Sierras, Henry gave up his plans to search for gold and instead made a fortune by developing a cattle ranch in San Mateo, a hay farm in Milpitas, and orchards in Los Altos. By the early 1860s, he was a major land owner and well on his way to becoming a wealthy man. In 1864, he married Christine Hassler and began a family that eventually included seven children, including a daughter named Christine, after her mother.

The Rengstorff House in Mountain View is haunted by several members of this pioneer family who appear in the windows of the second floor.

After the birth of their first child, Mary, in 1867, Henry and Christine built the twelve-room, 4,000-square-foot mansion.

When Henry Rengstorff died in 1907, at the age of seventy-seven, his daughter, Elise Rengstorff Haag, moved in with her husband and Perry, the orphaned son of Elise's sister, Helen. Perry inherited the house, and then sold it in 1959 to a development company. The place sat empty and fell into disrepair. Although it was scheduled for demolition in 1980, the local community saved the house, moved it, restored it, and opened it to the public in 1991 when it gained a reputation as being haunted.

Little information exists about events that may have occurred there that have led to ghostly activity. Henry, his wife, Christine, and Elise died in the house and no doubt other family members died there too.

For a few years in the 1960s, the house was rented to Max and Mayetta Crump. They experienced intense, frequent noises that seemed to emanate from inside the walls and the treads of the staircase.

The couple was also awakened by the sound of a child crying and heavy footsteps walking on the stairs. At times, these sounds were so loud that the Crump's German shepherd, a former police dog, would hide under the bed.

After a short stay, the Crumps moved out and the house remained vacant and derelict for many years. During restoration, a hidden staircase was discovered that led to the attic. Aside from scraps of junk, the attic contained a hospital bed with leather restraints. The meaning of this discovery remained obscure until renowned psychic Sylvia Browne visited the place. She perceived the spirits of two men. One of them had been crippled by arthritis while the other was described as being angry after losing a leg in a farming accident. It is possible that one of these men was housed in the attic. Browne also noted the presence of a man who had been strangled in a second-floor bedroom. Subsequent visits by ghost hunters have not generated reports of paranormal activity that might be attributed to these three men, but empathetic sensitives do encounter intense cold spots and isolated places that create feelings of intense sadness and anger.

The Rengstorff House is now available for rental for receptions and parties. Docent-led tours are conducted on Sunday, Tuesday, and Wednesday at 11:00-5:00, as an example of Victorian architecture and the local lifestyle of the 1860s in Mountain View.

BELLA SARATOGA

14503 Big Basin Way
Saratoga, CA 95070-6011
408-741-5115
www.bellasaratoga.wet

This charming, Victorian style house was built in 1895 by Samuel H. Cloud, who operated a grocery store next door. Not long after moving in, Sam walked into the street in front of the house to look around the neighborhood. Being unfamiliar with the sounds of traffic on the street, he failed to recognize the meaning of a clanging bell and the shouts of people standing nearby. Without seeing the impending danger, Sam was struck by a steam-powered street car as it careened down Big Basin Way.

A crowd quickly gathered that included a physician who found that poor Sam was near death. Not wanting the man to die in the street, the doctor enlisted several men to carry Sam into the house and up the stairs to a front bedroom. Within a short time, Sam died in his bed.

Sam's wife carried on with management of the grocery store and remained in the house with two of her children, who left the house after her death in 1910. Soon after the new occupants moved in, odd things began to happen. Throughout the 1920s and '30s, the place gained a reputation as a haunted house but the paranormal activity wasn't so bad that tenants were scared away.

In 1950, the place, which had been vacant for many years, was renovated into a boarding house, offices for the *Saratoga News,* and then a restaurant. In the 1970s, when the place opened as the Bella Mia restaurant, its reputation as a haunted place became more

The popular Bella Saratoga Restaurant was once a home in which two tragic deaths created ghosts who cannot leave the place.

widespread and attracted the attention of psychic Sylvia Browne. In 1994, the place changed hands and was renamed the Bella Saratoga. Since then, employees and patrons of the restaurant housed in the old Cloud house have experienced many strange things that can only be the haunting activities of ghosts. Many people have felt something swish by them without the possibility of an opened door or window. When least expected, doors and windows open by themselves, lights go on and off, and objects are moved or hidden. Several employees have seen the figure of a young woman dressed in white. This ghost has been spotted climbing the stairs to the second floor and standing next to the bar on the main floor. This woman may be Sam Cloud's wife, or one of his children, who remains to look after Sam. She has been described as a gentle ghost, but owner Bill Cooper admitted that her spirit may have frightened some employees into quitting.

Sam's ghost may be among those who cause so many odd noises and strange happenings at the Bella Saratoga. Psychic ghost hunters have told me they've seen a male apparition in the bar, gazing through the pocket doors to the dining area, and in the second floor banquet room, which was once Sam's bedroom.

EAP AT MADRONIA CEMETERY

14766 Oak Street
Saratoga, CA 95070
408-867-3717
www.madroniacemetery.com

One of my dearest friends is buried in Madronia Cemetery. We lived together on an estate in nearby Monte Sereno for more than five years before she died. During the twenty years since her death, I've visited her grave countless times, often hoping to make contact with her.

Knowing Aurelie's spirit as I did, I really don't expect her to be haunting this cemetery. Like so many visitors to cemeteries, I always hope for any sign that a loved one is free of whatever pain or distress that accompanied the transition from life to death. But I tend to agree with writer Troy Taylor and many paranormal investigators:

cemeteries are rarely haunted by the deceased. Exceptions occur when a grave is damaged or desecrated or the engraving on a headstone is erroneous or occupied by the wrong person. But none of this applies to Aurelie's grave. So, when I think objectively, I have to conclude that my dear friend would not make an appearance in this cemetery no matter how fervently I wished her spirit to be present. The place is beautiful, but Aurelie is elsewhere.

I have to report, however, that I've detected a lot of paranormal activity in this beautiful cemetery. Most of my visits have been at night when I've been the only living soul in the cemetery. On several occasions, when I've walked into the dark graveyard, I've heard several voices speaking in hushed tones. My first impression was that there must be a large group staging a memorial service by moonlight, but my search for other living souls has always turned up nothing.

I've heard a mix of male and female voices speaking unintelligibly yet seeming to carry on vibrant conversations. The voices continue for several minutes until my footfalls on the paved walk and my flashlight make them aware of my presence.

Audio recordings made in this cemetery have captured these ghostly voices. Bursts of paranormal sound are much longer than typical EAP, sometimes lasting a minute or more. However, most of the words are not spoken with sufficient clarity to reveal what these spirits are saying. The other atypical feature is that sensitives such as I can readily hear these hushed conversations. EAP or EVP are rarely heard through human hearing mechanisms while they are imprinted on audio recording devices through direct manipulation of the magnetic tape or electronic media.

GHOSTS OF THE FUNERAL HOME

Coggeshall Mansion
115 North Santa Cruz Avenue
Los Gatos, CA 95031

In 1890, the widow Mary Coggeshall moved from San Francisco to Los Gatos with her children and used her considerable charms to gain the attention of J. J. Hill. Local history has this wily lady connected with the raucous Mountain Charley as well, but contemporary historians dismiss those rumors while affirming that Mary and J. J. were involved in a relationship. Victorian sensibilities of the 1890s required that the affair be kept quiet, but when construction of the grand mansion was completed, it was clear that the widow had impressed someone with a lot of money.

Mary Coggeshall did not die in her grand mansion, but it is likely that one of her children passed away in an upstairs room. In the census of 1900, Mary is listed as a resident of Sacramento County and the mother of three children, "two of them still living." I could not find additional historical records that indicated the date of death of Mary's third child, but it is likely the tragic event occurred in Los Gatos. These meager historical notes are consistent with the experiences of countless people who, in later years, worked and dined in the old mansion after it was converted to a popular restaurant called the Chart House.

Restaurant staff and patrons reported seeing the transparent

The Coggeshall Mansion in Los Gatos was a funeral home before it became a popular restaurant.

apparition of a little girl in the basement and on two main floors of the mansion. The ghostly girl is credited with playing with the cash register and running up huge bar bills, turning bottles of wine so their labels face the wall, flipping light switches off and on, creating intense cold spots in the restrooms located in the basement, knocking plates and glasses off shelves, and unnerving diners by projecting her apparition on the windows.

Many locals believe the Coggeshall mansion is haunted by several other ghosts. From 1917 to 1971 the beautifully spooky house was the Place Funeral Home. Three generations of Place men operated the business and staged funerals for many of the town's most important people.

After sitting vacant for six years, the mansion opened as the Chart House restaurant in 1977. In the 1980s, I ate in the restaurant and enjoyed the bar many times. During most of those visits I detected the presence of a tall, thin man wearing a dark coat. This fellow showed up most frequently in the lower level of the house near the restrooms. Since part of the house was once the body storage area, it is possible that that spiritual entity was one of Place's funeral directors.

After a run of thirty years, during which the Chart House became known to locals as a haunted restaurant, the business closed. During the years I lived in Los Gatos, I met many people who said they would never enter the place because of all the ghosts it harbored. Between 2007 and 2009, two other restaurants opened in the haunted mansion. Their failure after a short run has been attributed by some locals to the paranormal activity in the house. One woman told me that the ghosts loved the Chart House but did not like the décor or staff of its successors.

In October of 2009 I visited the Coggeshall mansion and found it empty and up for sale. It is sad to see it unused particularly since Los Gatos is a very wealthy bedroom community for Silicon Valley software geniuses, including the people who brought us Netflix and the Apple computer company.

GHOST OF THE MISSING ACTRESS

Opera House
140 Main Street
Los Gatos, CA 95030-6814
408-354-1218
www.operahouseeventsite.com

The only performances that take place at the Los Gatos Opera House now are weddings, banquets, and lavish parties. Once a grand music hall, the 1904 vintage building has a history of hosting some of the most famous performers of the early twentieth century who staged operas, vaudeville, concerts, and plays. The ghosts that haunt this place may be actors, singers, or stage hands that fell in love with a leading lady. Psychics, disc jockeys who hosted parties, events managers, patrons, and staff have reported hearing disembodied female voices calling out their names. These people have heard the names Jane, Barbara, and Elizabeth. Some of the voices seemed to emanate from inside walls, leading to speculation that a female was killed and the body hidden inside a wall or that a female ghost is trapped in a specific spot at which a wall was later added to the building.

A clue to the ghost's identity may be found in the history of this grand opera house. Eugene L. Ford began construction of the place in 1901 and opened the doors to the first audience on October 10, 1904. Ed, a former stationmaster for Southern Pacific Railroad, purchased the land for a cheap price after a fire swept through Main Street structures. Funding for the project was obtained from Eugene's wife, Caroline. The 500-seat opera house was on the second floor while businesses such as an ice cream parlor, bookstore, and tea shop occupied the ground floor. The Fords prospered for several years before Eugene ran away with an actress whose name has been lost to history. This messy affair has led to speculation that Eugene ran for his life after Caroline confronted the actress and caused her sudden disappearance. Perhaps the ghost of the opera house is that of the actress whose body remains hidden at the site.

During the 1980s, I spent a lot of time inside the old opera house perusing the vast array of merchandise offered by an antique store. I always got the feeling that I was being watched by some unseen being, especially when I visited the mezzanine.

In 1989, the building was so severely damaged by the Loma Prieta earthquake that some engineers recommended demolition. Fortunately, the place was saved by a very expensive renovation and earthquake retro-fit. During the year-long restoration, paranormal activity increased. Workers reported tools missing, knocking sounds in the walls, unexplained puddles of water, and scratches on wood and drywall.

In 1992, after reopening in its current role as an event venue, photographer George Sakkestad snapped twenty-five shots of an employee in various locations throughout the building. When the film was developed, two frames revealed a shadowy figure standing on a balcony. The dark figure could not be the result of a film processing accident because a clear image of the white balcony is seen in front of the figure. This discovery, however, did not yield any information about this ghost. The shape of the figure cannot be distinguished as a man or woman. It could be the trapped spirit of an actress who had an affair with the building's owner, or a singer waiting to go on stage to receive the attention of visitors to Ford's Opera House.

SPIRITS FROM FORGOTTEN GRAVES

Village Lane Shops
North Santa Avenue at Highway 9
Los Gatos, CA 95030

In 1868, the little village of Los Gatos, nestled against the eastern slope of the Santa Cruz Mountains, faced a problem. An old woman had died of pneumonia after her cabin filled with a surge of cold water from a flash flood. At the time, Los Gatos had no official cemetery in which to bury her remains. Recognizing that this burial would be the first of many, a civic-minded farmer named John Mason donated a small tract of land at the east end of town to house the old woman's soggy body and those who would most certainly die after her.

The graveyard was opened and quickly filled as farm accidents, shootings, and hangings took the lives of the careless, the unlucky, and the criminal residents of Los Gatos. In addition, infectious diseases took the lives of the very young and old, adding to the number of residents in the oak tree shaded graveyard. By 1890, the cemetery was running out of space, but its borders could not be expanded because the town had also grown, crowding the fences of the graveyard on all four sides.

Meeting in closed session, the town council decided to move the cemetery to another site. Relatives of the graveyard's population were contacted and asked to move the remains of their loved ones. Many complied, but some family members could not be found while others refused to move the graves of their loved ones. Frustrated with the lack of speedy compliance and pressured by the economic boom that demanded land for shops and homes, the city council set a deadline for grave removal and hired a contractor to remove any remnants of graves or monuments. Eager to fulfill their contract and cash their paychecks, the contractors dislodged the remaining headstones, placed them over the underlying caskets, and began laying out new streets and constructing new buildings. The remaining graves were soon forgotten since relatives of the deceased either ignored requests to move their loved ones or had themselves died.

In the 1950s, a crew digging a new sewer line along Village Lane uncovered a small cast iron coffin containing the remains of a child. They also uncovered as many as seventeen gravestones of adults. Until this time, local residents and shop-owners had not realized that they occupied buildings that sat over the final resting place of many dead people. The discovery prompted historical research that concluded that as many as thirty additional graves lay under the shops of Village Lane.

The implications of these long-forgotten graves and their desecration by construction crews became clear when reports were made of strange noises, radios found blaring, and other strange happenings when a shop-owner arrived for work in the morning.

At Lisa's Tea Treasures (330 North Santa Cruz Avenue, 408-395-8327), a doorbell rings at odd times when no one passes through the door. Cesar Rivera-Valdez, an optician at Eye Contact (350 North Santa Cruz Avenue, 408-395-8046), reported an alarm system that sounds even after being disarmed. The control panel often indicates that the system is being turned on and off in rapid succession as if a ghost is playing with the electrical device. Several other shops situated in the charming micro-village bordered by North Santa Cruz Avenue, Village Lane, and Highway 9 have been the sites of haunting activity. Sometimes ghosts are seen such as the dark-haired woman who wanders through several shops. Perhaps she is the wife of John Mason, whose son, Paul, refused to move his mother's grave in 1890.

Evidence that the ghost of a little boy, Willie, haunts the area has been gathered by local ghost hunters. Willie died of pneumonia at the age of two, one day after coming home from a San Francisco hospital. He had been hospitalized for a long time in order to have his club-feet corrected by surgery. In 1958, at the corner of Highway 9 and North Santa Cruz Avenue, workmen uncovered little Willie's gravestone. He was buried in 1889, according to his sister, Nellie Turner Denning, who recorded pertinent information in 1958. She described Willie as a beautiful boy with "golden ringlets all over this head." He was playful and always seemed happy. Perhaps his ghost is the one that haunts the former Kid's Trading Company, a children's clothing and toy store, now occupied by Marbella Hair Salon.

Staff members at the Beau Chaveau hair salon, Joplin and Sweeney Music Company, and Omo 24 Hair Salon have all reported paranormal activity that includes secured items falling from the wall or shelves, doors opening and closing, and drawers moving in and out.

DOUBLE D'S SPORTS BAR

254 North Santa Cruz Blvd.
Los Gatos, CA 95030-6814
408-395-6882
www.doubleds.com

This popular eating and drinking establishment is one of many businesses located over the old Los Gatos Cemetery (see Village Lane Shops). Several graves were left on this plot of land at the intersection of Highway 9 and North Santa Cruz Avenue in 1890 when the town experienced a population explosion. Since the early 1900s, the entire block has been known as a site of frequent ghostly happenings. One of the curious things about the site occupied by Double D's Sports Bar is that all of the businesses previously located here failed in less than five years. Many were well-run, popular restaurants, but success eluded the owners, perhaps because the restless spirits whose bodies were buried beneath didn't like the owners, patrons, or the kind of business that occupied their graveyard.

Visitors to the sports bar have experienced the usual cold spots, the rush of wind, and the feeling that someone was looking over their shoulder. The latter happens most often in the men's room. Some people speculate that the ghost of little Willie (see Village Lane Shops) frequents the sports bar since it sits almost on top of his grave. I lived in Los Gatos many years and became curious about Double D's when three previous businesses failed in rapid succession. Being suspicious of the influence of ghosts on those businesses, I anticipated Double D's would close in less than two years. Contrary to that expectation, the business has flourished and may soon begin its third decade. That is not to say that spirits at the site are entirely happy. The last time I visited this bar, I entered the men's room and, noting that I was alone, I said, "Looks like ghosts like this place." At that moment a large mirror mounted on the wall broke free and flew three feet horizontally before crashing to the floor.

The manager and a bartender rushed into the room and asked me what had happened. I explained what I saw but did not mention that I had been talking to myself about ghosts. As the two men surveyed the shattered mirror, one of them said, "Looks like they're still here."

I get the impression that ghosts still roam the former graveyard but are willing to coexist with businesses.

GHOST OF THE RAILROAD MAN

Billy Jones Wildcat Railroad
Vasona Park
233 Blossom Hill Road
Los Gatos, CA 95032
408-395-7433

If you visit Vasona Park in Los Gatos you will see a miniature railroad coursing through the trees and across meadows. Construction of the tracks that came to be known as the Billy Jones Wildcat Railroad began in 1941 on land owned by William "Billy" Jones (1884-1968). In 1943, the first round trip was made through Jones's orchard with a 1906 vintage engine that had been used for thirty-six years to pull tourist-laden cars through the city of Venice in Southern California. In 1939, Jones rescued the engine hours before it was scheduled to be shipped to Japan as scrap metal. Jones ran his miniature railroad for twenty-five years, carrying children and adults who were thrilled to ride behind a real stream engine.

In 1969, a year after Billy passed away, a local non-profit corporation purchased the railroad and moved it to Vasona Park. A ticket booth and a small stations building were added together with a water tower, crossing gates, and a garage for the engine and cars. In 1972, the tracks were extended 2.3 miles and a 40-foot trestle was added. In the 1980s, the old 1906 steam engine underwent major overhaul and returned to limited service. A diesel engine was added to the railroad in 2006 to carry the large numbers of people who visited the park on weekends.

If you have ever known railroad hobbyists, you may have noticed their nearly fanatical devotion to trains and rolling stock. Love for the sound and smell of a well-lubricated steam engine and the rumble of the cars as they pass over the tracks is unyielding in railroaders and may account for the ghost that haunts the Billy Jones Wildcat Railroad.

The partial, transparent apparition of a tall man dressed in engineer's coveralls has been spotted standing near the water tower. Witnesses report that the apparition appears to be smiling. If this ghost is that of Billy Jones, he is probably happy that his 104-year-old locomotive has been lovingly restored and is still in service. This apparition is seen only when the old engine is running on weekends from mid-May through September. This ghost has not been seen when the newer diesel engine is in service.

GHOST OF THE OLD TOWN

New Almaden Hacienda Cemetery
21350 Almaden Road
San Jose, CA 95120
408-323-1107

In 1824, Mexican pioneers Luis Chabolla and Antonio Sunol discovered mercury deposits known as cinnabar on the eastern slope of the Santa Cruz Mountains. It wasn't until 1845, however, that a Mexican cavalry captain, Don Andres Castillero, recognized the value of the discovery and filed a formal claim to the crude diggings. With knowledge of modest gold discoveries made in several locations throughout California, Castillero understood that the mercury in cinnabar was an agent essential for extracting gold from quartz and other rock. With the Gold Rush of 1848, the cinnabar claim passed into the hands of the Barron Forbes Company and eventually the Quicksilver Mining Company. Throughout the ensuing twenty years, the size of the mining operation grew to include seven hundred buildings, three villages, three major mine shafts, a school, company stores, smelting facilities, and two cemeteries. The company's three villages—Spanishtown, Englishtown, and the Hacienda—were established to accommodate three principle ethnic groups. Today, a county park encloses the mines and preserves the village sites and remnants of the factories built to produce mercury for the nineteenth century mining operations in California and Nevada. Along Almaden Road, several houses built for mine supervisors and their families are still used as private residences. Many of these houses have ghost stories associated with them, but ghost hunters must get permission from residents before entering private property.

Like most mining operations, cinnabar mining was dangerous work. Fires, cave-ins, accidents, and infections that followed relatively minor injuries filled the graveyard with young people. Among the early dead were numerous children. Despite the beautiful setting that modern visitors encounter, life in the villages was hard, often challenged by privation. The medical clinic established by the mining company could do little for children poisoned by mercury-tainted water or those who were born with birth defects.

This historic building housed offices for the New Almaden Mining Company, a boarding house, and theater that have contributed to a large collection of ghosts.

Almost hidden from view on Bertram Road, the Hacienda Cemetery contains the remains of many Almaden children and their parents. The visible headstones represent only a fraction of the people interred there. Many grave markers made of wood were destroyed by brush fires that swept through the place while others, even stone markers, were washed away by winter floods from nearby Alamitos Creek. When the narrow road that winds past the cemetery was paved in 1928, several graves were covered. Some of the houses constructed nearby may also sit on unmarked graves. Residents may be willing to share stories of strange lights, cold spots, a sense of an unseen presence, and moving objects inside their homes.

The grave of little Jenny Danielson attracts a lot of visitors. She was born December 7, 1886, and died July 27, 1888. Her grief-stricken parents added, "She was blue-eyed and very beautiful." At this grave, ghost hunters have captured some fascinating EAP. Long periods of sobbing have been recorded. Sensitives also pick up intense emotions that include grief and anger. These paranormal phenomena are environmental imprints, or residuals, created by living people who made frequent visits to Jenny's grave. This is a common finding in cemeteries, particularly at the graves of children. Rarely are spirits of the dead present. Instead, visits by grief-stricken parents, made frequently over a period that may exceed many decades, create environmental imprints that are durable and often easily detected.

Another fascinating grave in the Hacienda Cemetery is that of Richard Bertram's arm. In 1898, at the age of thirteen, Bertram lost an arm in a hunting accident. By law, the member had to be buried. The family complied by creating a miniature plot complete with a formal headstone and a picket fence. When the rest of Richard Bertram died in 1959, burial was carried out at Oak Hill Cemetery in San Jose. There is an urban legend about Bertram's arm climbing out of the grave in search of the rest of the body, but ghost hunters dismiss it as they search the grounds for orbs, EVP, partial apparitions of mourners, and the head and arm that appear to belong to an angry grave digger.

GHOSTS OF THE KINDLY LADY AND THE MINERS

La Floret Restaurant
and other historic Almaden buildings
21747 Bertram Road
San Jose, CA 95120
408-997-3458
www.laforetrestaurant.com

The ghost of a kindly lady walks the floors of this popular French restaurant, but she is rarely noticed by eager patrons who come here from the nearby Silicon Valley. Sometimes only the swishing sound of her long skirts is heard through the din of animated conversation. Late in the evening, when the place is nearly empty of patrons and when staff move about quietly, sensitive people catch a glimpse of a lady in clothing typical of the nineteenth century. She moves through the dining rooms, appearing to float rather than walk. Witnesses told me they could not see the lower half of her skirt or her feet but, at times, her apparition displays amazing detail. The lady has curly gray hair, hazel eyes, and alabaster skin. She is short, perhaps five feet tall, and slim. When she reveals her hands, they appear deformed by arthritis.

La Floret Restaurant in New Almaden is still haunted by the ghost of a lady who served miners in the 1880s.

La Floret Restaurant is housed in a building constructed in 1848 as a boarding house for miners who worked at the Almaden Quicksilver Mines. Named the Hacienda Hotel, the building also housed visitors to the mines who rented rooms there while they conducted business with mine supervisors. When the mining company declared bankruptcy in 1912, only a few retired miners stayed on as boarders. By 1930, all of the boarders were gone and the place was converted to a restaurant called Café del Rio that served local farmers. At the time, the Almaden area was about fifteen miles from the heart of San Jose and isolated from the region's visitors and residents by vast orchards and unpaved roads.

The Café del Rio closed in the 1960s, leaving the building vacant for many years, but the explosive growth of San Jose in the 1970s brought it new life. In 1974, Santa Clara County opened Almaden Quicksilver County Park, bringing visitors and fostering construction of new houses on the site of the old miners' villages. In 1979, the old Hacienda Hotel building underwent another round of renovation and opened as La Floret. Today, La Floret is a popular destination for Silicon Valley locals who, while wanting to stay close to home, feel that they've left town for a few hours of dining in a remarkable historical setting.

I could not locate detailed historical records that might reveal the name of the kindly lady who walks through La Floret. She may have been the manager of the Hacienda Hotel when it served miners or an early owner of the Café del Rio. She seems happy with the modern restaurant, however, and does not appear distressed. Local ghost hunters believe that she is not alone. The ghosts of miners have also been seen on the second floor of the restaurant and the balcony. These ghosts are bearded and appear to be wearing dirty clothes. It is likely that these fellows died in their rooms at the Hacienda Hotel.

Ghost hunters should also visit the Casa Grande, the imposing brick mansion on Almaden Road. Constructed in 1854 as a residence for the mine manager and offices for supervisory personnel, the building has been used as a live stage theater and a museum. Ghost hunters might be interested in the historic homes sitting on a narrow strip of land between Almaden Road and Alamitos Creek. Built in the 1840s and '50s, most of them have a plaque that outlines their history, including the names of people who resided within. All of them are private residences, but access might be granted to serious ghost hunters.

PORTAL TO THE SPIRIT WORLD

Winchester Mystery House
525 South Winchester Avenue
San Jose, CA 95128-2537
408-247-2101
www.winchestermysteryhouse.com

Sarah Winchester's (1839-1922) massive, sprawling mansion in San Jose is a must for every Bay Area ghost hunter and for visitors to the region who have little time but an insatiable thirst for paranormal experiences. Known as the "house built by ghosts for ghosts," the mansion contains bizarre architectural features, dark hallways that lead nowhere, cold spots, and thick air that are all clear signs that ghosts live there in a world quite different from ours. Once composed

The world-famous Winchester Mystery House, in San Jose, stands as a monument to Sarah Winchester's bizarre collaboration with spirits.

of more than 700 rooms, the current 160-room Winchester Mystery House has stairways that disappear into the ceiling, doors that open from the upper floors into mid-air, and wandering corridors that caused many of the workmen who constructed the place to become lost. Built over a period of thirty-nine years at a cost of more than five million dollars, the place still contains 1,000 doors, 52 skylights, 3 elevators, 30 staircases, 47 fireplaces, and nearly 1,500 windows.

The house is dominated by the number thirteen; there are 13 bathrooms, 13 steps on many staircases, ceilings with 13 panels, chandeliers with 13 lights, and many rooms with 13 windows. But throughout the mansion there are only two mirrors, because mirrors were believed to frighten ghosts away and Sarah Winchester had no wish to be inhospitable toward her friends from the spirit world.

In 1883, at the age of forty-four, Sarah Winchester was widowed and inherited the Winchester Rifle fortune which amounted to twenty million dollars, plus an income of $1,000 per day. This fortune did not diminish Sarah's depression over the deaths of her husband and baby daughter, Annie. While seeking solace from a psychic in Boston,

Sarah was told that spirits demanded that she move to the West Coast and build a beautiful home of the most costly materials, and that construction must never stop, day or night. When she inquired about the last directive, Sarah was told that as long as construction continued, she would remain alive. The psychic added that this construction project, funded by profits from the sale of Winchester rifles, would be restitution to the many spirits who lost their lives to Winchester firearms during the Civil War and Indian Wars.

Frightened, yet dedicated to the psychic directives, Sarah moved to San Jose, purchased a small farmhouse that stood on 161 acres of land, and began building her monument to the spirit world. Construction continued, nonstop, for thirty-nine years as Sarah followed daily instructions from spirits who spoke to her in her séance room. Despite her obedience, she died on September 5, 1922. At the moment of her death, workmen walked off the job, leaving rooms unfinished and nails partially driven.

A labyrinth of hallways, secret passageways, dead-end staircases, and many oddly shaped rooms with low ceilings await visitors who tour Sarah's house. The séance room, the Daisy Room, and Sarah's bedroom containing her deathbed are the three most fascinating chambers. In these rooms, sensitive visitors have reported hearing chains rattling, whispers, and footsteps; feeling cold spots and icy breezes; and even seeing apparitions. Professional psychics and ghost hunters such as Sylvia Browne have reported these phenomena plus organ music and strange lights that flow across walls or flash out of nowhere. Sylvia Browne also reported seeing the ghosts of a man and woman, caretakers of the Winchester estate at the turn of the century, who are unhappy about the many visitors to the house. They watch over Sarah Winchester's home with great devotion.

Many investigators believe other ghosts inhabit the house, including Indians, soldiers, bandits, and cowboys from all over the Old West. After all, the place was designed by ghosts as a home for ghosts on earth.

The ghost of a workman has been spotted in the basement by staff and tourists. This fellow wears coveralls and is sometimes seen pushing a wheel-barrow. His presence received a lot of publicity during the 1980s when the basement was cleaned of rubble in preparation for its inclusion in the mansion's tours. Volunteers mentioned the helpful workman to their supervisor, who, in turn, revealed that no such man was employed at the mansion. Review of a historic photograph of mansion staff in the early 1900s resulted in identification of this ghost.

The switch-back staircase that conveys visitors from the ground floor to the second floor sits over a source of intense electromagnetic energy that is easily detected by sensitives or EMF instruments. Every time I walk these stairs, mid-way through each of the five stair segments I feel intense dizziness and nausea. These symptoms are brief, lasting a few seconds until I step beyond the mid-way treads. Many believe the staircase sits over a lei line of electromagnetic energy which is used by ghosts to move from the spirit world to our physical world. In fact, the entire mansion may sit on an intersection of several lei lines that enabled Mrs. Winchester's daily communication with spirits.

Many people insist that Sarah's ghost is not present inside the mansion. Her body is buried in New Haven, Connecticut, in a grave she shares with her infant daughter, Annie, and her husband, William (1837-1881). The commercial atmosphere of the large gift shop and concessions create the impression that the place is too busy and noisy for spirits. However, in 2008 I was sent a copy of an amazing

One of the most haunted places inside this San Jose mansion is the bedroom in which Sarah Winchester died in 1922.

photograph that suggests Sarah Winchester is on the premises. This photograph reveals the head of Sarah at a level that is appropriate for her height when seated. In life, she stood only 4 foot 10 inches.

Near Sarah's bedroom, the ghosts of a man and woman appear as shadows. They often stand back against the wall as visitors gaze into the room in which Sarah died.

A number of investigators have spent the night inside the huge mansion but remained sequestered in the Daisy Room. Sarah slept in this room the night of April 18, 1906. When the great San Francisco earthquake struck at 5:12 the next morning, Sarah was not only terrified but also trapped in the room for hours. The door frame was thrown out of square so badly that the door was stuck and could not be dislodged by several carpenters. Eventually, Sarah was freed but she was so shaken by the experience that she ordered her carpenters to seal the room. Ghost investigators who have spent the night in this room reported that the atmosphere is spooky and chilling, creating a sensation of being watched by an unseen person. From this spot, the sound of a distant piano is often heard.

A guided tour is the only way to gain entry into the Winchester Mystery House. Great adventures in this haunted house take place on the Friday the Thirteenth candle-light tours and on the flashlight tours offered weekends in October and ending on the Halloween tour. Either way, this place is one of the best houses in the Bay Area, accessible to the public, with a documented presence of ghosts.

GHOSTS OF THE SUICIDE ROOM

Former Le Baron Hotel
Wyndam Hotel and Resort
1350 North First Street
San Jose, CA 95112-4709
408-453-6200
www.wyndam-san-jose-pacifichost.com

On February 5, 1982, a UPI story published in a San Francisco magazine described a tragic suicide that took place in room 538 of the Le Baron Hotel in San Jose. The story reported that a traveling salesman, whom the desk clerk described as haggard and stressed, checked into the hotel and proceeded to room 538. The next morning, his lifeless body was found stretched out on the bed, the victim of suicide by an overdose of sleeping pills. Not long after the man's death, his apparition was seen by housekeeping staff members who entered the room. Occasionally, guests who occupied room 538 reported problems with flickering lights, a radio that turned on and off, and bizarre sounds. As sightings became more frequent, the apparition was spotted floating through the corridors and occasionally at the front desk.

Many years after the UPI story was published, information began to surface about a preceding suicide in the same room. According to staff members who work at the front desk, in November of 1979 a young woman committed suicide in room 538 after her groom failed to appear for the wedding. Devastated, she checked in, went to the room, and overdosed on pills. After the body was removed, housekeeper Lupe Moncivais had the unpleasant task of cleaning the room. Apparently the ghost of the jilted bride was still in the room and took a liking to Lupe. For months after the tragic death, Lupe felt someone pulling her hair and speaking her name. Lupe and other housekeepers often found the water running in the bathroom and the radio on. While cleaning the hallway, another housekeeper spotted a young woman entering room 538 on a day it was not rented. When the supervisor checked the room, it was found empty.

The similarity between these stories aroused my suspicions that reports of two tragic deaths in the same room might be nothing more than an urban legend. The UPI story was found to be genuine, however, and based on a police report. As for the young woman who committed suicide, that was easier to confirm. She was rumored to have worked as an American Airline flight attendant, but my source recalls that she worked as a ticket agent at San Jose Airport and had graduated from Saratoga High School in 1976. I learned of this suicide soon after it happened because the woman I dated at the time had been invited to the wedding. She flew from Los Angeles, where we were living, to San Jose to attend the event but called me later that night to report that the groom had failed to show. A few days later, we learned of the bride's suicide.

In 1996, the Le Baron Hotel underwent extensive renovation and reopened as the Wyndam Hotel. In spite of the remodeling, room 538 is often booked far in advance of Halloween and Fridays the thirteenth. Local paranormal enthusiasts find it particularly thrilling and believe their chances of a ghostly encounter are greatest on those dates.

GHOSTS OF THE INMATES

Old Agnews Mental Hospital
Sun Microsystems Campus
4150 Network Lane
Santa Clara, CA 95054
Press contact: 408-884-4980

For most of the twentieth century, residents of the East Bay Area thought of Napa and Santa Clara as strange places distinguished by insane asylums. In fact, when I was a kid, some of my teachers admonished rowdy students to shape-up or they would be sent to Napa. No one thought of grapes, vineyards, or wineries, but the notion of being sent to the Napa where crazy people were kept was scary. As a teenager, when I traveled south from Alameda to San Jose or Santa Cruz, I saw signs along the highway that pointed to the Agnews State Hospital, and the idea of being close to insane people made me avoid stopping in Santa Clara. Today, Napa is a world-class destination for wine lovers while Santa Clara is the home of Sun Microsystems and other high-tech companies. Both are attractive communities and desirable places to work and live, yet Napa's State Hospital continues to house more than a thousand patients and some of the Agnews buildings still stand, reminding many of the insane asylum.

Opened in 1885, the Agnews State Hospital housed mentally ill patients from around the state, many of them for life. While many patients were docile, some criminally insane persons were also incarcerated there. It is unknown how many environmental imprints were created by the hospital's patients during their lengthy stay. In 1998, Sun Microsystems purchased the 90-acre site and spent $10 million restoring the grounds and the four historically significant buildings, but many people still think of the place as a former asylum.

Occasionally, stories are leaked by employees who see or hear bizarre things, but virtually all of these reports are anonymous. Paranormal experiences have occurred in newer buildings that sit on the former sites of patient dormitories or treatment rooms. Apparitions of people dressed in hospital gowns appear for seconds, foul odors are detected, and sounds are heard that include screams, sobbing, moaning, bizarre laughter, and unintelligible shouts. Occasionally, cabinet doors fly open and contents fall to the floor. Investigation by ghost hunters is not possible due to the company's security policies and limited entry to most buildings on the campus, but visitors walking the grounds have had similar experiences.

The expansive campus includes a central treatment building capped by a clock tower that stands eight stories above the ground. In 1889, this building was the primary treatment center where patients were subjected to ice water baths, electric shock, and surgeries such as prefrontal lobotomy. It is likely that hundreds of patients died in this building during these unimaginably stressful procedures. The 1906 earthquake added another 119 patients to the death toll. This un-reinforced concrete structure suffered major damage that included walls collapsing onto patients and some staff members. Frequent paranormal activity is experienced by people working in this building, but only a few reports have been publicized.

In 2004, three telephone technicians worked inside the clock tower building installing new phone lines and switching equipment inside a closet. While they worked, strange noises were heard coming from an adjacent small room. After several minutes of hearing knocks on the door, tapping on the walls, and whistling, one of the telephone technicians opened the door and found the transparent apparition of a young girl standing with her arms out-stretched. When the tech fell back onto the other workers, all three regained their composure and peeked into the small room. The sight of the apparition shocked all three of them, and they immediately ran from the building.

I've obtained reports of paranormal experiences from others who have entered the building to perform various renovations that included plumbing, furniture installation, and electrical work. In many instances, paranormal activity is limited to unexplained movement or disappearance of tools and supplies, but some workers have reported seeing apparitions of people dressed in gray gowns.

Ghost hunters may walk the campus searching for environmental imprints created by the thousands of patients who suffered years of incarceration at this site. Entry to the clock tower building may be obtained by permission of the security staff. Nearby, the nineteenth-century auditorium, executive mansion, and administration building stand as monuments to the old Agnews asylum.

After touring the old Agnews asylum campus, take a short drive to the site of the old cemetery at 1250 Hope Drive. The cemetery is located less than half a mile from the asylum's haunted clock tower and is surrounded by residential housing. A chain link fence prevents entry, but inside the small museum is a viewing platform that allows visitor to view the site where an unknown number of patients are buried. There are no grave markers and no accessible records that allow an estimate of the number of bodies buried there. However, it is unlikely that many of the deceased patients were claimed by relatives and buried elsewhere. In the nineteenth century, mentally ill people were most often ostracized by their families, sent away to institutions, and forgotten. From 1885 until the 1960s, when more humane treatment was afforded patients, it is likely that more than 5,000 deceased patients were cremated and the ashes buried in the Agnews Cemetery.

GHOST OF THE GUARD

Trials Pub
265 North First Street
San Jose, CA 95113
408-947-0497
www.trialspub.com

Looking quite out of place in the capitol of the Silicon Valley, Trials Pub is anything but a franchised, high-end watering hole for venturing capitalists, software entrepreneurs, and chip engineers. That is not to say that San Jose State University computer engineering students and other locals who aspire to high-tech industry careers don't drink there, but the place is as far from classy and modern as one can get in Santa Clara County. Many bars in the nearby Santa Cruz Mountains have more amenities and attractive architecture than Trials Pub. But, if you ask patrons, they will tell you that the lack of pretension, twenty-first century glitz, and intrusion of anything high-tech make this place comfortable and enjoyable. The pub is so down-to-earth that I felt self-conscious when others at the bar noticed when my iPhone lit up with an in-coming call.

Aside from good beer and a fascinating collection of patrons, the pub is known as a haunted place. Looking at the nineteenth-century exterior, visitors get the immediate impression that the place is spooky even if the idea of ghosts never occurs to them. The place was built by Giuseppe Tagnazzi in 1894. The first floor was used as a grocery while the Tagnazzi family lived on the second floor. Early in the twentieth century, the place was sold and converted into a hotel for workers who maintained the local railroad. By 1920, the second floor was a busy brothel that served men who staggered upstairs from the first floor bar. In the 1930s, the building was renovated once again and used as an auxiliary jail for law breakers who were awaiting trials at the court

The ghost of an old jail guard haunts the basement of this popular San Jose pub.

house a few blocks away. It is rumored that during this period, the most incorrigible prisoners were housed in the basement and beaten by guards. In the early 1950s, downtown San Jose was a hovel of derelict buildings and pot-holed streets. During its renaissance, which began in the 1970s, the streets were cleaned up, historically significant buildings were restored, and places like Trials Pub opened, preserving local history.

The ghosts of the Trials Pub are believed to be derived from the building's period as a jail. In the basement, the brooding shape of a man has been seen moving through the remnants of jail cell doorways. Witnesses believe that this ghost was the head guard or warden and that he was killed during a prisoner revolt. This fellow doesn't break anything or make sounds, but his large size and dark features can be frightening. Staff members have refused to go into the basement without a companion.

SAINTE CLAIRE HOTEL

302 South Market Street
San Jose, CA 95113
408-295-2000
http://larkspurhotels.com/collection/sainte-claire/accommodations

San Jose is a very old city. Following the orders of the Spanish Viceroy of New Spain, Lieutenant Jose Moraga founded the settlement of Pueblo de San Jose de Guadalupe on November 29, 1777. Throughout the two centuries that followed, San Jose evolved from a Spanish military outpost to a Mexican pueblo, an American agricultural community, a state capital, an industrial center, and finally, the capital of the world-famous Silicon Valley and birthplace of many high-tech industries. Throughout these transitions, buildings in the heart of the city were modified, renovated, torn down, and replaced by newer structures. Because of this recurrent process of urban development, ghosts found in existing buildings may have their origins in structures that no longer exist. The spiritual entity is often unaware of the newer structure and moves about as if it were still in its home or workplace or place of death.

Some of the ghosts that haunt the Sainte Claire Hotel may have been residents or workers in previous structures. Before the hotel was built in 1925 and opened on October 16, 1926, the site was occupied by a huge brick building that housed the Eagle Brewing Company. The brewer had stood for seventy years, providing opportunities for fatal accidents and for the creation of lingering ghosts.

Reports of construction costs earned the Sainte Claire the moniker of San Jose's "million dollar hotel" and attracted luminaries such as Clark Gable, Judy Garland, Eleanor Roosevelt, and Bob Hope. By the end of the 1960s, however, the Sainte Claire had become a run-down flop house surrounded by urban decay. Until the first round of renovation began in 1980, victims of substance abuse died on the premises. Additional renovations in the 1990s brought the hotel into step with San Jose's urban revitalization as the capital of the Silicon Valley. By the mid-1990s, the Sainte Claire was well-known as a haunted hotel.

There are reports that most of the paranormal activity takes place on the third and sixth floors, but staff members told me that ghosts have been heard and seen on every floor including the lobby. Some staff have been so frightened by their ghostly encounters that they have refused to enter certain rooms or work on a particular floor unless another worker accompanies them.

A boy described as ten or twelve years old has been spotted sitting on the stairs at various locations between the third and fifth floors. His clothing appears dirty and rough, inviting speculation that he was a child laborer in the old brewery. Men and women in early twentieth-century clothing have been seen walking through the lobby and entering the lounge.

On the second floor, guests have reported excessive noise arising from a room that was once a private club for alumnae of the Santa Clara University. Nearby, in room 215, the amorous activity of newly married couples has been overheard by people passing the honeymoon suite. During my visits to the Sainte Claire, I heard a female voice laughing and soft moans emanating through the door at a time when the room was not rented. I also spotted the transparent apparition of an old man dressed in dirty coveralls. He appeared to have a small bucket in his right hand. I suspect he was once a worker at the Eagle Brewing Company.

MISSION SAN JOSE

43300 Mission Blvd.
Fremont, CA 94539
510-657-1797 extension 100

This large mission was founded by Father Fermin de Lasuen on June 11, 1797, and named in honor of Saint Joseph. The mission was established at a site fifteen miles north of the city of San Jose to avoid interaction between Spanish soldiers stationed in the South Bay and local Indians converted by the priests to mission life and the Catholic faith. At one time, Mission San Jose had more Indians than any other northern California mission while thousands of cattle roamed grasslands now covered by the city of Fremont. In accepting the mission lifestyle dictated by the Franciscan priests, the Indians came under the rule of Spanish priests that were sometimes harsh. Neophytes were also exposed to measles and smallpox brought by Spanish soldiers and others who visited the mission. In 1805, a devastating epidemic began which ultimately killed one third of the mission's Indian population. Many of these unfortunate people were buried in unmarked graves in the cemetery adjacent to the north wall of the church.

Despite this tragedy, the Indian population grew to almost 2,000 by 1825. This population explosion created friction between the Indians and the priests, who had established themselves as absolute rulers over all Native Americans associated with the mission including a group of Indians who retained their autonomy. In 1828, their leader, tribal elder Estanislao, gathered his loyal followers and turned against the priests who had tried to bring these Indians into the mission community. Estanislao led thirty Indians in an armed attack on the mission, causing the priests to barricade themselves and loyal neophytes inside the church. Several soldiers, who rushed to the mission from the town of San Jose, were killed along with many of Estanislao's followers. Estanislao survived the conflict and, with the intervention of Father Duran, escaped punishment. Taking up residence at the mission, Estanislao lived there another ten years before he died. His body remains buried in an unmarked grave near the church he once attacked.

Today, Mission San Jose has several sites for ghost hunting. The patio and church cemetery are good places to search for spirits. Many Indians worked at mission trades in the patio and lived in quiet desperation while longing for their old, beloved lifestyle. Most ended up in unmarked graves in the shadow of the tall adobe church that they built. The cloister, a long building fronting the street, has a broad porch that offers many shady spots for lingering spirits to watch the modern world roll by.

Sightings have been reported at the unique, half-circular steps at the front of the church. These steps, built by Indian labor, were covered with the soil of passing decades and forgotten until they were revealed during a restoration in the 1980s. On these steps, late in the afternoon, cold spots have been experienced with occasional areas of "heavy" air, suggesting the presence of ghosts sitting upon the steps. It is possible that some of the Indians who built the steps, and all the mission buildings, have claimed this place as their own, having paid with their lives and their culture. Or, perhaps, the Spanish soldiers killed by Estanislao and his warriors sit upon these steps, clinging to the church they defended in 1828.

WHITE WITCH OF NILES CANYON ROAD

Niles Canyon Railroad Depot
6 Kilkare Road
Sunol, CA 94586
925-862-9063
www.ncry.org

I've heard stories about the White Witch since I was a kid growing up in Alameda. When I was a teenager, the stories circulated as a warning not to venture into the Oakland hills on Friday and Saturday nights. It was said that the White Witch attacked young couples who parked at scenic spots to admire the view of the city below. I never met anyone who was attacked, but several people reported to me that they thought they saw a humanoid, vaporous white cloud pass over their car. The witch was believed to be the ghost of Granny Norton, who died near Clayton when her buggy tipped over in 1879.

Years later, people claimed that the White Witch was haunting Niles Canyon Road near Fremont. The story was the same: the ghost was that of a woman who died when her buggy tipped over. Since the story was taking on the traits of an urban legend, I dismissed reports of a haunting in Niles Canyon until recently. A friend who is a skeptic of the paranormal told me that while cycling through Niles Canyon, he found it to be terribly spooky, even in broad daylight. When I questioned him further, he denied seeing anything that might be paranormal, but he admitted that when passing through a segment of the canyon near the Sunol train station, he felt frightened for no apparent reason. This discussion occurred at the same time I discovered a report that world-renowned psychic Annette Martin had encountered the spirit of a young women near the train depot. Martin based her investigation on vague reports of a fatal auto accident in the canyon in 1938, not on a nineteenth century buggy accident.

Reports by Annette Martin and my friend the skeptic prompted me to search for historical proof of a fatal accident in the area that involved a young woman. Various Internet postings mentioned the year 1938, but writers had no further details. My search for an accident report included a name perceived by Annette Martin—Mary Anne. Another writer mentioned the surname Lowerey. I had no luck locating a Mary Anne Lowerey who in Alameda County in the 1930s. I tried different spellings of the surname, but I still had no success in finding a dead woman who might be the White Witch of Niles Canyon.

Taking a unique tack, I gained access to the 1930 U.S. Census for Alameda County. In those records, I discovered a Mary Catherine Lowery who was born in San Francisco in 1920. The 1940 Census did not list this person. With the name Mary Catherine instead of Mary Anne, I searched obituaries in Livermore area newspapers for the 1930s. That search failed, but I was directed to a list of burials in area cemeteries. Scanning Pleasanton Cemetery records, I found Mary Catherine Lowery, who died in February of 1938. Burial records included the notation "killed by cars."

The plural word "cars" was an important element of my search. An obscure notice in a San Francisco newspaper mentioned that Mary C. Lowery was killed in Niles Canyon when her horse-drawn buggy over-turned. The accident occurred because a car passed close to her horse, causing it to bolt, tip the buggy, and toss Mary into the road where a second car ran over her: a two-car accident.

The story gets even stranger. Some writers report that the ghost of Niles Canyon appears life-like to some motorists, who stop and offer her a ride. Upon stepping up to the car, she says she needs a ride to an address in San Francisco, the city in which Mary C. Lowery lived until the age of ten when she moved to the Sunol area.

The White Witch appears alongside the road a few hundred yards from Sunol Depot on Kilkare Road. Her appearance ranges from fully life-like to a diaphanous white cloud that barely resembles human form. She may be unaware of her death and still trying to travel to the home of her fiancé. People who have seen her report that she appears quite sad and distressed.

OTHER PLACES TO HUNT GHOSTS:

GHOST OF SAM THE PIZZA MAN

Bronco Billy's Pizza Palace
3940 Smith Street
Union City, CA 94587-2616
510-489-4601

The ghost of an old timer named Sam has been reported by patrons of Bronco Billy's Pizza Palace. Astonished witnesses have experienced a husky voice whispering in their ear, cold spots, and a gloomy, scary sensation in the party room. I questioned two managers and a waitress about paranormal activity but they had no experiences of their own to report. The building is more than a century old and once housed a hardware store, feed store, and a restaurant. One of the managers told me the second floor was once a brothel. There is no information available about the identity of this ghost. Patrons and staff have named him Sam for reasons which no one could tell me.

W. E. MASON CAROUSEL

Vasona Park
233 Blossom Hill Road
Los Gatos, CA 95030
408-395-7433

More than a few ghosts have become attached to this historic carousel. They may be trying to relive some of the best moments of their lives when, as children, they rode the dazzling wooden horses and stages in make-believe races. Built in 1910 in England, the carousel was shipped around Cape Horn to Los Angeles and then sent north by rail to San Francisco where it was reassembled in 1915 for the Panama-Pacific Exposition. At the close of the Exposition, it became part of a traveling circus until 1967, when it was disassembled and placed in storage. In 1980, a group of Los Gatos citizens headed by Bill Mason, Charles Dewey, Paul Seaborn, and Jerry Kennedy raised $50,000 to purchase the carousel and begin restoration. In July of 1990, the carousel was dedicated to the memory of Bill Mason. Peter Panacy, executive director of the Billy Jones Wildcat Railroad and W. E. Mason Carousel, has reported many "weird things" that have occurred at the carousel that point to a ghost. Panacy has heard gates opening and noticed lights turning on without explanation. A bell that sounds when the carousel starts moving has been heard when the machine is shut down. It is suspected that the ghost responsible for all of that is Paul Seaborn, who died in 1990. Seaborn volunteered hundreds of hours designing and building the carousel's modern mechanical and electrical systems and he may still be on the site insuring that everything runs well. It is possible that the spirits of Bill Mason and volunteer Al Smith haunt the old carousel together with other wayward spirits who climbed aboard sometime during the past 100 years.

YSHIHIRO UCHIDA HALL

Old San Jose State University Gymnasium
South 4th Street at East San Carlos Street
San Jose, CA 95112
408-924-1000
http://www.sjsu.edu/

From the moment I first stepped into this old building, I knew it was haunted. I was eighteen years old and visiting the campus for a swim meet. Something about the place gave me goose bumps and made my heart beat faster. Years later, I learned that the ghosts of detained Japanese citizens and Japanese Americans roamed the building. Designed to reverse the unemployment created by the Great Depression, the gymnasium was built in 1933 as one of President Franklin Roosevelt's Works Progress Administration projects. At the outbreak of WWII, the gymnasium was used as a temporary detention center for Japanese. As many as 6,000 Japanese were processed in this building before being transported to permanent centers in Arizona, Nevada, and California's Central Valley. Faced with unprecedented extraction from their homes and businesses, many of the people incarcerated there lost everything but the clothing they carried. Their fear and torment have left many indelible imprints on the environment that may be detected by EAP investigations. Sensitives who pass by this building hear voices speaking in Japanese and women and children crying.

The two-story building now houses the departments of kinesiology and intercollegiate athletics. It was named for the college's legendary judo coach, Yoshihiro Uchida, who served in the U.S. Army throughout WWII.

LORD BRADLEY'S INN

43344 Mission Blvd.
Fremont, CA 94539
510-490-0520

This charming inn is easy to overlook if visitors are focused on the Mission San Jose located nearby on the same street. I found this place in 1990 and rented the entire inn for my wedding. At the time, I was unaware of its haunted history, but the historical ambience was something I noticed. The history of the place has been difficult to research because of multiple owners and diverse uses of the space over a period of one hundred years. Starting as a farm house, and then undergoing expansion to a boarding house, store, bar and brothel, and finally reverting to an inn, the building's ghosts may be remnants from several eras. When I spent my wedding night there, I didn't detect anything paranormal. Subsequent overnight guests have reported incessant heavy footsteps, sounds of glasses touching as if spirits are toasting their continued presence in the place, and the sound of baggage being dragged across wood floors. I am not aware of any paranormal investigation of this inn, but bizarre, unexplained sounds are so frequently reported that ghost hunters would likely have success in capturing ghostly activity on audio recorders.

Chapter 5

East Bay Area

The East Bay Area has a rich history, well-preserved in hundreds of Victorian mansions, old office buildings, hotels and resorts, wharves and docks, airplanes, boats, bars, and cemeteries. Local Indians, Spanish explorers, Yankee sailors, writers, pirates, and fishermen have left an indelible mark on the land and a lingering echo of their lives that is easy to detect. The under-appreciated charms of Oakland, the excitement of Berkeley, and the peaceful ambience of small towns such as Pleasanton, Alameda, and Clayton provide a wide variety of ghost hunting experiences.

CASA PERALTA

384 West Estudillo Avenue
San Leandro, CA 94577
510-577-3492

Seventeen-year-old Luis Maria Peralta (1759-1851) never dreamed that his service as a soldier in one of the earliest explorations of California would result in fame, fortune, and a lasting mark upon the East Bay's communities. Enlisted in the regiment of Juan Bautista de Anza, Luis arrived in Alta California in 1776, accompanied by his parents and three siblings. After settling his family in Monterey, he served as corporal of the guards at Mission San Jose, Mission Santa Clara, and at Mission Santa Cruz. In 1805, he attracted the attention of the Spanish governor of Alta California by leading troops in a victory over renegade

Indians and suppressing other uprisings. After Spain relinquished Alta California to Mexico, Luis was rewarded with 44,000 acres of land that comprises several East Bay cities now. Today, the name Peralta graces parks, streets, hills, schools, and other landmarks. Over the ensuing decades, Don Luis's lands were sold or given to relatives.

In 1874, Peralta's granddaughter, Ludovina Peralta, received land in the area known as San Leandro. By 1901, a nine-room Victorian house stood on the property. Ludovina lived there with her sister, Maria, and a niece, Herminia Peralta. When Ludovina and Maria passed away, Herminia inherited the house and lands, and stayed there throughout her marriage to publisher William Dargie. When he died, Herminia traveled in Europe, gathering ideas for remodeling her home. She brought a dashing twenty-one-year-old architect from Spain, Captain Antonio Martin, to San Leandro in 1926 to transform her house into a Spanish estate.

Antonio Martin knocked out walls, created arched passageways, and added colorful Moorish tiles and decorative murals to parts of the house. When his work was completed, he remained in residence on

The Peralta House in San Leandro was the scene of a legendary love affair that has left at least one ghost that may be waiting for the return of its lover.

the estate in a small apartment. There is no historical evidence, but many have speculated that Herminia and Antonio had quite a torrid affair. The fact that Herminia left her house and half her lands to him lends credence to the idea. Also, his apartment was a short distance across an elevated walk from the sunroom, one of Herminia's favorite parts of the house.

Added drama came after Herminia's death when her will was contested and Antonio lost all claim to the estate he had called home, due to bitter disputes with Herminia's relatives. Later, the land was sold in parcels and the house passed through the hands of several Peralta descendents. In the 1940s, Casa Peralta served as a hospital for treatment of alcoholism and later became a nursing home.

Today, Casa Peralta is restored and opens for tours and special events. It is a fascinating museum depicting Herminia's life through displays of furniture, art, clothing, and photographs. Antonio's artistic and architectural additions to the house are highlighted as well. Local ghost hunters believe that Antonio's ghost is still in residence at his beloved Casa Peralta. Perhaps he put so much of his soul into its architecture and art that his spirit could not let go of the place. He may have remained on the earthly plane to enjoy the place with Herminia, too, for the presence of a female spirit has also been detected there. Observers have seen the pale image of a small woman dressed in a Victorian gown in the garden and in a second floor bedroom. Other spirits, from the Casa's days as a hospital, may also inhabit the place.

GHOSTS OF THE OLD TRAIN STATION

Former site of Spellbinding Book Store
1910 Encinal Avenue
Alameda, CA 94501

Alameda is full of century-old buildings that retain the charm of the Victorian era and a large number of ghosts. At the corner of Chestnut Street and Encinal Avenue sits a large two-story building constructed in 1904 by John L. Ansel. Originally designed as a commercial center to house a meat market on the ground floor and private apartments on the second floor, the place was converted in 1906 to a train station when Southern Pacific Railroad installed standard gauge tracks on Encinal Avenue. The structure was designed with an alcove to accommodate a pre-existing shelter for street car patrons. The shelter may be seen in historic photographs of Alameda's Chestnut Street Station posted on the Internet. The station proved to be a busy enterprise serving residents who traveled to the ferryboat pier at the west end of the island and then on to San Francisco. The shelter, which covered most of the sidewalk in front of the building, was removed in 1933 because its twin-peak design, resembling two Asian-style straw hats, appeared old-fashioned to the island's city council members. Train service ended in 1941 as tracks on Lincoln Avenue proved better for handling WWII traffic to the Alameda Navy Air Station. The old station was converted to shops but failed to prosper as Park Street become the city's prime commercial district. When I was a kid, my friends and I always avoided these stores because there was something about the place we considered spooky.

In 2007, the former train station was renovated and rededicated as a commercial center for the residents of the neighborhood. That event followed the failure of several businesses that had struggled to succeed at this location since the 1940s. One of those businesses was one of my favorite bookstores, Spellbinding Tales. Featuring books about the occult, this place was known to be haunted by at least three ghosts. Investigators from Spirit-Speak, Ghost Trackers, Central California Paranormal Investigations, Southern Wisconsin Paranormal Research Group, Haunted and Paranormal Investigations, and several independent paranormal enthusiasts have hunted for ghosts in this bookstore. The store's owner hosted a book signing for me in 2006 and allowed me an opportunity to do an EAP sweep.

During its short run, staff and customers of the bookstore reported dark figures that seem to walk the aisles between stacks of books, sounds that included banging, cracking wood, pounding that emanated from inside walls, and books that flew off the shelves. Psychics and sensitives detected the presence of two female entities on the mezzanine. These spirits moved fast, rushing up the stairs as paranormal investigators walked the aisles. One EAP recording captured a female voice that said, "I'll get in the apartment." The ghost may have used the mezzanine or loft as a portal to the second floor apartments.

Among the spirits that occupy this old building was a man identified as a German shopkeeper named Helgar or Heimer. Another male spirit was found under the stairs. This fellow creates cold spots and conveyed to psychics that he is afraid to move onward to the next level that many describe as "the light."

A female spirit named Louisa came to the store with an antique chair. She has been heard on audio recordings speaking in a sweet voice while expressing her interest in the books. Since the store's closing, this chair has been removed.

Since November of 2009, the old Chestnut Street Station has housed a clothing consignment store. I questioned the shop owners about unusual events in their renovated store. They denied having experiences that might be called paranormal, but they said they've been too busy with the store to notice if items are moved or hidden or if unexplainable sounds have occurred.

CROLL'S 1883 RESTAURANT AND BAR

1400 Webster Street
Alameda, CA 94501
510-748-6075

For over one hundred years, Croll's bar was a popular drinking and eating establishment for boxers, sailors, longshoremen, and fishermen residing in Alameda. The place opened in 1883 with financing provided by Comstock silver baron James Fair. Fair recruited John G. Croll, then manager of the Union Pacific Restaurant in Oakland, to develop the place as a prominent feature of the famous Neptune Gardens Amusement Park and Baths (swimming pools) located at the foot of Webster Street in Alameda. Fair allowed Croll to name the place and set up a training resort for boxers. Within months, outdoor exercise areas, practice rings, massage tents, and dining rooms were opened. Boxers and their trainers had priority, but John Croll wisely opened the place to the general public, making it an Alameda landmark business. Several of boxing's greatest fighters trained at Croll's, including Gentleman Jim Corbett (1892-97),

Croll's Bar in Alameda was the site of a training center for boxers before it became a popular drinking establishment for sailors.

John L. Sullivan (1892-95), Ruby Bob Fitzsimmons (1898-99), and Jim Jeffries (1899-1905).

Croll became so successful that he bought the entire establishment from James Fair in 1891, enlarged the facilities, and established stronger business ties with Alameda's Neptune Beach, also known as the Coney Island of the West. All of this came to an end when the great earthquake shook the place on April 18, 1906. Tourism declined to near zero while boxers looked for other, less seismically active places to train and stage fights.

By the late 1920s, Croll's had become a bar that catered almost exclusively to military personnel. Many sailors, soldiers, and marines stationed at the Alameda Naval Air Station had their last drinks there before shipping out to foreign ports or combat zones of WWII, Korea, and Vietnam. The bar's close proximity to the air station and naval harbor made it a first stop for many of the military returning from those historic events. In the 1990s, pool tables and rock bands attracted a younger, civilian crowd, but the bar's reputation for trouble spread through the East Bay Area. When I was in high school, my friends and I always avoided passing by the place on a Friday or Saturday night, because the riotous atmosphere within often spilled out onto the streets. After I turned twenty-one, I patronized the place occasionally, but I always felt unsafe and often got pushed around and soaked with beer.

Over the years, local legends developed about fights, robberies, and shootings that supposedly took place there. There are no official records available confirming fatal shootings, but the eerie atmosphere of the place suggests that something bad happened there. Croll's Bar closed in 1998 and sat vacant for a few years before reopening in 2005 as an upscale restaurant with garden seating. The laughter, music, and wild banter of the long-deceased drinking crowd can still be heard, though, by those sensitive people who visit the site. These sounds can be detected by psychics and captured on audio recorders late in the evening at the threshold of the Webster Street entrance. They come as brief but unmistakable audible remnants of ghosts that still hang out at the old Croll's Bar. A dark figure is often seen standing in the doorway looking out to the street. This ghost may be waiting for long lost friends to return from a war so they can drink a few rounds at Croll's Bar.

USS *HORNET*

Former Alameda Naval Air Station
Atlantic Avenue entrance
707 West Hornet Avenue
Alameda, CA 94501-1147
510-521-8484
www.uss-hornet.org

It has been said that all ships are haunted, especially those that served in combat. Fear and anger experienced by dedicated crew members during battles would produce intense environmental imprints detectable as paranormal activity. Accidents in engine rooms, fires in fueling stations, explosions in ammunition holds and in gun turrets, bullets, shells, and torpedoes fired by the energy, and aircraft crashes on a flight deck would naturally produce ghosts confused by the end of life while still feeling the need to remain on duty. Many of the dead would be young men, fiercely loyal to their ship and shipmates and so devoted to service to their country that they would not let death keep them from defending their homeland and defeating an enemy. The WWII aircraft carrier USS *Hornet* has a history that includes the horror of battle, tragedy of countless accidents, misfortune of numerous fatal illnesses, and overwhelming personal stress and mental anguish of many crew members. So it isn't any wonder that the USS *Hornet* is one of the most haunted ships in America.

Commissioned on November 29, 1943, the USS *Hornet* was sent to the South Pacific to avenge the loss of her namesake, the aircraft carrier *Hornet* that was sunk by the Japanese in 1942 at Guadalcanal. Pilots flying from her deck sank seventy-three Japanese ships totaling 1,269,710 tons and destroyed 1,410 enemy aircraft. She was a key element in every amphibious landing after March of 1944 and is credited with initiating the attack on the Japanese battleship *Yamato*, flagship of the fleet that attacked Pearl Harbor. During the bloody battles of Okinawa and Iwo Jima, the *Hornet* came under heavy attack fifty-nine times, sustaining severe battle damage but always remaining sea-worthy and capable of aircraft operations. This combat record was

The USS Hornet *in Alameda is reputed to be one of the most haunted ships in America.*

not accomplished without considerable loss of crew. During twenty-seven years of service, more than 300 crew members died aboard this ship. Flight deck operations resulted in decapitation of at least three crewmen by aircraft arresting cables. More than thirty sailors were killed by contact with aircraft propellers while an unknown number were ingested by jet engine intake vents or burned by jet exhaust. More than fifty aircraft crashed on the *Hornet*'s flight deck, killing air crew and flight deck workers. Aside from combat and accidents, the stress of long voyages severely stressed some crew members, leaving the *Hornet* with the dubious distinction of having the highest suicide rate of any ship in the U.S. Navy.

The last mission of this warship was a peaceful one, however. On July 24, 1969, she recovered the Apollo 11 astronauts upon their return from the moon. The 900-foot long ship was decommissioned in 1979 and sat many years awaiting restoration. It was during this time that caretakers began noticing strange sounds and other odd events. At times, when no other living soul was aboard the old ship, watchmen heard loud tapping sounds reverberating through the steel hull. Heavy steel doors would slam shut or swing open. The possibility that these events could result from movement of the ship was dismissed, for the 42,000-ton vessel sat in placid, protected waters at Hunter's Point Naval Shipyard off of San Francisco. Wind and tide could not cause rocking or other motions of the huge ship.

After the old *Hornet* opened as a museum in August of 1998, staff members who continued the restoration and maintenance of the ship noticed the slamming doors, movement of objects, and the sounds of footsteps on the metal deck. Suspicions that the old ship was haunted spread quickly and attracted the attention of serious paranormal investigators and TV producers. The *Hornet* has been featured in several movies including *XXX: State of the Union,* in TV shows such as *JAG,* and in numerous paranormal shows including *Sightings, Scariest Places on Earth,* and *Ghost Hunters.* Psychics such as Sylvia Browne have visited the ship and affirmed that the Gray Lady is, indeed, most haunted. Some paranormal investigators believe there may be as many as 300 ghosts on this ship.

The USS *Hornet* has been investigated by several paranormal organizations including Ghost Trackers, The Atlantic Paranormal

Society (TAPS), Sonoma SPIRIT headed by Jackie Ganiy, and Ghost. Since the *Hornet* is berthed in my home town, I've investigated ghostly activity on the ship many times. There are numerous dark passageways, dimly lit rooms, and dark spaces on a ship this size, but I've seen the most vivid apparitions in the well-lit sick bay. I've spotted the ghosts of sailors resting in the berths and lying unconscious on the operating table. I've also seen ghostly physicians and corpsmen moving around the sick bay. Other hot spots for ghostly activity are the pilots' ready room and the chapel.

Hundreds of visitors to the *Hornet* have reported paranormal experiences. These include sightings of apparitions of deck hands and pilots on the flight deck, officers on the bridge, officers wearing "dress whites" in the passageways, men in the medical wing and sick bay wearing khakis or operating room garb, engine room workers wearing protective gear that resembled firefighting suits, sailors in blue uniforms, and injured men who appear burned or missing an arm or head.

Sounds have been heard or captured on audio recording at several locations throughout the ship including the flight deck, forecastle,

The catwalk in the forecastle of the USS Hornet *has been the sight of ghostly activity.*

hangar deck, engine room, fantail, restrooms, sailors' racks (sleeping quarters), sick bay, and chapel. US Coast Guardsmen, *Hornet* museum staff members, and others who were on board to help maintain the ship have reported hearing disembodied voices offer them advice, bark orders, call for help, and scream as if they are in pain. Lockers, doors, and hatches have been heard opening and closing. Footsteps have been heard on the decks when no one can be seen moving about.

Photographic indications of paranormal activity have been posted at several Web sites, but the best evidence was shown to me by Jackie Ganiy, president of Sonoma SPIRIT. In the engine room, Jackie and her team captured an infrared image of a man wearing protective gear similar to that worn by firefighters. The image is so detailed that it is easy to see creases in the man's sleeve at his left elbow. On the flight deck, the team captured one of the best orb photographs I've even seen. The orb floats over the approach end of the flight deck in the vicinity of the aircraft arresting cables. Inside the orb, a skull can be seen. If this orb represents a spirit presence, it may be the result of decapitation of a crew member by the arresting cable. Official ship's record indicate that three crew died in this gruesome way.

The *Hornet* is open for self-guided tours, although some parts of the ship may be entered only with a docent. Overnight stays can be arranged.

HEINOLDS FIRST AND LAST CHANCE SALOON

48 Webster Street
Jack London Square
Oakland, CA 94607
510-839-6761
www.heinoldsfirstandlastchance.com

In the 1880s, the Oakland waterfront was a wild place. Ships came to call from all over the world. Their crews would hit the town with money in their pockets and lust in their hearts. Ships were often abandoned by their officers and crew, leaving the docks congested with derelict vessels that were scavenged by crews of other ships who

228 ⌐ Ghost Hunter's Guide to the San Francisco Bay Area

might have needed additional hardware, ropes, sails, or wood for fuel. In addition to crowds of sailors, the docks were full of longshoremen and naval personnel, all of whom supported a bustling community of bars and brothels and kept the jail full.

In 1879, the crew of a whaling ship was incarcerated for several weeks, leaving their ship unattended. The old vessel became grounded on the Oakland mud, and soon local scavengers stripped her of wood, metal, and other valuable building materials. Much of her timber was used to build a solid structure that served three years as a boarding house for sailors.

In 1883, the place was purchased by Johnny Heinold for $100 and transformed into a bar. Johnny's bar became a popular waterfront gathering place for oyster pirates and the lawmen that pursued them on San Francisco Bay. The curious name—the First and Last Chance Saloon—was derived from the bar's location. The place stood at the

For more than 120 years, the Last Chance Saloon on Oakland's waterfront has been a popular drinking establishment for sailors, including Jack London.

foot of a pier from which ferryboats carried passengers across the Oakland Estuary to the dry town of Alameda. Johnny's bar was the last chance for a drink before passengers departed for Alameda and their first chance upon returning to Oakland.

In 1886, a boy named Jack London sat on the stool selling newspapers to the bar's patrons. Later, he sat at a corner table to do his school work. Not only was young Jack London inspired by the exciting stories of adventure told by the men drinking at the bar, but at the age of sixteen, Jack made a deal to purchase his first sailboat while seated at a corner table.

Over the years, sailors, soldiers, marines, aviators, and others embarking on far reaching adventures have made Heinold's bar a last stop before departure, and a first stop upon returning home. Many of these adventurers have returned only in spirit. The warped floor boards, century-old chairs, stools, and tables offer an atmosphere of timelessness that is comforting to the living as well as the dead. Some ghost hunters have sensed the spirit of Jack London and members of his oyster pirate gang. Others have experienced the touch of the long-departed Johnny Heinold. Several cold spots in the tiny bar could be the spirits of famous visitors from long past decades including Robert Louis Stevenson, Earle Gardner, Ambrose Bierce, Robert Service, and Joaquin Miller. The old photographs and other maritime souvenirs mounted on the walls document the history of this old bar and provide hints of the identity of the many spirits who still visit the First and Last Chance Saloon.

CAMROM-STANFORD HOUSE

Lake Merritt
1418 Lakseside Drive
Oakland, CA 94612-4307
510-444-1876
www.cshouse.org

This ornate Italian-style Victorian mansion is the last of many grand houses that once stood on the shores of Lake Merritt. It is named for the two most prominent families that occupied it during the first thirty-one years it served as a private residence. Will and Alice Camron built the mansion in 1876 and moved in for a brief stay in 1877. Later in the year, the family of David Hewes moved in and staged the biggest social event in the house's history—the marriage of his daughter, Franklina Hewes, which took place in the parlor in October of 1877. Among the notables who attended the wedding was Lucy Webb Hayes, First Lady of the United States. From 1881 to 1902, the mansion was home to Josiah Stanford, brother of Leland Stanford, and his wife, Helen.

In 1907, the City of Oakland bought the mansion and renovated it for use as a museum. It served in this capacity until 1967 when the new city museum opened nearby. The City of Oakland then began a lengthy preservation process to restore the ornate house to its former glory as a home for some of Oakland's wealthiest citizens. Through the efforts of more than 1,000 volunteers, artists, craftsman, and historians, the Camron-Stanford house regained the atmosphere of the 1880s. Sensitive visitors experience a time-warp there now and feel the texture of another age. Some of them also feel the presence of ghosts.

As a child, I visited this old house many times, always fascinated with the artifacts on display as part of the old Oakland Museum. At the age of twelve, I thought I saw a young woman descend the staircase and pass through the foyer, then disappear as she entered the parlor. The amazing experience left an indelible mark on my memory. Many years later, after I started investigating the reports of paranormal activity in the San Francisco Bay Area, I returned to the Camron-Stanford House to confirm my suspicion that the experience I had as a child was an encounter with a ghost. I spent a long time in the foyer and parlor, keeping an eye on the staircase, but I did not detect anything that was ghostly. After about an hour inside the old house, I discovered a few vertical streaks of light that resembled wisps of fog. As I watched, these wisps of fog coalesced and became the partial apparition of a woman who appeared to be dressed in a white Victorian gown. This apparition stood facing the interior of the mansion's front doors. She did not move during her brief manifestation, but I noted the fragrance of flowers. Psychically tuning into this apparition, I got the impression that the young woman was waiting for someone to return home to this fascinating portal to the 1880s. Suspicions run high that this ghost is Franklina Hewes.

GHOSTS OF THE TWO LADIES

Pardee Home
672 11th Street
Oakland, CA 94607-3651
510-444-2187
www.pardeehome.org/tourinformation.htm

Built in 1868, this magnificent mansion stands as a monument to one of California's great families. Full of original furnishings, clothing, personal items, and a vast collection of souvenirs gathered by the matron of the house, the place also contains the spirits of at least two former residents.

With riches panned in Sierra creeks during the Gold Rush, Enoch Pardee obtained an education in San Francisco and then built a grand house in Oakland. With a medical degree and specialization as an eye doctor, Pardee developed a successful practice in Oakland that earned him the admiration of the community. In 1870, he used his fine reputation and social status to launch a political career that included mayor of Oakland, state assemblyman, and state senator. With his wife, Mary, Enoch raised his only child in this house. Like his father, George Pardee became an eye doctor before embarking on a political career that culminated with his election as governor of California in 1902.

With Enoch's death in 1897, George, his wife, Helen, and their four girls moved into the house and made it the social and political hub of Oakland. Helen used the wide hallways and some of the rooms to create a museum that contained a huge collection of artifacts from Pacific Rim nations—candlesticks, scrimshaw, and shells—and territories and California fine arts. Much of the collection remains on display today and may account for the attachment of a female spirit to the house.

Sensitives who visit this place often detect the presence of at least two female spirits. One of them may be Helen Pardee (1857-1947), who

Once the home of a California governor, the Pardee House in Oakland is haunted by the ghosts of three women.

has found it impossible to leave her grand house and the collections she loved. People who stand quietly in front of Helen's curio cabinets often hear the swish of her Victorian skirts and notice the fragrance of perfume that is not encountered elsewhere in the house.

My impressions of the spirits suggest they are two young females, probably Carol and Florence. Florence died on September 11, 1910, at the age of twenty-two years, from injuries sustained in a motor vehicle accident. While traveling in San Rafael, the car in which she was a passenger rolled over an embankment, throwing her out. Her body was brought home and kept in the front parlor for viewing and a wake.

Carol died on March 4, 1920, at the age of twenty-nine years, from the Spanish flu that killed 100 million people world-wide. Her wake was held in the same parlor, but it was sparsely attended due to fears that the dead could still transmit the disease.

I believe the ghosts of these two young ladies still walk the rooms and halls of their beloved home. At times their apparitions appear as they did in their teenage years. Ghost hunters should study a photograph of the

Pardee family that can be found online. Since the apparitions are usually fragmented, identification might be made by comparing features of the spiritual entities with those displayed in the photograph.

Some paranormal investigators believe the two female spirits may be sisters Madeline (1890-1980) and Miss Helen (1895-1981), named for her mother. After the deaths of sisters Carol and Florence, and parents George in 1941 and mother Helen in 1947, these inseparable, spinster sisters remained in the house until their deaths. As elderly ladies, they spent their evenings in the front parlor watching TV. The house then sat vacant from 1981 to 1991, offering spirits time to re-establish themselves before the place was repaired and opened as a museum.

REMILLARD HOUSE

California Preservation Park Historic District
1233 Preservation Park Way
Oakland, CA 94512
510-874-7580
www.preservationpark.com

In the late nineteenth century, Oakland was the second largest city in California. Known for its thriving industries and as a commercial center of the state, its citizens enjoyed great personal success amid the gentle climate and park-like atmosphere of old Oakland. Many private citizens used their new-found wealth to subsidize a public transit system, excellent public schools and academies, several parks, and paved streets. Oakland's upwardly mobile residents also established magnificent neighborhoods in which the streets were lined with trees and nearly every home was surrounded by decorative fences and large gardens. Oakland was truly a land of oaks and other trees and homes that reflected the success of its citizens.

After a century of exposure to a climate that included long, wet winters, many mansions of Oakland's wealthy families fell into disrepair while some were left vacant. Others were situated in the path of projected freeways, shopping centers, sport arenas, and schools.

Rather than tear down these aging but valuable architectural treasures, the city's planning department designated a park in 1970 that would be dedicated to the preservation of these homes. Eleven homes were moved from locations throughout the city, joining five homes that were original to the site. Completed in 1991, the park was transferred to the ownership of the Oakland Redevelopment Agency in 1995.

Today, the collection of sixteen Victorian homes is one of the finest in America. All of these beautiful buildings have been restored to their original grandeur. Several are open to the public, accessible by special tour, or available for parties or meetings.

The Remillard House offers an interesting history that connects a wealthy family with the region's most famous author. Pierre Remillard arrived in Oakland from Montreal in 1881. In just five years, he rose from a hired hand to the wealthy owner of a brick manufacturing company. In 1887, he built a twenty-room mansion in the Queen Anne style. Pierre's daughter, Lillian, was popular among local high school students. She tutored many of them who struggled to learn the French language. Her most ardent student was a kid from a poor neighborhood. She enjoyed working with him because, in spite of his social position, he was well-mannered and highly disciplined in his study habits. His name was Jack London. Lillian and Jack spent many hours studying French together in the parlor of the Remillard House. In later years, he used this experience as a model for several passages in his novel *Martin Eden.*

Lillian became the Countess Dandini and ran the family brick business until her death in 1963. Local ghost hunters have detected her presence on the porch of her magnificent mansion. Admirers of Jack London have searched the place for his ghost as well.

Other homes in Preservation Park are believed to be haunted. Ghost hunters have investigated Nile Hall, built in 1911 as the Nile Social Club, and James White House, built in 1875 by the founder of the Seventh Day Adventist Church. The ghost of a child playing with a stick and barrel ring has been seen by some visitors at the 1873 Latham-Ducel fountain.

GHOST OF THE OLD PROFESSOR

Faculty Club Room 219
Cyclotron Road
University of California #6050
Berkeley, CA 94720-6050
510-540-5678
E-mail: info@berkeleyfacultyclub.com

The University of California at Berkeley boasts an academic community that has demonstrated intense loyalty to students, colleagues, and the institution for more than 140 years. Even after retirement from teaching, members of the faculty often remain in their professorial positions for decades as emeritus professors. The university's most dedicated professor may be Henry Morse Stephens, who joined the faculty in 1902 and remains an active member of the university community to this day. His death on April 16, 1919, has not diminished his interest in the university nor has it dampened his love of the Faculty Club where he resided for seventeen years.

Born in Scotland on October 3, 1857, Professor Stephens (known to his friends as Morris) joined the UC Berkeley faculty in 1902 as a history professor. Within a few years, he was promoted to the department's chair and became known as one of the university's most popular teachers. Stephens's greatest accomplish may be the acquisition of the Bancroft Library of California antiquities and manuscripts. This success led to his promotion of Dean of the College of Arts and Sciences in 1918. In spite of Stephens's distinguish career as a professor and enterprise as a speaker at off-campus events, he lived simply in room 219, known as the Tower Room, of the faculty club. On April 16, 1919, Stephens died in that room. I could not find the cause of death in any biographical material, but some sources say the professor died "mysteriously."

Not long after the professor's death, reports began circulating among students and staff of the faculty club that something strange was happening in room 219. The most vivid experience was reported by Noriyuki Tokuda, a visiting scholar from Japan. On March 9, 1974, Tokuda awakened from a late afternoon nap by "some kind of psychological pressure" and found a "very gentlemanly" figure sitting in a bedside chair staring at him. The apparition remained for a minute and then vanished. Others who have occupied this room have reported light switches that flip off and on, doors that swing open and closed, and the sound of footsteps. At times, the temperature in the room changes from very cold to hot even when heating and air-conditioning systems are off. Old editions of the student newspaper contain reports from students who claim to have seen the professor's apparition standing at the window of room 219.

When I was a student at UC Berkeley, the story of Professor Stephens's ghost was just one of several I heard. I've been told that the attic of the Faculty Club was used to store the personal belongings of professors until relatives could claim them. This led to hauntings that include knocking on the walls and ceiling of rooms below the attic, and widespread fear among staff members who refuse to enter the space unless all available lights are turned on and they are accompanied by another living soul.

In his *History of the Faculty Club*, James Paltridge recounts student reports of hearing professor Stephens standing at his opened window late at night reciting his favorite lines from the poet Rudyard Kipling: "Lord God of Hosts, Be with us Yet; Lest we Forget, less we forget!" Ghost hunter might want to use this information when hunting for the ghost of Professor Stephens. If you recite the lines incorrectly, you may capture EAP which contains the professor's rebuke or correction of your recitation. Photographs of Stephens can be found on the Internet. He wore wire-rim glasses and a full beard.

CLAREMONT RESORT AND SPA

41 Tunnel Road
Berkeley, CA 94705
510-843-3000
www.claremontresort.com

Only a few of thousand of the 400,000 "gold rushers" of the 1850s ever found their fortune in the streams and mines of California.

One lucky man who struck it rich was a Kansas farmer named Bill Thornburg. In 1848, Thornburg traveled overland to California by wagon, spending several months crossing desolate country and enduring hardships that we cannot imagine. Lured westward by the promise of fertile farmland, it is almost certain that Thornburg was unaware that California's streams and rocky canyons were full of gold. The Spanish and Mexicans had discovered gold in California as early as 1810, and it is possible that Thornburg had heard of these discoveries. Nonetheless, his timing was perfect as he arrived in California only weeks after Marshall discovered gold at Coloma. In order to convince his wife and daughter to undertake the arduous journey to California, Thornburg promised that the riches he would garner by establishing a vast farm in the San Joaquin Valley would be used to build the English castle his wife had always dreamed of having. Soon after arriving in California, however, Thornburg discovered a gold-laden stream as his oxen drank the cold water. Dreams of a profitable farm vanished as he fished gold nuggets from the stream.

With bags of gold dust and boxes of gold nuggets, Bill found suitable land in the Bay Area and purchased 13,000 acres. He built a sprawling castle, stables, barns, training areas for pedigreed horses, and facilities for a large staff. The fascination Mrs. Thornburg held of English society resulted in the marriage of her daughter to a British lord. After the daughter moved to England, Mrs. Thornburg became ill and died. A few months later, Bill sold the property. On July 14, 1901, a mysterious fire destroyed the castle along with several outbuildings.

The land passed through the hands of many people before another successful gold seeker, Eric Lindblom, built a sprawling Mediterranean hotel with riches he discovered in the Alaska gold rush of 1898. His opulent hotel opened in time for the Panama-Pacific Exposition of 1915. Several renovation projects over the years have created a modern, luxury resort that maintains the romantic style of Mrs. Thornburg's beloved castle. In fact, her ghost has been seen wandering the verandas and walkways of the Claremont Resort. Dressed in a Victorian gown, she glides around the gardens and seems quite pleased with the way her castle has been transformed into a beautiful hotel.

Local ghost hunters believe another female ghost haunts the terrace

The world-famous Claremont Resort has several ghosts, including a young woman who haunts the bar.

bar. In the 1930s, a law prohibited the sale of alcohol within one mile of the University of California. A young lady took it upon herself to measure the exact distance from the university to the front steps of the Claremont Resort. At the time, the Claremont did not have a bar because everyone assumed it fell within the one-mile limit, but she found that the Claremont was a few feet beyond. As a consequence, a bar was opened and the young woman was granted free drinks for life. She may be enjoying this reward at the terrace bar throughout her death, as well.

Several rooms of the resort have been the scene of paranormal activity, but none are as haunted as room 419. The ghost that inhabits this room turns lights on and off, opens and closes the bathroom door, and manifests as an apparition standing at the foot of the bed. Guests have described this apparition as a "foggy specter." The bed often shows signs that someone has reclined on it, and chairs have been moved into positions that suggest a ghostly meeting has taken place in the room. At times, people in adjoining rooms have called the front desk to complain of noise coming from room 419. Hotel staff offer assurance that the noise makers will be quieted, but they don't tell guests that they've been disturbed by a ghost that seems to be hosting a party in a room that was not rented for the night to any living soul.

Room 422 is also haunted. The ghost of a little girl, described as being six to eight years old and having long, curly hair, plays on the floor of the room and wanders the hallway. She is shy and creates a presence that guests have described as "unthreatening" and "pleasant."

BURLINGTON HOTEL

5 Canyon Lake Drive
Port Costa, CA 04569
510-787-1927

In the latter decades of the nineteenth century, the Sacramento River region between Rio Vista and the Carquinez Strait was a vibrant economic entity. The town of Benicia, once the state capitol, was still a major economic hub for ranchers, farmers, land developers, and travelers. The agricultural ports of Suisun City and Martinez were developed by brokers who transported the region's huge farm produce to distant markets, contributing to California's moniker as the nation's vegetable garden. Port Costa earned its distinction by serving as the landing point of the railroad ferryboats *Solano* and *Contra Costa* that provided a vital link in the transcontinental railroad that had its terminal in the San Francisco Bay Area. At its peak, the town had a population of more than 3,000; most of these were stevedores, sailors, or railroad workers. According to the 2000 census, only 232 called this place home.

Today, some historians consider these cities to be mere shadows of their former selves. Benicia, Martinez, and Suisun are largely residential communities with little in the way of industry that is reminiscent of the past. Port Costa seems to be hanging on by proverbial fingernails. Without a railroad or a highway, the town seems cut-off from the twentieth century. The winding two-lane road that meanders from

Crockett is too challenging for some travelers who simply can't negotiate the sharp curves while ignoring steep slopes that promise severe bodily injury to careless drivers. Sitting only a short distance from bustling communities, Port Costa seems isolated and inhabited by folks who seldom venture out of town. The population of the tiny enclave does swell on weekends as bikers and other brave souls roll into town to eat and drink at the Warehouse Café and Bar and then sleep it off in the Burlington Hotel across the street. Several blogs tell of R-rated encounters in the bar that ended in X-rated activity in the old hotel. The venue may be entirely appropriate for this kind of activity since the old three-story building was once known as one of the best brothels in the state.

Inside, the old Burlington retains much of the richness of its storied past while showing its age and evidence of a debauchery most of us cannot imagine. Ornate woodwork can be found throughout the place including stairway spindles and railings, wall paneling, doorway trim, and

The bizarre Burlington Hotel is haunted by ghosts from the 1920s, including women who practiced the world's oldest profession and some of their customers.

chair rails. Velvet flecked wallpaper is reminiscent of the early twentieth century, but some of it retains the stains of wild parties that occurred here not long ago. Creaky iron beds and a super-creepy porcelain doll that stands watch over the stairway evoke suspicions of ghosts.

Many bloggers have written about mysterious stains on the ceilings, headboards that were decorated with unidentified substances, and even food remnants on blankets, chairs, and carpets. Cobwebs in the windows and sparse amenities take patrons back to the early twentieth century. Among the remnants of the brothel days are pictures of children on the walls and as many as six doors that open to a single room. There is speculation that these are pictures of children born to the prostitutes who worked in the old Burlington. Further evidence of the hotel's legacy as a den of iniquity is found on the doors. Instead of a number, patrons find that each room is named for the young lady who did her business there.

Is the Burlington Hotel haunted? Many bloggers have answered in the affirmative. However, by their own admission, many of these bloggers retired to the hotel after a night of drinking at the Warehouse Café across the street. Several ghost hunters who have spent a night in the place have told me that they believe spirits roam the second and third floors. Convincing EAP and the reports of reliable psychics compose most of the evidence. Others have told me of dramatic EMF spikes and intense cold spots.

If the Burlington is haunted, who are the ghosts? No identification has been made of the spirits. Most ghost hunters who have investigated this place conclude that former prostitutes haunt the rooms in which they did their business. There is a vague story of a murder that allegedly took place at the Burlington Hotel, but I was unable to confirm that. It wouldn't surprise me to learn that more than a few people were killed in this place between 1880 and 1930. After all, Port Costa was a wild riverfront town. Conflicts between armed men were probably common, and if a murder was committed, frequent boat traffic on the river would have provided a quick escape.

Ghost hunters who plan to visit this place should understand that the hotel is not quiet on weekends. Access is reserved for those who have rented a room for the night. I do not recommend a solo investigation. Take one or two colleagues with you. Also, note that the hotel has no phone. Patrons must call the Warehouse Café and Bar across the street and leave a message for Howie, who acts as agent or manager for the hotel. Howie, who will not divulge his last name, sleeps until 2:00 p.m., so expect a return call late in the day. If Howie doesn't return your call within two days, just show up in town, stand in the middle of the street, and shout "Howie!"

All transactions are in cash.

ROSE HILL CEMETERY

Black Diamond Mines Regional Park
5175 Sommersville Road
Antioch, CA 94509-7807
925-757-2620

Noah Norton arrived in eastern Contra Costa country in 1855. Having considerable experience in the mining industry in Nova Scotia and Virginia, he founded a coal mining operation that included modern machinery, a company store, and a village for the workers and their families. By 1856, the place was home to more than sixty Welsh miners and their families. Living in the shadow of Mount Diablo didn't discourage these people from establishing a thriving community. Stories of spectral figures flying over the slopes of the strange mountain and sightings of the devil didn't scare them off. By 1905, however, the coal mine had played out and the village, named Nortonville in honor of its founder, lay deserted. All that remained were crumbling shacks, rusted machinery, and a rather full cemetery. My research produced a list of all those unfortunate souls who were buried in the mining company's Rose Hill Cemetery. About 250 people are buried in this tiny cemetery; nearly a third of them were under the age of ten when they died. With this fact in mind during my visits to the area, it has been difficult to imagine how illness and accidents could have taken the lives of such young people. The climate in this region is generally mild with the exception of warm summer days. There are no hurricanes, tornadoes, blizzards, ice and snow, or monsoons that might bring illness to those with compromised immune systems.

Judging from the average age at the time of death, life in Nortonville was hard for many folks. When the coal played out, survivors moved on, looking for a better life in the San Francisco Bay Area, while the victims of coal mine injuries, lung disease from coal dust, and infectious diseases that had rampaged through the small community in the 1870s were left in Rose Hill Cemetery.

Over the years, desecration of the graves and vandalism got to be too much for residents of the cemetery. Angry, unsettled spirits began harassing visitors to the area, especially those who picked up a souvenir of carved stone. Hundreds of visitors have experienced bizarre paranormal activity they have attributed to a poltergeist activity. This includes being struck by small rocks and sensations of being pushed, slapped, kicked, and scratched. For many, their experiences are less dramatic and include ghostly, disembodied sobbing and laughter. Cold spots, orbs in photographs, unexplained audio phenomena captured on recorders, and the sound of bells tolling are common experiences reported by visitors to the Rose Hill Cemetery and old Nortonville. Almost everyone who visits the cemetery experiences a feeling of ghosts watching them or hovering close by.

More than one hundred exorcisms have been performed at the graveyard in an effort to settle some of the most malicious spirits who were angry that their headstones were stolen or graves opened and robbed of valuables. There are reports of some people screaming and running from the cemetery with fright before completion of an exorcism or other ceremony that would quiet the spirits. I interviewed one person who reacted that way during an exorcism. She told me that she felt as though an evil spirit were trying to penetrate her body. Ghost hunters who visit this cemetery may want to equip themselves with protective agents such as crosses, Bibles, and holy water.

One of the ghosts of Nortonville's Rose Hill Cemetery has attained status as a local legend. Sarah Norton, also known as Granny Norton, served her community as a mid-wife from 1855 until her death on October 5, 1879, at the age of sixty-eight years. Granny Norton died when her buggy tipped over as she raced to assist a woman about to give birth in the nearby town of Clayton. The story tells of a sudden, strong wind that descended the slopes of Mount Diablo, frightening Granny's horse and tipping her buggy.

In her will, Granny had stipulated that there be no religious ceremony at her funeral, but the people of Nortonville felt obligated to gather at her grave site, say a few words about her life, and read a few scriptures from the Bible. Apparently, this angered Granny's spirit because the ceremony was cut short by a freak storm that rolled through the area. A few days later, Granny's friends gathered to finish the ceremony, but another storm hit the valley ending all attempts to memorialize her life and death. The attempt to include a quasi-religious ceremony to the burial may have aroused Granny's indignation, because she continues to haunt the cemetery and nearby areas to this day. In fact, her ghost, known as the White Witch because she wears a white gown and appears to have a pointed nose, has been reported as far as the Oakland hills and the Niles Canyon.

Some of the residents of the town of Clayton dress up as Granny Norton on Halloween, and her buggy ride is reenacted through the streets of Clayton. Some locals tell me that they fear this angers Granny's spirit and results in more haunting activity around the Rose Hill Cemetery.

If you visit Rose Hill Cemetery, plan your visit carefully. The hike from the parking areas to the cemetery is one mile, mostly uphill. Take water, food snacks, and a cell phone. I recommend that you avoid visiting this area when the weather is hot. There is little shade and cooling breezes from the nearby Sacramento River do not penetrate the hills to the former site of Nortonville.

MORESI'S CHOP HOUSE

(formerly La Cocotte Restaurant)
6155 Main Street
Clayton, CA 94517
925-672-1333
www.moresischophouse.com

In the 1880s, Clayton was a country town with none of the sophistication or civility that characterized the large cities on San Francisco Bay. Mining and ranching were the principle economic activities, and the local population was largely transient and as wild as the countryside. On weekends, the bars were full of gamblers and drunks. Local peace officers stayed busy while the upstanding citizens stayed indoors with their heads down.

One late Saturday afternoon, two miners became involved in a heated argument inside a bar known as the Growler. Each packed a revolver. They became itchy for a gunfight as they traded insults and accusations. At last, one of the miners reached his limit. He pulled his gun and fired his gun at the man who had aroused his indignation. The shooter missed his target, but his bullet penetrated the flimsy plank wall and struck a little girl as she stood on Main Street. The bleeding child was taken inside the bar where the patrons attempted to save her life, but the wound was fatal. She died on the floor amid a crowd of miners full of sorrow over such a terrible accident.

Over the years, the Growler was sold to various people whose businesses failed in the old building after a short time. The place stood empty for many years, during which stories spread about cries and moans rising at times from the silence of the deserted barroom.

In the 1980s, while the building was undergoing renovation, strange red stains were discovered on the floor. Strong cleaning solutions and hard work removed them but they would soon reappear. Local ghost hunters believe these stains are remnants of blood from the wounds of the unlucky little girl. The frustrated owners of the building placed a carpet over the stains and opened for business. Sensitives have seen the little girl inside the restaurant or standing on Main Street where she was struck by the miner's bullet 120 years ago.

Today, the former Growler bar is a popular restaurant called Moresi's Chop House. Many visitors inquire about red stains on the floor, but the spot has been covered by a carpet that cannot be lifted. Renovation of the interior has been so extensive that the place no longer resembles the Growler. The addition of interior walls to create private dining nooks and high-end color schemes and table amenities have erased any resemblance to the rowdy bar of the 1880s, but several antique photographs placed on all the walls, including a few of the old Growler, make patrons wonder about the old days when Clayton was a wild town.

THE LADY IN BLUE

Gay 90s Pizza Company
288 Main Street
Pleasanton, CA 94566
925-846-2520
www.gayninetiespizza.com

The ghost of a lady dressed in a blue Victorian gown has been spotted walking the floors of this popular pizza restaurant. It is believed that she was a madam who operated a brothel on the second floor of the building. Based on descriptions of her appearance and the history of the building, it is likely that she lived in one of the second-floor rooms in the late nineteenth century.

The two-story building that now houses the Gay 90s Pizza Company was constructed in 1864 to serve as a station for Wells Fargo stage coaches. The first floor was set up as a bank, office, and café while the second floor contained ten small rooms in which travelers would

This popular pizza restaurant, housed in a former Wells Fargo stage coach station, is haunted by a woman with red hair who appears life-like.

This young ghost hunter is looking for the ghostly message that often appears in this mirror at the Gay 90s Pizza restaurant.

spend the night. By 1890, stage service through the area had been replaced by a railroad, and Wells Fargo moved its banking services to a larger building. The old stagecoach station was renovated as a bar on the first floor while the second floor rooms were retained and designated "gentleman's quarters" where ladies of the evening would ply their trade. The second-floor business was overseen by a madam who many believe is the mysterious lady in blue.

The ghost has been seen by many people, including former owner Rob Earnest and his family. After renovation of the second floor into a two-room apartment, Rob's son noticed a woman standing near a window. Earnest says that he and his parents and son saw the apparition but she appeared completely life-like. He described her as voluptuous, showing cleavage, and wearing a gown typical of "dance hall girls" of the nineteenth century. Others have mentioned that this ghost has "big hair" that is curly and dull red and that she appears to be about forty years old. The ghost lady has made contact with many people and often smiles as if she approves of visitors in her brothel.

Restaurant staff members have describe the lady in blue as mischievous. She has been blamed for misplaced items that turn up later in bizarre places, lights that flicker, unexplained footsteps, doors that swing open and closed, cold spots, and the fragrances of perfumes. This ghost has left the word "boo" on a mirror near the women's restroom. It isn't clear why the ghost wrote this cliché, but it is likely that she overheard someone scoff at the idea of spirits haunting the old stage coach station. "Boo" was her response, and it appears to have had a lasting effect on everyone who visits the restaurant. Attempts to erase the word from the mirror have not been successful.

I've seen the lady in blue on two occasions. I get the impression she remains in the old building because she enjoyed managing a successful business that had many loyal, regular customers. She is not eager to move on in spite of her tendency to stand near windows and gaze at the street. Instead of thinking about leaving, it is likely that the lady in blue keeps a watch for her special customers.

As a side note, this pizza restaurant is also known as a great place for pregnant woman who wish to get on with labor. It is said that after eating a slice of Frank's Special Pizza, women who have passed their due date without giving birth suddenly develop labor pains that lead to a successful and happy outcome.

JOHN MUIR HOME

4202 Alhambra Avenue
Martinez, CA 94553
925-228-8860
www.nps.gov/jomu/

The John Muir home, built in 1882 on a knoll overlooking the farming community of Martinez, was actually built by the naturalist's father-in-law, Dr. John Strenzel (1811-1890). A Polish immigrant who arrived in America in 1831, Strenzel fulfilled his American dream by becoming a physician and a pioneer in the California fruit growing industry. He is most remembered, however, for granting John Muir permission to marry his daughter, Louisa (1847-1905), and for construction of the magnificent house that is now known as the John Muir Home, a National Historic Site. Built in the Italianate style, the 10,000-square-foot house had running water, marble fireplace surrounds, magnificent woodwork, and 13 foot high ceilings. Original furnishings and other period features, including an array of papers, books, and artifacts that fill John Muir's second-floor study, give the impression that the Muir family still lives in the house.

Many visitors to this mansion enter the place anticipating an encounter with the ghost of John Muir. My investigations of this house indicate his spirit is not there, however. Knowing his tendency to wander and his love of nature, I suspect the ghost of John Muir is likely somewhere in the Sierra Nevada, perhaps perched on a rocky outcropping where he can watch over his beloved Yosemite Valley. I have not encountered the ghost of Dr. Strenzel, either. The ghost I've encountered during every visit to this house resides in the child's bedroom on the second floor.

The bedroom includes a child's games and books scattered on the floor, giving the impression that one of Muir's little girls has just stepped out the room. I have not found light anomalies in my pictures of this room, but I always capture audio phenomena on my digital recorder.

Muir and Louisa had two daughters. Wanda (1881-1942) and Helen (1886-1964) were born in a modest ranch house, known as the "little house," less than a mile from the Strenzel-Muir mansion.

The John Muir House in Martinez is not haunted by the famous environmentalist, but a second-floor bedroom is haunted by the ghost of a little girl who plays with the toys scattered on the floor.

When Dr. Strenzel died in 1890, the doctor's widow asked the Muirs to move into the "big house" to keep her company. The girls were no doubt thrilled with the large parlors and bedrooms, and it appears that one of them left indelible audio imprints of her happiest moments.

Ghost hunters cannot enter the middle bedroom on the second floor, but the open doorway makes it easy to take pictures, check EMF levels, and perform an EAP sweep. On my recorder, I've captured audio of a little girl's laughter and humming. I have not found direct replies to my questions, but I've heard the girl's voice say "Go" when I asked if I could stay and watch her play. My recordings also include the sound of footsteps on the wood floor and the chilling words "Come play." My psychic investigation of this room suggests that it was occupied by Helen Muir, who was only four years old when she and her family moved into the big house.

Helen continued to use this bedroom until her marriage to Buel Funk in 1910. The death of her mother, Louisa, in 1905 occurred in this house, and Helen doubtless spent many days in her room grieving her loss. In spite of that, I found no environmental imprints of sobbing or crying on my audio recorder.

A doll that lies in a tiny cradle has eyes that seem to follow visitors who move across the doorway. This doll adds a spooky element to the room and seems to be most noticeable when the visitor stands alone at the doorway. During my second visit to this room, I was transfixed by the eyes of that doll when I saw the transparent apparition of a little girl kneel at the side of the cradle. The apparition was visible for only thirty seconds, but details of the girl were clear. On subsequent visits, I saw only partial apparitions of a girl's head and right shoulder.

OTHER PLACES TO HUNT GHOSTS:

THE FARMER RESTAURANT

(formerly the Pleasanton Hotel)
855 Main Street
Pleasanton, CA 94566-6668
925-399-6690
www.pleasantonhotel.com

The old Pleasanton Hotel is a landmark left over from the 1860s when the region was full of wild ranch hands and miners. Opened in 1865 as a "house of entertainment," proprietor John Kottinger offered patrons gambling tables, a well-stocked bar, musical entertainment, and fourteen rooms on the second floor that could be rented for private parties. The place burned in 1889 and again in 1915 but each time it would rebuild with modern amenities. Today, the place is known as the Farmer Restaurant. Ghosts of prostitutes, gamblers, and bandits are believed to roam the second floor. Loud, disembodied footsteps are often heard that sometimes blend with hushed conversations. Some staff members have reported seeing misty forms in the corridors of the second floor that sometimes resemble a partial apparition of a woman. A local psychic sensed the presence of a woman and a man in a military uniform.

MEEK MANSION AND CARRIAGE HOUSE

240 Hampton Road
Hayward, CA 94541
510-881-6700

Located in the heart of Hayward, it is difficult to imagine that the Meek Mansion was once surrounded by a great expanse of farmland. William Meek built the place in 1869 with money he earned from a nursery he founded in Oregon's Willamette Valley in 1847. His continued success in Alameda County earned him the distinction as the county's "first farmer." In 1880, Meek died in his grand mansion, but it is believed that his spirit continues to wander the rooms of the big house, gazing out the windows at the city that encroached on his farm. The ghost of a former housekeeper haunts this place too.

SPIRITS OF THE OLD INDIAN SHELL MOUND

Mound Street
Between Adams Street and Encinal Avenue
Alameda, CA 94501

Mound Street in Alameda has always had a reputation as a strange place. I grew up a few blocks away and all of the kids I knew avoided walking or biking on that street because of rumors that included scary shadows, screams that came out of nowhere, and the sudden disappearance of kids. When I was twelve, I visited the local museum and learned the street was named for a large Indian mound that was discovered in the 1890s as the city grew. Opened in 1908, archeologists removed the remains of 450 Indians, hundreds of stone implements, shell ornaments, and thousands of shell fragments. The mound measuring 400 feet long and 150 feet wide extended from the present day Adams Street to Encinal Avenue. Several houses in the area have been visited by apparitions of Indians who are probably disturbed by the desecration of their graves. Added to that, many people believe that not all remains were excavated and reburied elsewhere. Ghost hunters might encounter these spirits by walking Mound Street late at night while performing EMF and EVP sweeps. Several residents in this area have reported hearing disembodied voices speaking in a language that is unrecognizable.

SITE OF A-7 JET CRASH

1814 Central Avenue
Alameda, CA 94501

In the evening of February 7, 1973, a Navy Corsair jet fighter plummeted from 28,000 feet and slammed into an apartment building at 1814 Central Avenue. Residing only a few blocks away, I heard the horrific crash and raced to the scene as fire fighting vehicles and ambulances arrived. The impact of the jet and the explosion and fire destroyed the building and damaged adjacent structures. In addition to the pilot, ten people on the ground were killed. Within months, the apartment building was demolished and a new structure erected. Residents of the new building reported strange lights, moving doors and windows, and occasional apparitions believed to be the ghosts of crash victims. Paranormal activity has diminished considerably since the late 1980s, but sensitives who walk the halls of this building still pick up impressions of the tragedy. Residents I spoke to declined to comment when questioned about ghostly activity.

Appendix A

Sighting Report Form

Photocopy and enlarge the form on the next page to a standard 8.5 x 11 inch format. This form should be completed right after a sighting. If the ghost hunt is performed by a group, a designated leader should assume the role of reporter. The reporter is responsible for completing this form.

The reporter and each witness should make a statement, either audio or written, describing in full their experience at the site. Date, sign, and label these statements with a reference number identical to the report number on the sighting report form. Attach the statements to the report form.

SIGHTING REPORT

SITE NAME _____ REPORT # _____
LOCATION _____ DATE: _____
                         TIME: _____
REPORTER _____ SITE # _____
WITNESSES _____

_____

DESCRIPTION OF APPARITION: _____

temperature change	[] YES	[] NO
auditory phenomena	[] YES	[] NO
telekinesis	[] YES	[] NO
visual phenomena	[] YES	[] NO
other phenomena	[] YES	[] NO

Description: _____

_____

Use the reverse side for diagrams, maps, and drawings.
SPECIFIC LOCATION WITHIN SITE: _____

_____

PREVIOUS SIGHTINGS AT THIS SITE?:   [] YES   [] NO
Reference: _____
Summary: _____

_____

RECORDS:
audio	[] YES	[] NO	Ref. No. _____
video	[] YES	[] NO	Ref. No. _____
photo	[] YES	[] NO	Ref. No. _____

Summary of records: _____
Disposition of records: _____

_____

WITNESS STATEMENTS—Summary: _____

_____

audio	[] YES	[] NO
written	[] YES	[] NO

Disposition of statements: _____

_____

Appendix B

Suggested Reading

BOOKS

Allison, Ross and J Temples. *Ghostology 101: Becoming a Ghost Hunter*. Seattle,WA: AuthorHouse, 2005.

Auerbach, Loyd. *ESP, Hauntings, and Poltergeists*. New York: Warner Books, 1986.

___. *Ghost Hunting: How to Investigate the Paranormal*. Oakland, CA: Ronin Publishing, 2004.

___. *A Paranormal Casebook: Ghost Hunting in the New Millennium*. Dallas: Atriad Press, 2005.

Browne, Sylvia. *Adventures of a Psychic*. New York: Penguin Books, 1990.

Coustier, C., S. Marino, K. Zimmerman. *True Ghost Stories of Alameda: the Hidden Side of the Island City*. InstantPublisher.com, 2005.

Dwyer, Jeff. *Ghost Hunter's Guide to the San Francisco Bay Area*, 1st ed. Gretna, LA: Pelican Publishing, 2005.

___. *Ghost Hunter's Guide to Los Angeles*. Gretna, LA: Pelican Publishing, 2007.

___. *Ghost Hunter's Guide to New Orleans*. Gretna, LA: Pelican Publishing, 2007.

___. *Ghost Hunter's Guide to Seattle and the Puget Sound*. Gretna, LA: Pelican Publishing, 2008.

___. *Ghost Hunter's Guide to California's Wine Country*. Gretna, LA: Pelican Publishing, 2008.

___. *Ghost Hunter's Guide to California's Gold Rush Country*. Gretna, LA: Pelican Publishing, 2009.

___. *Ghost Hunter's Guide to Monterey and California's Central Coast*. Gretna, LA: Pelican Publishing, 2010.

Hauck, Dennis William. *Haunted Places: The National Directory*. New York: Penguin Group, 2002.

Hawes, Jason, Grant Wilson, and Michael Jan Friedman. *Ghost Hunting: True Stories of Unexplained Phenomenon from the Atlantic Paranormal Society*. New York: Pocket Publishers, 2007.

Holzer, Hans. *Real Hauntings*. New York: Barnes and Noble, 1995.

___. *True Ghost Stories*. New York: Barnes and Noble Books, 2001.

___. *Ghosts I've Met*. New York: Barnes and Noble Books, 2005.

May, Antoinette. *Haunted Houses of California*. San Carlos, CA: Wide World Publishing, 1993.

Ramsland, Katherine. *Ghost: Investigating the Other Side*. New York: St. Martin's Press, 2001.

Reinstedt, Randall. *California Ghost Notes*. Carmel, CA: Ghost Town Publications, 2000.
Richards, Rand. *Haunted San Francisco*. San Francisco: Heritage House Publishers, 2004.
Southall, R. H. *How to be a Ghost Hunter*. Woodbury, MN: Llewellyn Publications, 2003.
Steiger, Brad. *Real Ghosts, Restless Spirits, and Haunted Places*. Detroit: Visible Ink Press, 2003
Sweet, Charlotte. *How to Photograph the Paranormal*. Charlottesville, VA: Hampton Roads Publishing, 2004.
Taylor, Troy. *Ghost Hunter's Guidebook*. Alton, IL: Whitechapel Productions Press, 1999.
Van Praagh, James. *Ghosts Among Us: Uncovering the Truth about the Other Side*. New York: HarperOne, 2009.
Wlodarski, Robert and Anne. *California Hauntspitality*. Alton, IL: Whitechapel Productions, 2002.

ARTICLES

Associated Press. "Ghost buster: Ohio woman inspires CBS' supernatural series." *Boston Herald*, July 4, 2005.
Barrett, Greg. "Can the living talk to the dead? Psychics say they connect with the other world, but skeptics respond: 'Prove it.'" *USA Today*, June 20, 2001.
Benfell, Carol. "Bodega's spooky schoolhouse." *Santa Rosa Press Democrat*, October 31, 2001.
Cadden, Mary. "Get spooked on a walking tour." *USA Today,* October 17, 2003.
Clark, Jayne. "10 great places to get spooked by your surroundings." *USA Today,* October 26, 2007.
Delsol, Christine. "Historic ghosts of old Monterey." *San Francisco Chronicle*, October 14, 2009.
Dremann, Sue. "A haunting experience." *Mountain View Voice*, October 31, 2003.
Fox, Carol. "Ghostbuster to tell secrets of the hunt." *Los Angeles Times*, October 28, 1989.
Giovannetti, Joe. "Crossing over: Ghost hunter knows things that go bump in the night." *Fairfield (CA) Daily Republic*, October 18, 2007.
Hannah, James. "Who ya gonna call for the paranormal?" *San Francisco Chronicle*, June 8, 2008.
Harmanci, Reyhan. "Get in the Spirit. San Francisco Ghost Society." *San Francisco Chronicle*, March 15, 2007.
Hill, Angela. "Paranormal expert say it's not all funny." *Oakland (CA) Tribune*, October 18, 2002.
Huffman, Jennifer. "Ghost hunters: Local couple sees dead–all the time." *Napa Valley Register*, October 31, 2006.
Irwin, Richard. "Jeff Dwyer's ghost stories aren't just for Halloween." *Long Beach Press Telegram*, June 17, 2007.
Jenkins, Chris and Colin Fly. "Haunted hotel has baseball players walking." *San Francisco Chronicle*, July 26, 2009.
Kirby, Carrie. "Ghost hunters utilize latest in technology." *San Francisco Chronicle*, October 31, 2005.
Kovner, Guy. "Apparitions don't spook couple: departed loved ones haunt home." *Santa Rosa Press Democrat*, October 31, 1995.
Kurhi, Eric. "Investigating the eerie historic Hayward mansions." *Oakland Tribune*, December 13, 2009.
"Loyd Auerbach Shares Tales from the Dark Side." *San Francisco Chronicle*, October 30, 1998.

Massingill, T. "Business of ghost busting." *Contra Costa Times,* October 8, 2000.

McConahey, Meg. "Local haunts: believe it or not ghosts, some old can't seem to escape the past." *Santa Rosa Press Democrat,* October 29, 2005.

McMahon, Regan. "S.F. pioneer cemeteries: where the dead lived." *San Francisco Chronicle,* October 29, 2009.

Moran, Gwen. "Real-Life Ghost Busters." *USA Weekend,* October 31, 2004.

Nolte, Carl. "Merchant seaman forgotten in death; mariner's cemetery buried in debris, used as parking lot." *San Francisco Chronicle,* November 25, 2006.

Nolte, Carl. "150th anniversary of duel haunts California." *San Francisco Chronicle,* September 7, 2009.

Nyholm, Christine. "Haunted Sainte Claire Hotel in San Jose, CA." *San Jose Mercury News,* September 26, 2007.

O'Brien, Matt. "Angel Island's Ghosts Linger." *Contra Costa Times,* February 7, 2009.

Parker, Ann. "Ghost bust'er."*Santa Cruz Sentinel,* May 14, 2006.

___. "Spirited dining at the Brookdale Lodge." *Santa Cruz Sentinel,* September 14, 2005.

Pierleoni, Allen. "'Ghost Whisperer' consultant speaks out." *Sacramento Bee,* January, 2, 2008.

Schoolmeester, Ron. "10 great places to go on a haunted hike." *USA Today,* July 28, 2006.

Sichelman, Lew. "Plenty of spooky sites around the nation." *San Francisco Chronicle,* October 28, 2007.

Smith, David. "Pacific ghost hunters charged with burglary." *San Francisco Examiner,* January 17, 2007.

___. "Spirits, Specters and Strange Sightings Abound at America's Most Haunted Hotels." *Los Angeles Times,* October 15, 2003.

Speckert, Corinne. "Fabled Brookdale Lodge holds 'spirit tour.'" *San Cruz Sentinel,* July 15, 2008.

Stanley, Pat. "Ghost on second west." *Napa Valley Register,* September 30, 2005.

Templeton, David. "Ghost stories: everyone knows one." *Sonoma Independent,* June 13-19, 1996.

Thompson, Ian. "Tracking things that go bump in the night." *Fairfield (CA) Daily Republic,* October 29, 2000.

Wach, Bonnie. "The Dead Zone." *San Francisco Chronicle,* October 31, 2004.

Wheat, Christine. "Haunts near home: author chronicles ghost stories in Solano." *Fairfield (CA) Daily Republic,* October 30, 2005.

Appendix C

Films, DVDS, and Videos

Fictional films may provide you with information that will assist you in preparing yourself for a ghost hunt. This assistance ranges from putting you in the proper mood for ghost hunting to useful techniques for exploring haunted places and information about the nature of ghostly activity.

An American Haunting (2006). Directed by Courtney Solomon. Starring Donald Sutherland and Sissy Spacek.

Dragonfly (2002). Starring Kevin Costner and Kathy Bates.

Ghost of Flight 409 (1987; made for TV). Directed by Steven Hilliard Stern. Starring Ernest Borgnine and Kim Bassinger.

Ghost Story (1981). Directed by John Irvin. Starring Fred Astaire and Melvyn Douglas.

Haunted (1995). Directed by Lewis Gilbert. Starring Aidan Quinn and Kate Beckinsale.

Haunting Across America. Documentary (2001). Produced by Linda Lewis. Hosted by Michael Dorn.

Haunting in Connecticut (2009). Directed by Peter Cornwell. Starring Virginia Madsen and Martin Donovan.

Haunting of Seacliff Inn (1995). Directed by Walter Klenhard. Starring Ally Sheedy and William R. Moses.

Hereafter (2010). Directed by Clint Eastwood. Starring Matt Damon.

Living with the Dead (2000). Directed by Stephen Gyllenhaal. Starring Ted Danson and Mary Steenburgen.

Paranormal Activity (2009). Directed by Oren Peli. Starring Katie Featherston.

Paranormal Activity 2 (2010). Directed by Tod Williams. Starring Katie Featherston.

Sightings: Heartland Ghost (2002). Directed by Brian Trenchard-Smith. Starring Randy Birch and Beau Bridges.

Stir of Echoes (1999). Directed by David Koepp. Starring Kevin Bacon.

The Others (2001). Directed by Alejandro Amenabar. Starring Nicole Kidman Christopher Eccleston.

The Sixth Sense (1999). Directed by M. Night Shyamalan. Starring Bruce Willis and Haley Joel Osment.

White Noise (2005). Directed by Geoffrey Sax. Starring Michael Keaton.

13 Ghosts (2001). Directed by Steve Beck. Starring Tony Shalhoub.

1408 (2007). Directed by Mikael Hafstrom. Starring John Cusack.

The following movies are not about ghosts but they are worth watching before visiting the San Francisco Bay Area. They will give you a sneak preview of the some of the scenery and a bit of local culture.

The Birdman of Alcatraz (1962). Directed by John Frankenheimer. Starring Burt Lancaster.

Dirty Harry (1971). Directed by Don Siegkle. Starring Clint Eastwood.

Just Like Heaven (2005). Directed by Mark Waters. Starring Reese Witherspoon and Mark Ruffalo.

The Pursuit of Happyness (2006). Directed by Gabriel Muccino. Starring Will Smith and Jaden Smith.

The Rock (1996). Directed by Michael Bay. Starring Nicholas Cage and Sean Connery.

Vertigo (1958). Directed by Alfred Hitchcock. Starring James Stewart and Kim Novak.

Zodiac (2007) Directed by David Fincher. Starring Jake Gyllenhaal and Mark Ruffalo.

Appendix D

Special Tours and Events

Alcatraz Island Federal Penitentiary Tour. Now a U.S. National Park, Alcatraz Island Penitentiary operated from 1934 to 1963. Known as "the rock," it housed notorious criminals that included Al Capone and the Birdman Robert Stroud. Guided tours take visitors to the cells once occupied by famous inmates, solitary confinement, the laundry, and other buildings that date from the Civil War. Featured on several TV shows as a haunted place, ghost hunters will have opportunities to take photographs and attempt to capture electronic voice phenomena recordings. Day and night tours are offered. $26.00 (day), $33.00 (night). Pier 33, Hornblower Alcatraz Landing, San Fransciso. Call 415-981-7625. www.alcatrazcruises.com.

Annual Ghost Walk in Clayton. Held only once a year on Halloween, this entertaining walk is hosted by historian Richard Taylor. He points out the best spots for seeing ghosts and tells some fascinating stories about this historic village. Tours starts at 8:00 p.m. at Endeavor Hall in Clayton. Contact: Richard Taylor, 925-672-6171.

Annual Petaluma Cemetery Walk. Petaluma's early history and some of its ghosts are revealed in this annual October event. Established in 1871, Calvary Cemetery has all the elements for a chilling brush with spirits. Costumed re-enactors, representing the town's pioneers, will tell you about local history and where the bodies are buried. This is a good orientation for ghost hunters who want to return to this location later for a serious investigation of paranormal phenomena. No fee. Contact: Petaluma Historical Museum, 707-778-4398. www.petalumamuseum.com.

Benicia Ghost Walk. Staged on Fridays during the months of October, this tour takes visitors to several nineteenth century buildings in this historic town. Call 707-745-9791.

China Town Ghost Tour. This tour of San Francisco's famous China Town brings to life tales of a supernatural past and present. Chinese legends, myths, and modern-day appearances of ancient spirits make this one of the most popular tours in the city. 731 Grant Avenue, San Francisco. $16.00 to $24.00. Fridays and Saturdays at 7:30 p.m. Call 415-793-1183 or 1-877-887-3373. www.sfchinatownghosttours.com.

Ghost Walk at the Palace. Focusing on the fabled Palace Hotel, this tour recounts stories of gunshots in the hallways, the deaths of kings and presidents, and tragic romances that contribute to ghostly lore. Meet in the lobby, at the main entrance, of the Palace Hotel, 2 New Montgomery Street, San Francisco. Free for groups of nine or less. Call 415-557-4266 or e-mail: tours@sfcityguides.org.

Ghost Walk at San Francisco City Hall. Offered only in October, this tour reveals the bizarre history and sites of ghostly activity in and around the city hall and civic center. Stories about disinterred remains from the former cemetery now covered by the civic center and assignations are told by knowledgeable tour guides. Meet at South Light Court (Polk Street) entrance to San Francisco City Hall. Free for groups of nine or less. Call 415-557-4266 or e-mail: tours@sfcityguides.org.

Haunted Haight. This award-winning, two-hour walking tour takes visitors to the core of the Hippie Movement of the 1960s. The tour passes more than 150 Victorian homes, where ghostly activity and macabre history have been recorded, and ends at a haunted pub. $20.00 includes guideline book and map. Meet at 1206 Masonic Avenue (Coffee to the People café), San Francisco. Call 415-863-1416.

Petaluma Downtown Walking Tours. Offered on Saturdays and the first and third Sundays, May through October, this tour includes historic buildings, gardens, streets, and bridges. Led by costumed docents, this is an entertaining and efficient way for ghost hunters with limited time in town to learn of local history, legends, and lore that point to where ghosts may be found. Adults $20.00. Contact: Petaluma Historical Library and Museum, 707-778-4398. www.petalumamuseum.com.

San Francisco's Barbary Coast Trail Tour. See the plaza where Sam Brannan shouted the news that gold was discovered at Sutter's Mill in 1848. Walk the streets that over-lay the remains of hundreds of Gold Rush-era ships that were abandoned by their crews. Visit a saloon where sailors were once "shanghaied" into service. Tours by appointment. $22.00. Call 415-454-2355. e-mail: info@barbarycoasttrail.org.

San Francisco Ghost Hunt. This is the foremost ghost tour in the San Francisco Bay Area. Led by the incomparable Jim Fassbinder, the haunted history of the City by the Bay is described by a master story teller and magician. The tour starts at the famous Queen Anne Hotel and winds through the spooky back streets still haunted by Flora Sommerton and Mary Ellen Pleasant. Adults $20.00. Meet at the Queen Anne Hotel, 1590 Sutter Street, San Francisco. Every night, except Tuesday, at 7:00 p.m. Contact: 415-922-5590. E-mail sfghost@yahoo.com. www.sfghosthunt.com.

San Francisco Maritime National Park. Take a self-guided tour through seven historic ships including the haunted 1886-vintage square rigger *Balclutha* and the ferryboat *Eureka*. Docked at the foot of Hyde Street in San Francisco, this floating museum offers ghost hunters a great opportunity to spend several hours aboard historic vessels that still harbor the ghosts of their crews and passengers. $5.00 fee allows entry for seven days. Call 415-447-5000.

Stories from a Silent City: A Cemetery History Walk. From 1852 to the 1940s, San Francisco's largest cemeteries once occupied ground now covered by modern structures in the Laurel Hill, Jordan Park, and Lone Mountain areas. Tour guides will tell fascinating stories of grave removal and how ghostly activity may be the result of bodies that were left behind as the city grew over undetected burial plots. Meet at the southwest corner of Euclid and Collins Streets in San Francisco. Offered only in May and October. Free for groups of nine or less. Call 415-557-4266 or e-mail: tours@ sfcityguides.org.

USS *Hornet* Tour. Docked in Alameda, this historic fighting ship is a popular destination of paranormal enthusiasts and has been featured on several TV shows. Visitors may take a self-guided tour through several areas including the hangar deck, flight deck, officer's country, crew berthing areas, galley, sick bay, and pilot ready rooms. Guided tours are conducted on the bridge, engine room, and combat information center. Adult, $12.00; children (5-17), $6.00. 707 West Hornet Avenue, Alameda. Call 510-521-8448. www.uss-hornet.org.

Vampire Tour of San Francisco. If you are into the macabre history of San Francisco, this tour is for you. Mina Harker guides visitors on a two-hour nighttime adventure that combines Nob Hill history of the rich, famous, and infamous, with vampire fantasy. Friday and Saturday nights at 8:00 p.m. Meet at the corner of California and Taylor Streets, San Francisco. Adults $19.00. Contact: 650-279-1840 or 866-4-BITTEN.

Winchester Mystery House Tours. Guided tours of the great house built by Sarah Winchester, at the direction of spirits, offer visitors an opportunity to see the famous séance room and sixty other rooms constructed over a period of thirty-nine years. The Behind the Scenes Tour includes the mansion's basement which is haunted by the ghost of a workman. On Fridays the Thirteenth, lights inside the mansion are extinguished and tours are conducted by flashlight, adding to the mysterious atmosphere of this haunted house. $26.00 for adults; $20.00 for children (6-12). 525 South Winchester Blvd., San Jose. Call 408-247-2101. www.winchestermysteryhouse.com.

1906 Earthquake and Fire Tour. Visit the scene of the most devastating earthquake of twentieth century California. Roam the streets south of Market Street while you hear tales of horror and misery, and then escape to the safety of Union Square only to encounter the fire that consumed much of San Francisco. Tours are conducted June through September, on the first and third Mondays, at 10:00 a.m. Meet at the benches between 555 and 525 Market Street, San Francisco. Guide: Kathy Martin. Free for groups of nine or less. Call 415-557-4266. e-mail: tours@sfcityguides.org.

1906: Presidio and Earthquake Tour. This walking tour conducts visitors to several historic, Civil War-era buildings and other venues that played a prominent role in training troops before deployment to the battlefields of WWI and WWII. Included in this tour are locations that served as temporary housing for 200,000 San Franciscans displaced by the destructive earthquake of 1906. Offered June through September on Fridays and Saturdays at 1:00 P.M. Meet at the Officer's Club at the Presidio, San Francisco. Free for groups of nine or less. Call 415-557-4266. e-mail: tours@ sfguides.org.

Appendix E

Organizations

You may contact these organizations to report ghost phenomena, obtain advice, or arrange for an investigation of a haunting. Many of these organizations conduct conferences, offer training, or list educational opportunities for those seeking to become paranormal investigators.

Amateur Ghost Hunters of Seattle, Tacoma (AGHOST)
No mailing address
Contact: 253-203-4383
E-mail: aghost@aghost.us
Website: www.aghost.us/index.html

American Society for Psychical Research
5 West 73rd Street
New York, New York 10023
212-799-5050

Berkeley Psychic Institute
2436 Hastings Street
Berkeley, CA 94704
510-548-8020

Committee for Scientific Investigations of Claims of the Paranormal
1203 Kensington Avenue
Buffalo, NY 14215

Ghost Trackers
P.O. Box 89
Santa Clara, CA 95052
408-244-8331
E-mail: ghostrackers@yahoo.com
Web site: www.ghost-trackers.org

Haunted and Paranormal Investigations
www.hpiparanormal.net
1-888-709-4HPI
Institute for Parapsychology
Box 6847
College Station
Durham, NC 27708

International Society for Paranormal Research
4712 Admiralty Way
Marina del Rey, CA 90292

International Ghost Hunter's Organization
www.ghostweb.com/ondex.html

Napa Valley Paranormal Investigations
Cherilyn Hays and Troy Hutchins
www.nvpi.org
e-mail: ghosts@nvpi.com
707-224-1655
707-631-5482

Parapsychology Foundation
228 E. 71st Street
New York, NY 10021
212-628-1550

Psi Applications
Steve Moreno, director
P.O. Box 1964
Suisun, CA 94585
e-mail: director@psiapplications.com
www.psiapplications.com

Psychical Research Foundation
C/o William Roll
Psychology Department
West Georgia College
Carrolton, GA 30118

San Francisco Ghost Society
www.sfghostsociety.org

Appendix F

Internet Sources

www.bayareaparanormal.com. Members of Bay Area Paranormal Investigations (BAPI) will look into anything that falls outside the realm of conventional scientific research.

www.darknessradio.com. This internet radio interview program streams Sunday night from 10:00 p.m. to midnight. Guests range from ghost hunters to trance channels. Host David Schrader adds announcements about meetings for paranormal enthusiasts.

www.ghosthunter.com. Web site of ghost hunter and lecturer Patti Starr.

www.ghostresearch.com. Web site for information about ghost hunting methods and equipment and on-going investigations.

www.ghostresearch.org. Ghost Research Society was established in 1971 as a clearinghouse for reports of paranormal activity. Members research homes and businesses and analyze photographs and audio and video recordings to establish authenticity. This society is headed by well-known ghost researcher Dale Kaczmarek.

www.ghost-stalker.com. Richard Senate is a well-known author, lecturer, and ghost investigator who focuses mainly on Southern California locations.

www.ghosttowns.com. Informative Web site that gives detailed information about ghost towns in the U.S. and Canada.

www.ghost-trackers.org. Ghost Trackers is a professional research group based in the San Francisco Bay Area. Among their members are scientists and expert technicians. E-mail: ghost-trackers.org.

www.ghostweb.com. International Ghost Hunters Society, headed by Drs. Sharon Gill and Dave Oester, researches spirits to produce evidence of life after death. The society offers a home-study certification for paranormal investigators. Membership exceeds 15,000.

www.hauntings.com. Web site for the International Society for Paranormal Research.

www.historichotels.nationaltrust.org. Historic hotels of America are detailed here.

www.historychannel.com. Official Web site of the History Channel.

www.hollowhill.com. A ghost information Web site that display reports, photographs, eye-witness accounts, location information, and information about ghost hunting techniques.

www.hpiparanoermal.net. Haunted and Paranormal Investigations is a highly active group of ghost hunters who have considerable experience with Sacramento-area and Gold Rush country spirits. E-mail: ghost@snmproductionsco.com.

www.jeffdwyer.com. Web site of author, paranormal investigator, ghost hunter, and writer Jeff Dwyer.

www.mindreader.com. Office of Paranormal Investigations directed by internationally known author and researcher, Loyd Auerbach. The office investigates a variety of paranormal activity for a fee.

www.nvpi.org. Napa Valley Paranormal Investigations, headed by Cherilyn Hays and Troy Hutchins, conducts investigations of paranormal phenomena throughout the Wine Country.

www.paranormal.com. This Web site has a live chat room and links to news articles about paranormal activities.

www.prairieghosts.com/ghost_hunt.html. Official Web site of the American Ghost Society, founded by ghost researchers Troy and Amy Taylor. This site provides information about ghost research, paranormal investigations, and books written by Troy Taylor.

www.psiapplications.com. PSI is a north California organization dedicated to the investigation and documentation of anomalous events, including the paranormal.

www.sfghostsociety.org. The San Francisco Ghost Society conducts investigations, stages special events for paranormal enthusiasts in haunted San Francisco locations, and supports a Web cast called Supernatural San Francisco found at www.sfgs.podomatic.com.

www.sonomaspirit.com. Headed by Jackie Ganiy, this organization maintains a Web site that serves as a great research utility.

www.technica.com. This is a catalog of electronic detectors and recorders that may be used in ghost hunting.

www.the-atlantic-paranormal-society.com. Official Web site of the Atlantic Paranormal Society (TAPS). This group of ghost investigators gained fame through the SyFy Channel's *Ghost Hunters*. This organization has more than fifty groups spread through the U.S. and has demonstrated excellence and discretion in its investigations of the paranormal.

www.theshadowlands.net/ghost. Directory of reports of unsubstantiated hauntings and other paranormal events organized by state. This is a good Web site for findings places that might be hot spots for ghostly activity.

www.warrens.net/. The New England Society for Psychical Research is the official Web site for famed researchers and demonologists Ed and Lorraine Warren.

Regional newspapers: access archives to search for articles about haunted places and local ghost hunters and learn about special events and tours.

www.arguscourier.com. the *Petaluma Argus-Courier*

www.contracostatimes.com. the *Contra Costa Times*

www.insidebayarea.com/oaklandtribune. the *Oakland Tribune*

www.marinij.com. *Marin Independent Journal*

www.mercurynews.com. *Silicon Valley Mercury News*

www.sfgate.com. the *San Francisco Chronicle*

www.timesheraldonline.com. *Vallejo Times Herald*

Appendix G

History Museums and Historical Societies

Historical societies and museums are good places to discover information about places that figure prominently in local history. They often contain records in the form of old newspapers, diaries, and photographs about tragic events such as fires, hangings, train wrecks, and earthquakes that led to the loss of life. Old photographs and maps that are not on display for public viewing may be available to serious researchers.

Alameda Historical Society
12324 Alameda Avenue
Alameda, CA 94501
510-5231-1233
www.alamedamuseum.org

Belmont Historical Society
1219 Ralston Avenue
Belmont, CA 94002
650-593-4213
wwwbelmont.gov.orgs/BHS/

Benicia Historical Society
P.O. Box 773
Vallejo, CA 94590
707-745-1822
www.beniciahistoricalsociety.org

Berkeley Historical Society
931 Center Street
Berkeley, CA 94704
510-848-0181
www.ci.berkeley.ca.us/histsoc/

Burlingame Historical Society
900 Burlingame Avenue
Burlingame, CA 94010
650-340-9960
www.burlingamehistorical.org

California Historical Society
687 Mission Street
San Francisco, CA 94105
415-357-1848
www.californiahistoricalsociety.org

Chinese Historical Society
965 Clay Street
San Francisco, CA 94108
415-391-1188
www.chsa.org

Clayton Historical Society
6101 Main Street
Clayton, CA 94517
925-672-0240
www.claytonHS.com/

Concord Historical Society
1601 Sutter Street #EF
Concord, CA 94520
925-827-3380
www.conhistsoc.org

Crockett Historical Museum
900 Loring Avenue
Crockett, CA 94525
510-787-2178

Fremont Museum of Local History
190 Anza Street
Fremont, CA 94539
510-623-79-7
www.museumoflocalhistory.org

Hayward Historical Society
22701 Main Street
Hayward, CA 94541
510-581-0223
www.haywardareahistoru.org

Los Gatos History Club
123 Los Gatos Blvd.
Lops Gatos, CA 95030
408-354-9825

Marin County Historical Society
1125 B Street
San Rafael, CA 94901
415-454-8538
www.marinhistory.org

Oakland Museum
1000 Oak Street
Oakland, CA 94611
510-238-2200
www.museumca.org

Palo Alto Historical Association
P.O. Box 193
Palo Alto, CA 94302
650-326-3355
www.pahistory.org/

Petaluma Historical Museum
20 Fourth Street
Petaluma, CA 94954
707-778-4398
www.petalumamuseum.org

Pittsburg Historical Society
515 Railroad Avenue
Pittsburg, CA 94564
925-439-7501
www.pittsburgca.net

Presidio Historical Association
Presidio of San Francisco
San Francisco, CA 94129
415-921-8193
www.presidioassociation.org

Richmond Museum of History
400 Nevin Avenue
Richmond, CA 94801
510-235-7387
www.richmondmuseumorhistory.org

Saratoga Historical Museum
20350 Saratoga-Los Gatos Road
Saratoga, CA 95070
408-867-4311
www.saratogahistory.com

San Jose Historical Museum
1300 Senter Road
San Jose, CA 95112
408-277-2757
www.historysanjose.org

San Mateo County History Museum
777 Hamilton Road
Redwood City, CA 94063
650-299-0104
www.sanmateocounmtyhistory.com

Santa Clara Valley History Society
580 College Avenue
Palo Alto, CA 94306
650-857-0765
www.siliconvalleyhistorical.org

Sausalito Historical Society
420 Litho Street
Sausalito, CA 94965
415-289-4117
www.sausalitohistoricalmuseum.org

Tracy Historical Museum
1141 Adams Street
Tracy, CA 95376
209-832-7278
www.tracymuseum.org

Vallejo Naval History Museum
734 Marin Street
Vallejo, CA 94590
707-643-0077
www.vallejomuseum.org

Western Aerospace Museum
Oakland Airport
8260 Boeing Street
Oakland, CA 94521
510-638-7100

Wells Fargo History Museum
420 Montgomery Street
San Francisco, CA 94104
415-396-2619
www.wellsfargohistory.com

Index